Cutting to the Heart

This is a book that both young and seasoned preachers will find themselves returning to again and again. Here is real practical help which is theologically informed on one of the great challenges in preaching. Those who want to understand just what we mean when we talk about applying the text of the Bible in teaching and preaching, and how to do this in a faithful and effective way, will benefit greatly from Chris Green's labours.

Mark Thompson, Principal, Moore College, Sydney

Cutting to the Heart

Applying the Bible in teaching and preaching

Chris Green

INTER-VARSITY PRESS
Norton Street, Nottingham NG7 3HR, England
Email: ivp@ivpbooks.com
Website: www.ivpbooks.com

First published 2015

British Library Cataloguing in Publication Data
A catalogue record for this book is available from the British Library.

ISBN: 978-1-78359-293-7
         978-1-78359-294-4 (ePub)
         978-1-78359-295-1 (mobi)

Set in Monotype Garamond 11/13pt
Typeset in Great Britain by CRB Associates, Potterhanworth, Lincolnshire
Printed and bound in Great Britain by Ashford Colour Press Ltd, Gosport, Hampshire

Inter-Varsity Press publishes Christian books that are true to the Bible and that communicate the gospel, develop discipleship and strengthen the church for its mission in the world.

Inter-Varsity Press is closely linked with the Universities and Colleges Christian Fellowship, a student movement connecting Christian Unions in universities and colleges throughout Great Britain, and a member movement of the International Fellowship of Evangelical Students. Website: www.uccf.org.uk.

The word of God is alive and active. Sharper than any double-edged sword.
(Hebrews 4:12)

For Dick, who persistently asks what is in the text,
and for Richard, who persistently asks what he is supposed to do with it.

CONTENTS

PREFACE

To be invited to give the annual Moore College Lectures is a daunting honour. These public lectures, inaugurated in 1977 by F. F. Bruce's series on biblical theology and later published as *The Time Is Fulfilled*,[1] have produced a stream of significant contributions, including at least two books on preaching: Klaas Runia's *The Sermon Under Attack*,[2] and Peter Adam's *Speaking God's Words*.[3]

Runia's and Adam's books reflect on and feed into the enormous range of contemporary literature on preaching, from the dauntingly complex issues of hermeneutics, through careful exegetical practice, to current debates about communication and style.

But I accepted the invitation to lecture about preaching because in that range there is still only a handful of books on the issue of application; and if we ask what God intends to *do* through his inspired Word, the comparative gap on the shelves becomes rather obvious and embarrassing. My goal is to place something at that point in the preacher's study, and to encourage the discussion further. As I hope to show, the issues that application touches range both deeply and widely,

---

1. F. F. Bruce, *The Time Is Fulfilled: Five Aspects of the Fulfilment of the Old Testament in the New* (Exeter: Paternoster, 1978).
2. Klaas Runia, *The Sermon Under Attack* (Exeter: Paternoster, 1983).
3. Peter Adam, *Speaking God's Words* (Leicester: Inter-Varsity Press, 1996).

and will need many more conversation partners. I have deliberately kept the focus on personal and corporate application to Christians; the questions of application to wider society or to those who are not Christians (other than in evangelism) are significant in themselves, but are distinguishable from how God changes his people to become like his Son. Similarly, I have not explored issues of pastoral counselling, although a number of books I refer to have that issue at the forefront and it is a directly related issue.

I was also keen that the format of the lectures did not turn into a forbidding book that would not help the normal preacher preparing normal sermons in a normal church. So I have split the lectures into short chapters, given the ideas more room to breathe, put in material I did not cover in Sydney and included a number of diagrams. These are tools I use myself whenever I prepare a sermon, and I hope others find them useful. I have also included discussion questions at the end of each chapter, because many churches have small teams of preachers, and these issues are helpful to work through together.

So I am enormously grateful to the faculty, students and graduates of Moore College who listened to and engaged with this material, and showed me such warmth and hospitality. I am particularly grateful to the then principal, Dr John Woodhouse, both for extending the invitation and for being such a kind and warm host, together with his wife, Moya.

Much of this material has been developed over the years at Oak Hill Theological College in London, and I am also grateful to its principal, Dr Michael Ovey, for giving me the permission to use the material, and encouragement to accept the invitation, and then to bring it to this point. Now I have moved back into a regular preaching ministry, I am thankful to the members of St James, Muswell Hill, for their continued encouragement and support as we learn from God's Word together.

My wife and children put up with extended absences from me, and managed not to be too obviously envious of my trip to Australia; it is a privilege to know their love and support in ministry.

But opening God's Word before his people is an even more daunting honour than flying in to give some lectures, and it is one that many of us know well and could easily become familiar with. My prayer as a preacher is almost always the same: 'Lord, would you open your Word to our hearts, and open our hearts to your Word. Amen.'

Chris Green
Sydney 2012, London 2014

1. THE BLUNT SWORD

The words of the wise are like cattle prods . . .

(Eccl. 12:11)[1]

Summer

It was a humid summer's evening at the end of a long summer's day, and the people had come to church. They fanned themselves cool with their notice sheets, stood a little further apart than usual when they sang, and tried, unobtrusively, to separate themselves from their sticky clothing. They dozed.

I cannot remember what passage I preached on that night, but the details are still painfully clear to me. Because halfway through the sermon my mind's eye saw a little banner scroll across the bottom of my eyesight, and like the breaking news element on a website it told me quite clearly, 'This is very boring.'

I could see it in their faces. I could feel it in my head. I can still see the page of my notes in my mind's eye to this day, because although I cannot remember what I was preaching on I do know I was midway through an illustration about a Russian tsar of which I was very proud. But just as I remember seeing the newsflash, so too I remember going home and vowing that never ever would I allow myself to preach like that again. I have failed on many occasions, of

---

1. Unless otherwise noted, the translation used below is the New International Version (NIV), and occasionally the English Standard Version (ESV), but this quote is from the New Living Translation.

course, but that experience has burned into me my dreadful responsibility for preaching the worst sermon I have ever heard.

What had gone wrong? Theologically, it is hard to say. 'The word of God is alive and active. Sharper than any double-edged sword' (Heb. 4:12), and God was no doubt waiting to wield it that evening among his people. The church was one with a long history of faithful Bible teaching, and the members were keen and well taught. I had spent my time in my study, reading, thinking and praying, and I had written it carefully. I know that because it is what I always did. That raises the rather discouraging thought that maybe I was equally as bad on every other occasion as well.

Somehow or other I had got in the way. God's Word is sharp, but I seemed to be making it blunt. It is fresh, but I was making it stale. It is living, but I was stifling it, and that was stifling God's people and me. It is designed to do deep soul-work and move lives, but I could not find the necessary leverage.

Self portrait

In the intervening years I have read almost any book about preaching I have laid hands on, from short pamphlets to multivolume dictionaries. The churches I have worked in have experienced each bend on the road of my journey, as I have tried to improve on the issue of helping them feed on God's Word. And I have discovered a tension.

The textbooks, whether by practising preachers or seminary professors, focus on the critical task of understanding the passage. They rightly insist, over and again, that our task is to bury ourselves in the text and then bring out its treasures.

However, the people who listen to sermons by those same preachers not only comment on the clarity and accuracy of those sermons, but even more on their relevance, timeliness and helpfulness. It's almost as though the daily round of being a pastor feeds into the sermon process and – without the preacher consciously realizing it – feeds into the sermon.

Curiously, the preachers claimed that they gave themselves to understanding the passage, but the listeners experienced that the preachers had given themselves to application.

That would not be a problem if we could assume that any preacher can reliably (if unconsciously) do the work of application. But as I have moved into teaching young preachers, I have noticed that they do not find this assumption helpful. They find many resources on the conscious, text-based work, but very few on the unconscious applicatory 'hunch'. And so they easily assume that only the conscious, written-about work is important. I noticed that it wasn't just their pastoral inexperience that made them dry and unapplied – they actually had an assumption that being dry and unapplied *was what they were supposed to be doing*.

My journey had led me to a different conclusion. The preachers I admired most were obviously drawing on their pastoral experience, and showing how the Bible helped make disciples. So I needed to find out more about how the Bible says that people are to change to become more Christlike. I needed to go back to the Bible, and discover what the Bible says about what the Bible is for.

What's more, in order to teach my students I not only had to be able to teach them how to handle the text, but also how to apply it, which meant that the process that had become unconscious for me I now had to make explicit so that they could see what I was trying to do. I had to make the task of application one that could be learned. And I found an unexpected helper deep in the Old Testament.

The preacher's self-portrait

There are only two Bible writers I am aware of who consciously reflect on why – *and how* – they wrote their parts of Scripture. One is Luke, who at the start of his Gospel (Luke 1:1–4), and more briefly in Acts (Acts 1:1), describes his research and writing style. It is useful material and, at a time when there is much assumed cynicism about the historical reliability of the biblical material, is important for us. Evangelists and apologists need Luke.

Less well known, though, is the writer of the book of Ecclesiastes. He is an enigmatic figure, whom various Bible translations call 'the Preacher' or 'the Teacher', and in the book he describes how he conducted a thought experiment. He examined the whole of life 'under the sun', as he calls it, and found it 'meaningless' or 'empty' (1:2). It is probably that verse that prompted Paul to write that the whole of creation is subject to 'frustration' until the return of Christ (the Septuagint, the Greek version of the Old Testament, and Rom. 8:20 use the same word).

Towards the end of his book the Teacher repeats his refrain that life is 'meaningless' (Eccl. 12:8), but then describes how he conducted his experiment. This passage was a turning point for me because it shows how a master teacher aimed to teach:

> Not only was the Teacher wise, but also he imparted knowledge to the people. He pondered and searched out and set in order many proverbs. The Teacher searched to find just the right words, and what he wrote was upright and true.

The words of the wise are like goads, their collected sayings like firmly embedded nails – given by one shepherd. Be warned, my son, of anything in addition to them.

Of making many books there is no end, and much study wearies the body. (Eccl. 12:9–12)

That conveys a sequence of activity. I am not claiming that this is *the* mandatory pattern for preachers, but it is worth watching carefully as a wise and Spirit-inspired master communicator thinks about his craft, and teaches us how he did it. The Teacher is unusual in being both a great communicator, and able to explain how he works, and so of all the books you have read and conferences you have attended this is the best teaching on preaching you could ever sign up for. Of course he is writing Scripture, so he has a level of certainty that belongs only to the biblical authors. He is inspired in a way no preacher today can claim. Nevertheless, he has a method, and it is that, rather than the claim to divine inspiration, that I suggest we follow step by step.

1. Wisdom: the process begins with the phrase 'Not only was the Teacher wise'. The first requirement is wisdom.

Ecclesiastes is, of course, an example of what is called 'wisdom literature', a class of writings marked by proverbs, catchy sayings and a quest for the meaning of life. But this is not another way of saying 'common sense'. Biblically, wisdom was associated in particular with God's gift to Solomon in 1 Kings 3, and it means something like 'thinking about life properly, given that God is on the throne'. As Solomon himself put it, 'The fear of the LORD is the beginning of wisdom' (Prov. 9:10). So although the Teacher did not have the equivalent of a seminary degree, he knew God, so he was 'wise', and that was his firm foundation. Knowing God and being wise are effectively the same thing.

But even though Ecclesiastes is in the Bible, we cannot just raid the Old Testament teachers of wisdom for practical tips on how to live life. The Bible has a plot, and God's gift of wisdom reached its highest trajectory in the person and work of Jesus. The theme of wisdom points to him directly, because Jesus himself said that 'The Queen of the South will rise at the judgment with the people of this generation and condemn them, for she came from the ends of the earth to listen to Solomon's wisdom; and now something greater than Solomon is here' (Luke 11:31).

And wisdom also points to Jesus' work, as Paul wrote:

Jews demand signs and Greeks look for wisdom, but we preach Christ crucified: a stumbling-block to Jews and foolishness to Gentiles, but to those whom God has called, both Jews and Greeks, Christ the power of God and the wisdom of God. For the foolishness of God is wiser than human wisdom, and the weakness of God is stronger than human strength. (1 Cor. 1:22–25)

The centrality to the Bible of the theme of wisdom, and the way Jesus underlines it about himself, means we are in an even more privileged position than the Teacher, because we know about the cross. The cross is the demonstration of God's wisdom, its highest peak; the Bible is the explanation of God's wisdom, its widest extent.

So our quest to understand God's wisdom will take us across the extent of God's Word, exploring its poems and stories, letters and visions, and seeing how they make sense in the light of the centrality of Jesus. Because this is not a textbook on exegesis, I have not covered all the usual material on sentence-flow diagrams, principal ideas, biblical theology, and so on, but that careful study of the text is the necessary foundation of proper preaching.[2] Being wise in a biblical sense begins with having a thorough grasp of the Bible.

But in itself even that is not enough, because it is possible to pass any exam in the Bible and yet be a fool. Jesus said that true wisdom is the decision to believe God, and act on what we know he has said. Here are his words on the subject of wisdom:

Therefore everyone who hears these words of mine and puts them into practice is like a *wise* man who built his house on the rock. The rains came down, the streams rose, and the winds blew and beat against that house; yet it did not fall, because it had its foundation on the rock. But everyone who hears these words of mine and does not put them into practice is like a *foolish* man who built his house on sand. The rain came down, the streams rose, and the winds blew and beat against that house, and it fell with a great crash. (Matt. 7:24–27)

Wisdom necessarily entails doing what Jesus said: without obedience, knowledge is foolishness. That is a foundational thought for understanding the work of application.

---

2. On a scale of rising technicality, see Haddon Robinson, *Expository Preaching: Principles and Practice*, 2nd ed. (Leicester: Inter-Varsity Press, 2001); J. Scott Duvall and J. Daniel Hays, *Grasping God's Word*, 2nd ed. (Grand Rapids: Zondervan, 2005); Kenton C. Anderson, *Choosing to Preach* (Grand Rapids: Zondervan, 2006); Robert B. Chisholm Jr., *From Exegesis to Exposition: A Practical Guide to Using Biblical Hebrew* (Grand Rapids: Baker, 1996).

2. Teaching: secondly, the Teacher is not a man who studies for studying's sake. He read theology, but not for a hobby, or to be well informed. He certainly knew his stuff, and if you had asked him for an answer to a question, simple or deep, you would have found he had knowledge. But he knew his full task was to have 'imparted knowledge to the people'. He is paying attention to other people.

There is apparently an easy test to distinguish good schoolteachers from poor ones: ask them what they teach. Poor ones reply, 'I teach French,' or 'I teach physics' or whatever their subject is. Good ones say, 'I teach children.' The Teacher here would have fallen into the second group: he taught knowledge to the people. Or better, he 'imparted' knowledge, meaning he passed it over, so that the people who learned from him knew the lessons for themselves. Poor teachers give long lectures and think that by doing that they have been teaching; but good teachers know that if people are not learning, they are not being taught properly. This Teacher studied for the sake of other people.

There is a little comment used in some Christian circles: 'So-and-so is a great Bible teacher' or 'After this song Fred is going to come and explain the Bible.' I know what is meant, but it worries me. It is true, but it is not true enough.

How does your preaching line up beside this so far? Is it wise, constantly pointing people to Jesus and his death? Does it teach people? Or do you just assume that if people are sitting quietly, they are soaking it all up? Are they learning, or are you like me on that dreadful summer's evening, speaking stodge into space?

3. Ponder: thirdly, the Teacher 'pondered . . . many proverbs'. In a busy week, with Sunday coming, this is one of the aspects of preaching we find it easy to avoid. But here is the Teacher, sitting in his chair with a cup of coffee, a pad of paper and a pen, and chewing things over, mulling, not rushing to read any more books, and certainly not rushing to write the first draft. This is not idle, lazy activity of course – it is a focused, praying, intentional time of thinking things through and jotting ideas down.

4. Research: fourthly, 'he searched out . . . many proverbs'. The Teacher had been involved in a deliberate piece of research to find out the world's wisdom on the meaning of life – he said at the outset that 'I applied my mind to study and to explore by wisdom all that is done under the heavens' (1:13), and the commentators often point out the similarities between parts of this book and the wisdom from surrounding cultures. The parallel with our task as preachers is not hard to see, because we also are to do careful study and research, but we should notice that the Teacher did that after he had pondered. His work is not a patchwork of other people's views but his own position, thought through and aware of alternatives.

5. Order: fifthly, he 'set in order . . . many proverbs'. This wise Teacher knew that to communicate well he had to think about the sequence in which his material would be presented, so that it would work logically. How could he seize people's attention? What would be the most striking way to begin?

> Meaningless! Meaningless! . . .
> Utterly meaningless!
>   Everything is meaningless.
> (Eccl. 1:2)

Will that do? Then, how will he build on it? And so the book weaves its subtle course, with prose and poetry, proverb and pun. This is careful, aware, intelligent and captivating communication. The result is that he defies us not to pay attention.

6. Words: sixthly, the Teacher 'sought to find just the right words'. The correct phrase, the proper adjective all combine to make an unmistakably clear piece of teaching. We preachers deal in words, but we do not normally have long in which to use them. Taking time to find the fresh phrase is yet again hard, but the right words will cut through a fog of inattention and thoughtlessness. The wrong words confuse.

7. Truth: seventhly, he made sure that 'what he wrote was upright and true'. He checked, and checked again. The equivalent for us is to make sure that we do not make theological blunders, and distort God's Word.

This passage is a biblical workbook on the communicator's craft. How many sermons have you heard, or preached, that were confusing? This Teacher 'set in order . . . many proverbs'. How many were true but deadly dull? This Teacher 'sought to find just the right words'. How many were shallow and manipulative? What this Teacher taught was 'upright and true'.

A journalist who is a Christian once commented that many preachers he hears could improve simply by taking more time in their preparation: not to squeeze more in, but to rework what they have. He wrote:

> a great many sermons are what an editor would call 'a good first draft'. All the
> material is there, the thinking has been done, it's in reasonable shape, but it's not
> actually finished (that is not surprising, since it was, in all likelihood, still being written
> at 11:30 pm on Saturday night). The tell-tale signs are: illustrations and stories that are
> funny and/or effective but only tenuously related to the point (i.e. that the preacher
> has spotted or thought of early in the sermon-writing process but that don't really fit
> into the finished product); extraneous points or cross-references that seem to have too
> little to do with the main flow of the argument; too much detail on an interesting side

issue or exegetical difficulty (about which the preacher is intrigued and has read quite a lot, most of which has found its way into the sermon draft); an overly long introduction or a too-brief conclusion (the introduction often being the first thing written, and the conclusion the last at 11:30 pm Saturday) . . . What is true of writing and editing articles is also true of sermons, I think: you must leave time for a re-write.[3]

8. Sermons that stick and sting: those lessons in themselves are priceless, and paying attention to them would improve many of our sermons. But the Teacher has more lessons for us, and uses three word pictures for them. It is possible they are variations of one image, but they play in slightly different directions.

'The words of the wise are like goads.' In my country and culture we do not use goads, and most Bible readers would have to look the word up in a dictionary. A goad is a stout stick, either sharp at one end or with a nail driven through it, which was used to whack cattle on the backside to make them move. A goad is a cattle prod. The Teacher wants us to think this one through for ourselves, which is why it is a proverb and not a straightforward statement. In what ways are 'The words of the wise . . . like goads'? Surely, goad words make people do things. There is intentionality about good teaching that means everyone feels they have to act in response.

So when someone asks, 'What was the point of that sermon?', we should have a mental image of a sharp stick, a stubborn cow and enough force to make the cow move in the right direction.

Notice too that this is no accident. The Teacher did not have three truths to communicate, with a general plan of leaving people feeling better informed, or feeling better in general. No, the image is of a deliberate, purposeful series of choices to sharpen his material to produce exactly the result he intended. I suspect the reason why so many sermons do not produce clear decisions is that we do not have the courage to dare to take this on our shoulders. We present truth clearly, but something inside us tells us that to make the implications clear, with the necessary consequences and life-changing results, would be pre-sumptuous. Not so, says the Teacher. Sharpen your stick and give them a prod.

The second image focuses on the nail itself: 'the collected sayings of the wise are like firmly embedded nails'. He could be continuing with the image of the nail through the cattle prod, or perhaps he has changed to someone hammering a nail deeply into a wall. In either case the emphasis lies on the phrase 'firmly embedded'. This nail will not come out.

---

3. Tony Payne, 'An Editor's Guide to Sermons', *Briefing* 323 (Aug. 2005), p. 17.

So the Teacher has put his material together in such a way that it stays in people's heads; they cannot forget it, so it is there when they need it. Once again this is no accident. This is his deliberate choice: he knows what will help people to remember, and he gives them every assistance. He is responsible for this.

So, preachers, we need to measure ourselves against these two pictures. Are our sermons designed to be easily memorable, so that people learn and act – do they stick? Are our sermons ruthlessly honed so that they move people to act – do they sting? Or do we too easily give people a lot of 'stuff' and leave them to work out what to do with it?

And finally, once we have reached the point of panicky bewilderment about the amount of work that goes into our task, the Teacher gives us a reassurance. The entirety of all these words of teaching is 'given by one shepherd. Be warned, my son, of anything in addition to them. Of making many books there is no end, and much study wearies the body.' This is difficult to translate exactly, but the title 'shepherd' was so associated with the Old Testament kings (Ps. 78:70–72; Jer. 10:21; 49:19; 50:44; Ezek. 34:1–6; John 10:11), and above them with God himself (Gen. 48:24; Ps. 23:1; Isa. 40:11; 53:6), that it makes sense to say the Teacher here says that truth is internally consistent, given us by one ruler, and that endless chasing after alternative ideas is a tiring, numbing process. But we, living after the Good Shepherd, who has promised us his voice in the Scriptures, can be even more confident than the Teacher (John 10; Rev. 7:17). Scripture is unified and unifying, and our task is simply to unpack it. That does not excuse our ignorance (remember that the Teacher's research covered many proverbs), but it does mean that we can ruthlessly prune our activity and content.

The preacher's self-portrait is a wonderful way to measure ourselves against one of the wisest teachers who ever lived, and is a quick and simple exercise for self-examination. But to make it even more effective, we need to gain more of his biblical wisdom. We need to move from the pressing deadline of making the next sermon, and even from asking about how and why we preach sermons. To understand why we preach sermons we need to ask the biggest question of all, and so set our smaller ones in their rightful place. Here is a question that requires biblical wisdom: Why did God bother to make anything at all? What is the ultimate point of anything?

Questions for reflection and discussion

- Chris Green shared the story of the worst sermon he has preached (so far!). What would be your 'worst sermon ever' story? Does it share any common elements with his?

- *Wisdom*: How well do you think you can explain how the whole Bible fits around the person and work of Jesus? Why do you think obedience is a central element of wisdom?
- *Teaching*: How could you check whether people are learning what is being taught in your church?
- *Ponder*: Do you have enough time to think about your sermon when you are preparing it? What might be a way to find the time to mull?
- *Research*: How do you make sure you have done enough reading and thinking in your preparation? And how do you know if you have done the right kind? How do you plan to keep ahead with your studies?
- *Order*: Look at, listen to or watch your last two or three sermons (if you are in a group, be kind but honest with one another). How carefully were they constructed to produce the desired end?
- *Words*: again, go back and check your vocabulary. Were you confusing?
- *Truth*: When did you last read through a book on Christian doctrine? What are the most tempting errors for your church?
- *Sting*: Did any of the sermons have a single aim that it 'prodded' people towards?
- *Stick*: Was any sermon constructed to be memorable? What are the sermons you can remember having had an impact on you? What made them stick in your mind?

PART 1

WHY HAS GOD GIVEN US A
RELEVANT BIBLE?

2. WHAT'S THE POINT OF PREACHING?

He is the one we proclaim, admonishing and teaching everyone with all
wisdom, so that we may present everyone fully mature in Christ.

(Col. 1:28)

God has a plan

When preachers become stuck in the weekly groove of preparing sermons and
talks, it can become hard to keep a clear view of why the work matters. Many
ministers know the sinking feeling that occurs in the pit of the stomach at half
past four on Sunday afternoon, as they realize they have to do it all again. Or
maybe it is you, three hours later, sitting in a pew and staring at the preacher,
or standing in a pulpit staring at the congregation, wondering why you are doing
this to each other.

God never wonders that. He never finds anything pointless, because he
knows exactly why he made it. He is an intentional God, and nothing we can
do, say or think will override his plan.

He says:

I make known the end from the beginning,
  from ancient times, what is still to come.
I say, '*My purpose will stand,*
  and I will do all that I please' . . .
What I have said, that I will bring about;
  what I have planned, that I will do.
(Isa. 46:10–11; see Prov. 19:21)

And he achieves what he wants, in his own way:

> As the rain and the snow
>   come down from heaven,
> and do not return to it
>   without watering the earth
> and making it bud and flourish,
>   so that it yields seed for the sower and bread for the eater,
> so is my word that goes out from my mouth:
>   *it will not return to me empty,*
> *but will accomplish what I desire*
>   *and achieve the purpose for which I sent it.*
> You will go out in joy
>   and be led forth in peace;
> the mountains and hills
>   will burst into song before you . . .
> (Isa. 55:10–12)

God does not hope for coincidences, or make a wish – he plans. And unlike every human plan, his absolute and unchallengeable sovereignty and will assure us it cannot fail. He can make promises and guarantee they will be kept. That is the power of his 'word'.

God's plan governs every corner of creation, throughout the history of space and time, and it is not about us at all. It is for his own glory:

> For from him and through him and for him are all things.
>   To him be the glory for ever! Amen.
> (Rom. 11:36)

And his plan does not just cover the vast sweeps of space in general ('all things'); it covers every detail of how we live in particular: 'So whether you eat or drink or whatever you do, do it all for the glory of God' (1 Cor. 10:31). That means we can be sure that everything God has made exists for the sake of his glory.

But not everything exists to bring God glory in the same way. 'Eating' and 'drinking' are similar actions, both capable of bringing him glory. And so is looking at a computer screen, talking to a friend or listening to some music. But they each do it in a unique way. Paul encourages me not to enjoy something merely for itself, but to align it with God's glory and to enjoy it for his sake.

So in order to understand the purpose of anything, and in order to enjoy it properly in line with the maker's plan, all I have to do is to answer the question 'How does this thing bring God glory?' To discover the proper purpose of preaching we cannot glibly assume that the answer is obvious, but we have to ask a much larger series of questions, and align the purpose of preaching with the purpose of everything God has made and done. To do that we will need to arc between the Old and New Testaments, and trace out God's plan for his glory.

Question 1: Why did God make us?

If we go to the creation account in Genesis 1, we find this description:

> Then God said, 'Let us make mankind in our image, in our likeness, so that they may rule over the fish in the sea and the birds in the sky, over the livestock and all the wild animals, and over all the creatures that move along the ground.'
>
> So God created mankind in his own image,
>   in the image of God he created them;
>   male and female he created them.
> (Gen. 1:26–27)

The origin of what it means to be human, built into our DNA in a way that makes us different from anything else, is being made in the image of God.

Much debate has surrounded that idea, but probably the best starting point is to look at what we see God doing in Genesis 1 and 2, and assume that therefore human beings will echo that. So we see God creating, ruling, naming, speaking – and in a derived sense we see the humans he has made doing the same kinds of things. The consequences of sin in Genesis 3 affect that idea, but they do not remove it, and so even radically evil human beings remain, in a shattered way, the image of God.

By contrast Jesus, unaffected by sin, is the perfect image of God, and the highest example of what a human being could ever be.[1] The New Testament writers repeatedly affirm that this 'image bearing' role has a unique focus in

---

1. He is also the eternal Son of God in human form, but that element of the equation is not one to explore here.

Jesus, as he not only takes up the responsibility Adam failed at, but does so on an altogether different level. He is, Paul says, 'the image of God' (2 Cor. 4:4), 'the image of the invisible God' (Col. 1:15), and Hebrews puts it even more clearly: 'The Son is the radiance of God's glory and the exact representation of his being, sustaining all things by his powerful word' (Heb. 1:3). God's glory takes visible form in Jesus.

So one way Paul describes our salvation is to say that *we are being remade in the image of Jesus, who is himself the glory-filled image of God*. He says it in various places: 'For those God foreknew he also predestined to be conformed to the likeness of his Son' (Rom. 8:29). It is something that one day will be complete: 'just as we have borne the image of the earthly man, so shall we bear the image of the heavenly man' (1 Cor. 15:49), but we can get a glimpse of it now: 'And we all, who with unveiled faces contemplate the Lord's glory, are being transformed into his image with ever-increasing glory' (2 Cor. 3:18). That last-day likeness is something we are to live in line with today. Paul said that we '*are* being transformed into his image with *ever-increasing* glory'. He puts it similarly to the Colossians: 'Do not lie to each other, since you have taken off your old self with its practices and have put on the new self, which is being renewed in knowledge *in the image of its Creator*' (Col. 3:9–10).

Let's tighten the focus to one letter. In Ephesians Paul constructs the whole of his argument about Christian change around that truth of our being like God. He moves from the general 'put on the new self, created to be *like God* in true righteousness and holiness' (Eph. 4:24) to a string of commands that conclude, 'Be kind and compassionate to one another, forgiving each other, *just as in Christ God forgave you*' (4:32). Then he continues with a double statement of being like God: '*Follow God's example*, therefore, as dearly loved children and live a life of love, *just as Christ* loved us and gave himself up for us' (5:1–2).

Our salvation lines us up with why we were created, which is to bear the image of our creator.

Question 2: Why has God saved us?

Let's zoom out again. At every point in the unrolling of God's salvation plan he made it clear why he was acting as he did. Among his people whom he rescued from Egypt, after an awesome moment of judgment, he said:

> Among those who approach me
>   *I will be proved holy*;

In the sight of all the people
>   *I will be honoured.*
(Lev. 10:3)

God is jealous for his glory. As he later promised the Jews who returned from exile, he made it clear that their return was for the same reason:

Bring my sons from afar
>   and my daughters from the ends of the earth –
everyone who is called by my name,
>   *whom I created for my glory,*
>   *whom I formed and made . . .*
>   the people I formed for myself
that they may proclaim my praise.
(Isa. 43:6–7, 21)

This is how you guided your people
>   to *make for yourself a glorious name.*
(Isa. 63:14)

The ultimate end of both the exodus and exile rescues was that God should receive glory, and since they were the prelude, the working models of the ultimate rescue on the cross, it is no surprise that in salvation too the ultimate end is God's eternal glory:

> In him we [Jews] were also chosen, having been predestined according to the plan of him who works out everything in conformity with the purpose of his will, in order that we, who were the first to put our hope in Christ, might be for *the praise of his glory.* And you [Gentiles] also were included in Christ when you heard the message of truth, the gospel of your salvation. When you believed, you were marked in him with a seal, the promised Holy Spirit, who is a deposit guaranteeing our [Jews' and Gentiles'] inheritance until the redemption of those who are God's possession – to *the praise of his glory.* (Eph. 1:11–14)

So there is constant interplay between God's glory, Jesus being the image of God's glory, and our defaced image being remade in his image to his glory. That is critical to answering our question. *In order to understand the purpose of anything, we have to understand how it brings God glory, and to understand the purpose of people we need to ask how they bring God glory – they bring him glory as they are remade in the image of his Son.* People bring God glory by becoming more like Jesus. Somehow preaching fits into that process.

Question 3: Why does God speak to us?

God, Adam and Eve spoke to each other, and we have already seen that that is a fundamental part of what it means to be made in God's image. Knowing God truly is what we were made for. The primary temptation from the serpent, therefore, was to do with God's word, to entice the man and woman to believe that God's word was a restrictive lie. 'Did God really say . . . ?' And 'You will not certainly die . . . God knows that when you eat from it . . . you will be like God' (Gen. 3:1–5). Satan's first tactic was to preach a lying sermon.

We live in the shadow of the ejection of Adam and Eve from the garden that followed their rebellion, and one of the consequences of that is that we do not know, and do not *want* to know, what God expects of us. In part that is wilful refusal, in part it is ignorance and in part it is his judgment on us. In Ephesians 4 Paul diagnoses this intellectual problem as a root cause of our moral problem:

> So I tell you this, and insist on it in the Lord, that you must no longer live as the Gentiles do, in the futility of their thinking. They are darkened in their understanding and separated from the life of God because of the ignorance that is in them due to the hardening of their hearts. Having lost all sensitivity, they have given themselves over to sensuality so as to indulge in every kind of impurity, and they are full of greed. (4:17–20)

'In the futility of their thinking . . . darkened in their understanding . . . ignorance': this issue plays itself out on the intellectual field. This is of course nothing to do with how clever people are, because the fundamental cause is 'the hardening of their hearts'. People, says Paul, are muddled over the issue of truth because of the deep issue of a sinful nature, or, as he puts it for Christians a few verses later, 'your old self' (4:22). In consequence, this sinful pattern plays itself out on the moral field too: 'every kind of impurity . . . full of greed'. Our news programmes and websites are therefore full of those issues, in both their apparent attraction and their dreadful consequences. But the reason it is futile to join a moral campaign to 'clean up the Web' is that you first have to win the battle to 'clean up the mind' – and to do that you have to win the battle to 'clean up the heart'.

That is precisely what the Lord Jesus has done for us. Paul continues:

> That, however, is not the way of life you learned when you heard about Christ and were taught in him in accordance with the truth that is in Jesus. You were taught, with regard to your former way of life, to put off your old self, that is being corrupted by its

deceitful desires; to be made new in the attitude of your minds; and to put on the new self, created to be like God in true righteousness and holiness. (4:20–24)

Three elements are changed for Christians. Instead of the 'old self' there is a 'new self'; instead of 'deceitful desires' there are 'true righteousness and holiness'; and instead of our previous 'ignorance' we are 'to be made new in the attitude of our minds'. It is that third element of the mind that Paul particularly stresses here, because he repeatedly stresses the matter of information we have been given and understood: 'learned . . . heard about Christ . . . taught in him . . . truth that is in Jesus . . . taught'. There is information here both about Jesus himself (we were 'taught about Christ') and how we are to live in consequence (we were 'taught . . . to put off . . . to be made new' and 'to put on'). *At each point God has replaced our ignorance with proper knowledge about who he is and what to do in consequence. And at each point we are to replace our ignorance with truth, and change our rebellious lives into obedient ones.* That is why he has spoken to us, and why we have the Bible (Isa. 42:21).

Why? Why has God done this? Elsewhere in this letter Paul roots it variously in God's loving nature, in his desire to establish the Lord Jesus as king of the cosmos, his plan to reconcile and reunite humanity in, with and under Christ, in his determination to defeat evil, and of course in his ultimate plan to gain glory for himself – but here there is another purpose revealed, new for Ephesians but by now no surprise for us: we have been 'created to be like God' (Eph. 4:24).

That means we are seeing a chain of consequences. The purpose of creation is that we bring God glory because we have been made in his image. The purpose of salvation is that we bring God glory by being remade in his image. The purpose of the Bible is to teach us how we bring God glory by living out being remade in his image.

Question 4: How does the church bring God glory?[2]

Paul is not the only New Testament writer who works with this chain of consequences. Peter's first letter, written to Christians on the edges of society, reminds them that although society may see them as marginal, they are central to God's plans. The theme runs through the letter, but it emerges at two points,

---

2. I have written more fully on this section of 1 Peter in Chris Green, *The Message of the Church: Assemble the People Before Me*, The Bible Speaks Today (Nottingham: Inter-Varsity Press, 2013).

one that sees the church from the perspective of God's eternal plan, the other at a local, relational level.

The eternal perspective comes at the end of a sequence of rich biblical quotations, and climaxes with a series of Old Testament promises being showered on the New Testament church:

> But you are a chosen people, a royal priesthood, a holy nation, God's special possession, that you may declare the praises of him who called you out of darkness into his wonderful light. Once you were not a people, but now you are the people of God; once you had not received mercy, but now you have received mercy. (1 Peter 2:9–10)

That is entirely consistent with what we have seen so far: God's eternal plan produces a people who praise him, or bring him glory. But we know now we have to be more careful – how exactly are we to bring God glory, and 'declare his praises'? Many Bibles put a major break here, but it is clear that Peter's thought flow continues. This is how we bring God glory: 'Dear friends, I urge you, as foreigners and exiles, to abstain from sinful desires, which wage war against your soul' (2:11). Once again, bringing God glory has to do with our obedience. But he goes on, 'Live such good lives among the pagans that, though they accuse you of doing wrong, they may see your good deeds and glorify God on the day he visits us' (2:12). Because we give God glory in this way, other people will give him glory too.

The second passage in 1 Peter comes later, in chapter 4, and it is apparently much more mundane and practical. This is the local, relational element:

> Above all, love each other deeply, because love covers over a multitude of sins. Offer hospitality to one another without grumbling. Each of you should use whatever gift you have received to serve others, as faithful stewards of God's grace in its various forms. If anyone speaks, they should do so as one who speaks the very words of God. If anyone serves, they should do so with the strength God provides, so that in all things God may be praised through Jesus Christ. To him be the glory and the power for ever and ever. Amen. (1 Peter 4:8–11)

Perhaps that sounds like the perfect church to you! If it does, remember that this is not meant to be an unattainable ideal, but what we are supposed to be like. Peter expects you to take this to your church prayer meeting, or to your elders, and say, 'How can we be more like this?'

At that point you would have asked the critical question. You would have identified that church is supposed to change people, and the church itself is supposed to change. That is a rather counterintuitive thought, because many of us live in a context where our cultures are changing rapidly, and changing in ways that are at best different from, and often hostile to, the gospel. Churches therefore default to resisting change, and being places identified with social and moral conservatism.

Now we are certainly not to change to ape our culture. Peter reminded these marginal Christians that they were 'foreigners and exiles' (1 Peter 2:11), unsurprised when insulted, misunderstood, abused or beaten. We will stand against a cultural tide. Nevertheless, that does not mean that we behave as if we are already perfect. No, we must see that the same fight goes on in our hearts, and we must 'not conform to the evil desires [we] had when [we] lived in ignorance' (1:14). But (here comes the church) the fight also goes on in our relationships, and so Peter addresses the realities of a church of grudges and grumbles, and some people with too much to do.

Why are we to engage in this fight? We could just be content to turn up for a church service, sing some hymns and listen to a talk, and then go home after a weak cup of coffee. What more is church for? Why bother with all the other stuff? Here is Peter's answer, for the second time: 'so that in all things God may be praised through Jesus Christ'. And a third: 'To him be the glory and the power for ever and ever. Amen' (1 Peter 4:11).

Churches bring God glory as we change each other to become like Jesus.

Question 5: How does preaching bring God glory?

The first time a dog meets a hedgehog it greets it like a willing playmate, perhaps taking it for an animated ball that will throw itself around for the dog's delight. One encounter with the prickles, however, and the dog learns to treat hedgehogs with more respect and caution.

The first time we meet the question 'How does preaching bring God glory?' we may respond with similar carelessness. We may respond with verbs like 'proclaim' and 'declare', or nouns like 'herald' and 'ambassador', but they will boil down to one simple answer: 'Preaching brings God glory because it talks about him a lot, and says how great he is.'

Preaching does indeed talk about God a lot and say how great he is, or at least it should, and the words 'proclaim', 'declare', 'herald' and 'ambassador' are biblical ones we should use with reverence and delight. But we now know to treat that question with more respect and caution – *how* exactly does talking about God in church bring him glory?

We need to return to Paul, this time to Colossians. Chapter 1 shows him explaining his theology of preaching. Here is his breath-taking panorama of God's glorious plan for the church:

> The Son is the image of the invisible God, the firstborn over all creation. For in him all things were created: things in heaven and on earth, visible and invisible, whether thrones or powers or rulers or authorities; all things have been created through him and for him. He is before all things, and in him all things hold together. And he is the head of the body, the church; he is the beginning and the firstborn from among the dead, so that in everything he might have the supremacy. For God was pleased to have all his fullness dwell in him, and through him to reconcile to himself all things, whether things on earth or things in heaven, by making peace through his blood, shed on the cross.
>
> Once you were alienated from God and were enemies in your minds because of your evil behaviour. But now he has reconciled you by Christ's physical body through death to present you holy in his sight, without blemish and free from accusation – if you continue in your faith, established and firm, and do not move from the hope held out in the gospel. This is the gospel that you heard and that has been proclaimed to every creature under heaven, and of which I, Paul, have become a servant.
>
> Now I rejoice in what I am suffering for you, and I fill up in my flesh what is still lacking in regard to Christ's afflictions, for the sake of his body, which is the church. I have become its servant by the commission God gave me to present to you the word of God in its fullness – the mystery that has been kept hidden for ages and generations, but is now disclosed to the Lord's people. To them God has chosen to make known among the Gentiles the glorious riches of this mystery, which is Christ in you, the hope of glory.
>
> He is the one we proclaim, admonishing and teaching everyone with all wisdom . . . (Col. 1:15–28)

There Paul is undoubtedly talking about God and his greatness, and proclaiming that greatness has been the centre of Paul's activity. And Paul has again identified the issue of God's glory as the gospel's bull's eye. But why? What is the purpose? How does preaching achieve that? Let him complete his sentence:

> He is the one we proclaim, admonishing and teaching everyone with all wisdom, *so that* we may present everyone fully mature in Christ. *To this end* I strenuously contend with all the energy Christ so powerfully works in me. I want you to know how hard I am contending for you and for those at Laodicea, and for all who have not met me personally. *My goal is that* they may be encouraged in heart and united in love, *so that* they may have the full riches of complete understanding, *in order that* they may know the mystery of God, namely, Christ, in whom are hidden all the treasures of wisdom and

knowledge. I tell you this *so that* no one may deceive you by fine-sounding arguments. For though I am absent from you in body, I am present with you in spirit and delight to see how disciplined you are and how firm your faith in Christ is. (1:28 – 2:6)

Paul had a clear goal in mind, which was to present the Colossians, individually and corporately, as mature and loving Christians, and to prevent the false ideas that would hinder that. His purpose in preaching was not only that the Christians should understand the gospel and reject its rivals (there is again a strong emphasis on the effect of his teaching on the Christian's mind here), but that it would be lived out as his 'body, the church' (Col. 1:18). The second half of Colossians is an extended application of this idea, worked out in every area of life.

So the purpose of preaching is the same as the purpose of the church, which is the same as the purpose of salvation, which is the same as the purpose of creation itself: to bring God glory by helping people to become more like Jesus.[3]

Sometimes preaching, even wonderfully rich, biblically sourced preaching, falls at this hurdle. People come, perhaps in large numbers, and go away again, much better informed but little changed. And even if they are changed, it is only at an individual level. Remember that Paul said his two goals were maturity and unity, and both of those are corporate activities. Preaching sells itself short if it thinks its task is to communicate information, or even transformation, into single lives. The proper step is to work at relationships within the body, and that has to be done together. At that point the taught Christians snap their notebooks shut, turn to each other, and ask what they are going to do about that morning's sermon, together.

So, preachers, why do you preach? What is the end you have in mind when you start your preparation? How do you intend to bring God glory? Is it by explaining a Bible passage with clarity, depth and force? Or is it by aiming to produce Christlike maturity and unity among the members of the church? And if you agree that it is the latter, how, in detail, will your next sermon achieve this?

Questions for reflection and discussion

How does Chris Green answer these questions?

- Why did God make us?
- Why has God saved us?

---

3. See chapters 20 and 21 below, on applying to one another and applying to the church.

- Why does God speak to us?
- How does the church bring God glory?
- How does preaching bring God glory?
- How does Chris Green suggest they are connected?

3. GETTING THE SERMON OFF THE MOUNT

Anyone who loves me will obey my teaching.

(John 14:23)

Making the Bible irrelevant

One thought that produces common agreement among many effective preachers is that the Bible does not need to be updated in order to be contemporary. As God's permanent word to his people it has a living force. So the megachurch pastor Rick Warren says, 'We don't have to make the Bible relevant. It is!'[1] Reformed theologian Sidney Greidanus, reflecting on years of thinking about the theology of preaching, says, 'The Word need not be *made* relevant because it *is* relevant.'[2] The Australian preacher and church planter Phillip Jensen says, 'The Bible does not need to be made relevant . . . The Bible is relevant because it addresses us, as we are, about the problems that most desperately plague us, and provides God's own remedy for our maladies.'[3]

---

1. In an interview with Michael Duduit for *Preaching* magazine, Sept. 2001 (http://www.preaching.com/resources/articles/11565775/page-4).

2. Sidney Greidanus, *Sola Scriptura: Problems and Principles in Preaching Historical Texts* (Toronto: Wedge, 1970), p. 23, italics his.

3. Phillip D. Jensen and Paul Grimmond, *The Archer and the Arrow* (Kingsford: Matthias Media, 2010), p. 95.

So what was going wrong in my sermon on that summer evening? Each of those authors is right, in the sense that the Bible is God's agenda for his church. It ensures that his identification of our problems is central, as are his analysis and solutions. I do not need to find out where people itch and then scratch it – I need to identify where God says they ought to itch, and get under their skin until they do, as Warren, Greidanus and Jensen do when they preach. We can call that the Bible's 'objective relevance', something it has in its very nature as God's Word, which it can never lose.

My problem on that warm Sunday evening was that in assuming the Bible's relevance I had begun to act as if I had no responsibility to show or explain its relevance, and as if it were automatically the case that people should grasp its significance. There is a little loophole for lazy or self-important preachers here that would allow me to preach a stodgy, theoretical sermon, and then if people were turned off by it, to assume no responsibility. After all, 'If the Bible is relevant, it must be relevant for you to know the things I have just told you.' There is an important gap between saying that the Bible is relevant, and saying that my sermon is relevant.

We can call this the Bible's 'subjective relevance', which is apparent when we are gripped by the meaning of God's Word for us here and now. When it happens, the preacher almost disappears, and we know that we have met with the speaking God.

No preacher can make that happen – it is God's sovereign prerogative. And in an absolute sense no preacher can stop the sovereign God speaking. But the careful interrelationship between God's sovereignty and our responsibility emerges here as well as in other areas,[4] because unless we are fatalistic and say we have no delegated responsibility at all, for anything, there must be a sense that we *can* make God's Word *appear* confusing, abstract and irrelevant. That is within the preacher's responsibility.

Obviously, we can do that by our words. There was once a famous cartoon of an earnest preacher declaiming to a bored congregation, 'I know what you're thinking. Sabellianism!' The cartoonist may have thought that Sabellianism is such an obscure irrelevance that it was a suitable butt for his joke, but he actually captured our dilemma better than he knew. Because quite possibly the preacher was right. Sabellianism is in reality a deadly heresy that collapses the three members of the Trinity into one being, with bizarre results such as Jesus praying to no one, the Father dying on the cross, and other nonsense. We end up not

---

4. D. A. Carson, *Divine Sovereignty and Human Responsibility: Biblical Perspectives in Tension* (Grand Rapids: Zondervan, 1994).

being saved. Perhaps the preacher had identified the error in a popular book or hymn the congregation loved, or he had been rightly stressing God's unity and was fearful of being misunderstood. A Sabellian understanding of the gospel is wrong, and the early church was right to condemn the error.

Now I'm as earnest as the poor preacher in the cartoon! But you see the problem: my communicator's task, if I have identified this wicked heresy, is to make it so transparently, unmissably clear that the congregation is ahead of me, and almost joins the dots for themselves. The cartoonist's point is that what was actually transparently, unmissably clear was that the preacher had woefully failed in that task. And although the cartoonist was not making this point, it is also clear that the evil lie of Sabellianism was unrebuked in the minds of that congregation.[5]

So first, we must work at being understandable, and it is the preacher's (not the hearers') job to do that work. In Corinth Paul was dealing with a church embedded in a culture that valued fancy oratory. One tradition of public speaking, or rhetoric, was basically concerned with the truth of the message and the genuineness of the speaker,[6] but another rhetorical style was more interested in the flamboyance of speech.[7] Crowds would applaud the clever phrases, and criminals would be let off because the defending lawyer had a better command of language. It is in that context that Paul faced a disappointed Corinthian congregation, let down by his simplicity. Many were rating him poorly compared to some fancy communicators elsewhere in town. So Paul defended himself: 'I do not think I am in the least inferior to those "super apostles". I may indeed be untrained as a speaker, but I do have knowledge' – knowledge of the cross, he means (2 Cor. 11:5–6). Earlier in the letter he had put it even more starkly for them:

> Therefore, since through God's mercy we have this ministry, we do not lose heart. Rather, we have renounced secret and shameful ways; we do not use deception, nor do we distort the word of God. On the contrary, *by setting forth the truth plainly* we commend ourselves to everyone's conscience in the sight of God. And even if our gospel is veiled, it is veiled to those who are perishing. The god of this age has

---

5. On Sabellianism and other heresies, see C. FitzSimons Allison, *The Cruelty of Heresy* (London: SPCK, 1994).

6. See Aristotle, *The Art of Rhetoric* (London: Penguin, 1991); Quintilian, *The Orator's Education*, Books 3–5 (Cambridge, Mass.: Harvard University Press, 2001).

7. Cicero, whose mature thought is in 'On the Orator (1)', in Cicero, *On the Good Life* (London: Penguin, 1971), pp. 236–336.

blinded the minds of unbelievers, so that they cannot see the light of the gospel that displays the glory of Christ, who is the image of God. (2 Cor. 4:1–4)

No one could deny that Paul was a formidable thinker with a wide grasp of God's Word and a brilliant use of language. Curiously, 2 Corinthians is one of the most rhetorically sophisticated letters he ever wrote, using irony throughout. But Paul's point is that this was not to make him look good. Instead, he bends every intellectual fibre to make the cross clear, even while he acknowledges that the battle is to be won by God, not him, and it is played out in the spiritual, not the mental, sphere.

But this goes deeper than words and concepts. Imagine I have laboured hard to find an explanation so that the congregation does indeed join the dots and corporately think, 'A-hah! Sabellianism!' They may go home thinking, 'What an interesting sermon today – I learned about the dangers of Sabellianism.' The critical moment, though, is what happens on Wednesday night at Bible study, when someone prays, 'Lord, we just thank you, Father, that you loved us so much, Father, and you died for us on the cross, Lord . . .' – would everybody say, 'Amen'? Or would someone have the courage to comment, 'Actually, Joe, that's what we heard about on Sunday . . .'?

My role as a preacher is to make the issue before us so clear that people can see its relevance, and use the information in their own lives, when they need it.

Paying attention to the Bible we read

The road used to have a speed limit of 40 miles per hour. I checked it later. I had driven down it safely for years. So on a busy Tuesday morning, when I was doing 39 miles per hour (because I am a law-abiding citizen, Rom. 13 and all that) I was first surprised, and then extremely irritated, to see a bright flash in my driving mirror and realize that I had been caught by a speed camera. This was the first time, which probably means it was the first time I had been caught, rather than the first time I had driven too fast, and so rather than facing court and a fine, I attended a day-long speed awareness course.

On the way back I made a detour, and revisited the road where I had been caught. It was littered with 30 miles per hour warning signs, speed camera warning signs, road markings, the camera itself was bright yellow – and from what I had learned that day even if all of those had been missing I should have been able to work it out from the presence of streetlights. I just had not noticed them.

Noticing – really noticing with care – is hard work. Take a look at what is called the Great Commission, in Matthew 28:18–20. What do you notice?

> Then the eleven disciples went to Galilee, to the mountain where Jesus had told them to go. When they saw him, they worshipped him; but some doubted. Then Jesus came to them and said, 'All authority in heaven and on earth has been given to me. Therefore go and make disciples of all nations, baptising them in the name of the Father and of the Son and of the Holy Spirit, and teaching them everything I have commanded you. And surely I am with you always, to the very end of the age.'

If you noticed nothing odd, find it in your own Bible and check. If you immediately noticed what I meant you to see, try Titus 1:10 – 2:1:

> For there are many rebellious people, full of meaningless talk and deception, especially those of the circumcision group. They must be silenced, because they are disrupting whole households by teaching things they ought not to teach – and that for the sake of dishonest gain. One of Crete's own prophets has said it: 'Cretans are always liars, evil brutes, lazy gluttons.' This saying is true. Therefore rebuke them sharply, so that they will be sound in the faith and will pay no attention to Jewish myths or to the merely human commands of those who reject the truth. To the pure, all things are pure, but to those who are corrupted and do not believe, nothing is pure. In fact, both their minds and consciences are corrupted. They claim to know God, but by their actions they deny him. They are detestable, disobedient and unfit for doing anything good. You, however, must teach sound doctrine.

Again, check against your own Bible. Or, how about Philippians 4:8–9:

> Finally, brothers and sisters, whatever is true, whatever is noble, whatever is right, whatever is pure, whatever is lovely, whatever is admirable – if anything is excellent or praiseworthy, whatever you have learned or received or heard from me, or seen in me – think about such things. And the God of peace will be with you.

Congratulations if you noticed what was wrong in that version in any of those three quotations, let alone all of them. One of the problems of becoming familiar with the Bible is that we tend to read it faster, and assume we know what it says. The result is that we *mis*read it. Because I work in a theological college I meet plenty of people struggling to learn Greek and Hebrew. As a half joke I say, 'I hope you don't get too good at it!' It's a joke because we will always need well-educated pastors and scholars, and I enjoy winding-up my language-teaching colleagues. But it is only half a joke, because there is a great advantage in struggling with the biblical languages in that it slows the reader right down, and you notice what previously you had sped by. I vividly remember the first time I limped through a translation exercise in Mark's Gospel, and came to Jesus' crucifixion: 'They crucified him.' It is only two words in Greek, brutal and stark. And compare the word 'crucified' (*staurousin*) with the word 'cross' (*stauros*). The physicality of Jesus' tortured death hit me with new force.

Slowing down to notice is a critical skill in reading the Bible properly. If you did not spot the mistakes in the passages I just quoted, Jesus actually said, 'teaching them to obey everything I have commanded you', Paul told the Philippians not just to think about his life and teachings but to put them 'into practice', and he told Titus to 'teach what is appropriate to sound doctrine'.[8] All three are explicit instructions to do what the Bible says.

Getting the Sermon off the Mount

Jesus' Sermon on the Mount stands at the opposite end of Matthew's Gospel to the Great Commission. When Jesus said, 'teaching them to obey everything I have commanded you', the disciples would have had this teaching as the bedrock. This is what people had to be taught to obey (not just taught, but taught 'to obey').

Henry Cloud and John Townsend look at the Sermon on the Mount with these lenses, and extract twenty-five clearly distinguishable instructions to obey from Jesus: some are directly actions to do or avoid, some are attitudes to God or to others, some are simply truths for us to remember, to guide us.[9] Twenty-five is a high number of commands to obey, and there is only one way to see if their sums are right. This will take several minutes, but take your Bible and a pen, and list the commands in the Sermon on the Mount that you notice.

Did you beat their target? If you tried, you would have discovered an important but easily missed point: there is a lot to do in the Sermon on the Mount. There is no need to be naive here, because there is plenty more in Matthew's Gospel that is truth aimed at understanding the gospel, and it would be wilful to take these chapters out of Matthew's overarching context, which is that everything leads to Jesus' cross and resurrection.

---

8. We will revisit Titus in chapter 9 below.

9. Henry Cloud and John Townsend, *How People Grow* (Grand Rapids: Zondervan, 2001), pp. 242–243.

Nevertheless, Jesus' conclusion is unmissable: 'Not everyone who says to me, "Lord, Lord," will enter the kingdom of heaven, but only the one who *does the will* of my Father who is in heaven' (Matt. 7:21). In case any reader does miss the unmissable, Jesus repeats it:

> Therefore everyone who hears these words of mine *and puts them into practice* is like a wise man who built his house on the rock. The rain came down, the streams rose, and the winds blew and beat against that house; yet it did not fall, because it had its foundation on the rock. But everyone who hears these words of mine and *does not put them into practice* is like a foolish man who built his house on sand. The rain came down, the streams rose, and the winds blew and beat against that house, and it fell with a great crash. (Matt. 7:24–27)

This sermon produced a change in people's view of Jesus. Matthew says, 'When Jesus had finished saying these things, the crowds were amazed at his teaching, because he taught as one who had authority, and not as their teachers of the law' (Matt. 7:28–29). But how would Jesus have known if hearers actually recognized his authority, unless they went away, got off the Mount, and changed their lives on the basis of what they had just heard? By the end of his book Matthew will have shown that Jesus' authority is indeed greater than that of the teachers of the law, because he has 'all authority in heaven and on earth' (Matt. 28:18). But there, as here, Jesus exercises that authority by requiring obedience to his words, to 'everything I have commanded you'. However, is that even possible?

Not WWJD but WHJD, and WDJS

The little question 'What Would Jesus Do?', shortened to WWJD, is a marketer's dream. Printed on bracelets, mugs and T-shirts, it is a simple way of remembering that Jesus is our moral guide and example.

Except that he is not. The honest answer to 'What Would Jesus Do?' in a given situation is that, unlike me, he would be perfect. He would sinlessly know whether to affirm or rebuke, how to align love and truth, when to scandalize by his love of sinners, or scandalize by his hatred of sin. He would know when to sit in the gutter with a prostitute and when to make his standards so high that a good person would weep.

The right reaction to trying to do what Jesus did is to collapse in despair at its impossibility. Not try harder – that makes him just a little bit better than us. No, despair.

It has been said that the gospel can be summarized in two words. It is a universal rule that every religion, philosophy, political platform or economic theory has one of them in common: *do* or *don't do* – it is the same principle. They are all about what we have to do. And my worry about the WWJD slogan is that it falls into the same trap. What would Jesus *do*, and so what must I *do*?

We will look at this in much more detail further on because it will arise every time we preach, but we must establish at the outset that that is not how the gospel works. Proper biblical Christianity is the only exception to that universal rule. The issue is not what must I *do*, but what has Jesus *done*? WHJD? He has died for my sins, my failure to keep his standards. He has removed the despair that his infinitely perfect standards have placed in me, as I have seen the depths of my rebellion against a holy God. He has done what I could never do: he has replaced my rebellion with his righteousness; he has judged me to be perfect.

Phew! So is the Sermon on the Mount just to show me my sin, and then as a forgiven sinner I can forget about obedience? Not at all. Jesus continually insists on our obedient attitude to him. Later in Matthew he says, 'For whoever does the will of my Father in heaven is my brother and sister and mother' (Matt. 12:50). In Mark he says, 'Whoever wants to be my disciple must deny themselves and take up their cross and follow me' (Mark 8:34). In Luke he says, 'Blessed rather are those who hear the word of God and obey it' (Luke 11:28), and after the parable of the good Samaritan, Jesus says, 'Go and do likewise' (Luke 10:37). In John he says, 'Now that you know these things, you will be blessed if you do them' (John 13:17). And, 'Anyone who loves me will obey my teaching. My Father will love them, and we will come to them and make our home with them. Anyone who does not love me will not obey my teaching' (John 14:23–24).

Jesus insists that we do what he says. In other words, the necessary partner to WHJD is WDJS – What Did Jesus Say? Or, as he puts the question, 'Why do you call me, "Lord, Lord," and do not do what I say?' (Luke 6:46).

The face in the mirror

Jesus' insistence that attention to obedience is a central aspect of discipleship was insisted on by his followers too. We have already seen that emphasis in both Peter and Paul, but other New Testament writers share it. Here is John in his first letter:

> We know that we have come to know him if we *keep his commands*. (1 John 2:3)

The world and its desires pass away, but whoever *does the will of God* lives for ever. (1 John 2:17)

Dear children, let us not love with words or speech but *with actions and in truth*. (1 John 3:18–19)

And in his second letter:

And this is love: that we *walk in obedience* to his commands. (2 John 6)

And in his third:

I have no greater joy than to hear that my children are *walking in the truth*. (3 John 4)

John is a famously allusive writer, whose themes interlock and develop in concert, and it is clear that for him, love, truth and obedience are necessary partners, summed up in his repeated image of 'walking'. So faced with a Christian who claimed to love truth, spending time in hours of study, but did not practically love people, John would say that that Christian did not actually love truth.

There are two obvious implications from John for today's preachers. First, if our preaching content and style encourage people to love truth, but do not equally encourage them to love obedience, we have not in fact encouraged them to love truth. What is even more worrying, if our personal pattern of ministry fits this as well, and we start to use study as an excuse to get away from people, then we are not loving truth either. There is a fine line between loving people so much that we spend hours in the study in order to feed them, and loving our study so much that we avoid people. Some preachers seem only to live in two places: the pulpit and the library, and both are solitary places – potentially quite selfish places.

James is the last writer to consider here, and he is notoriously blunt:

What good is it, my brothers and sisters, if someone claims to have faith but has no deeds? Can such faith save them? (Jas 2:14)

If anyone, then, knows the good they ought to do and doesn't do it, it is sin for them. (Jas 4:17)

A third verse is not only equally direct, but shows us that the problem lies in our attitude to the Bible:

Do not merely listen to the word, and so deceive yourselves. Do what it says. Anyone who listens to the word but does not do what it says is like someone who looks at his face in a mirror and, after looking at himself, goes away and immediately forgets what he looks like. But whoever looks intently into the perfect law that gives freedom and continues in it – not forgetting what they have heard but doing it – they will be blessed in what they do. (Jas 1:22–25)

So what is the right attitude to the Bible? First, says James, we need to 'look'. He underlines it, because he describes a person who 'looks intently' into the word. Secondly, we need to remember. Sometimes it is the press of our busy lives that makes us forget what the Bible says, and at other times we choose to forget it when it is inconvenient, but James says the Bible will be useful only if, 'not forgetting' what it says, we bring it to mind. And then thirdly, we need to put it into practice by 'doing it'. Look, remember, do. It is a simple but effective strategy.

Again, this addresses today's preachers. Lots of us work very hard at getting our hearers to look. Bibles are opened and referred to, passages printed out with relevant words underlined – many churches are quite deliberate at getting people to look intently. That is good. But are your sermons equally deliberate at helping people to remember? And are they equally deliberate at helping people to 'do'?

Let me be blunt. If you have been persuaded by James that the right pattern for approaching the Bible is to look, remember and do, what are *you* going to do about it? If your next sermon is unchanged by James's teaching, what is the consequence? At the best, we are colluding in people's sin, but at the worst we ourselves are sinning. 'If anyone, then, knows the good they ought to do and doesn't do it, it is sin for them' (Jas 4:17).

Questions for reflection and discussion

- Chris Green distinguished between the 'objective' and the 'subjective' relevance of the Bible. Why does he make that distinction?
- What were the three missing phrases in the passages he misquoted?
- Go through the Sermon on the Mount in your own Bible, highlighting all the commands to obey.
- Chris Green highlighted the sequence 'look, remember, do' from James. If you are a preacher, how much time do you spend focusing on each of those three elements? What do you think is, or should be, the most important?

4. WHO IS THE BIBLE ABOUT?

> Everything must be fulfilled that is written about me.
>
> (Luke 24:44)

The Bible is not a book about us

A pastor friend was on an extended sabbatical, during which he visited a number of churches and heard a number of sermons. Towards the end of his time he was taken out for a meal by the man in charge of a seminary, responsible for training hundreds of future pastors. The man leaned back in his chair and said, 'So, Paul, from all your visits and what you've heard, what should I be telling my students?'

Paul looked back at him and took a deep breath. 'I think', he said, 'that you should tell your students that the Bible is not a book about them.'

From what we saw in the last chapter that should be a shocking observation to have to make. We are not the hero of the Bible. God is, and it is his glory, not ours, that is his concern:

> Not to us, LORD, not to us
> > but to your name be the glory,
> > because of your love and faithfulness.
> (Ps. 115:1)

The Bible is the record of God's acts, his promises, his warnings and his blessings. He is the centre of every story, and even when there are eras or books where he is not met by name, the Bible authors are careful to hint that his controlling presence is guiding every step.

But yet, however shocking Paul's observation is, it is also easily recognizable as a problem. My life feels to me like a story in that, even if I am not the hero, I am centre stage all the time. So when I open my Bible, I naturally expect to find my life addressed, my questions answered and my hurts comforted. (As we will see, they are, although not necessarily in the way we expect.) The obvious temptation, though, is that if I start with the priority of my questions, hurts and needs, I run the risk of being blind to God's questions, his assumptions, arguments and values. Human beings, having rebelled against God, put themselves on the throne instead. And even when we place our trust in Christ, our daily experience is that our sinful hearts keep trying to put ourselves back on that throne again. God insists that he comes first; I have a vested interest in making sure that I come first. So I read the Bible as a book about me, and relegate God to the margins.

It is a widespread issue. The missionary and theologian Lesslie Newbigin returned to the UK after years overseas, and made this poignant observation:

> I suddenly saw that someone could use all the language of evangelical Christianity, and yet the centre was fundamentally the self, my need of salvation. And God is auxiliary to that . . . I also saw that quite a lot of evangelical Christianity can easily slip, can become centred on me and my need of salvation and not in the glory of God.[1]

We are all like the self-obsessed man at the party who at last gives way to the people he has been boring, 'But enough about me – let's talk about you. What do you think about me?'

Those of us who are pastors find ourselves in an even more insidious trap. Not only do we share the habit of reading the Bible as a book about me, but we speak to churches that also share that expectation. So quite understandably we fear that unless we name and address those questions and issues each time we speak, people will simply tune us out, and all the other things on their 'to do' list will flood their brains instead.

Of course if we are wise pastors and wise Christians, we see this danger coming. Since every sinful generation is self-obsessed, it goes with the job of the preacher to know that we have to force people to stop looking at the Bible as a mirror, and to see it as the doorway through which we meet God. At some

---

1. Quoted in Tim Stafford, 'God's Missionary to Us', *Christianity Today* 40.4 (9 Dec. 1996), p. 29.

point we have to say, 'Your questions are interesting, and God has answers to them – but he has questions to ask you too, and if you don't listen to them you'll miss him.'

So my friend Paul was quite right – I must remember that the Bible is not a book about me. But, curiously, it is not a book about God either.

The Bible is not a book about God

Does that shock you? There are lots of books that are about God sitting behind me as I write. There are dictionaries and encyclopedias, multivolume systematics and brief, intense monographs. They are a valuable resource, and I use them regularly. They are designed to give me information: true information, I hope, about God.

The Bible is different. Here is Moses' summary of the covenant God made with his people: 'The secret things belong to the LORD our God, but the things revealed belong to us and to our children for ever, that we may follow all the words of this law' (Deut. 29:29). Several consequences flow from that.

First, there are truths that have been 'revealed'. God has spoken, and explained himself, his character and his expectations. His unique ability to do that, flawlessly, even when he uses human language, is a wonderful reason to trust the Bible. Those dictionaries and encyclopedias are only ever partial collections, analyses and summaries of the Bible.

Secondly, there are other things that are 'secret'. This is in the context of a covenant with God, so Moses is not talking about future scientific discoveries or philosophical insights. These are secrets about God's relationships with people. Some of those would become clearer later, and it is a New Testament observation that with the coming of Christ some things have been made clear that were once mysteries (Eph. 3:1–13). But there are still many truths about God that have yet to be disclosed, and we will probably spend eternity delighting in them (Mark 13:32; 1 Cor. 13:12).

Thirdly, we can be sure that these 'secret things' will not be unpleasant surprises, or involve God's breaking his word. Moses said, 'The secret things belong to the LORD our God', and both the word 'LORD' (the covenant name of God) and the phrase 'our God' guarantee that what God has told us will be completely consistent with what he has not revealed, because the God who is hidden is the same covenant God as the one who rescued Israel and raised Jesus.

That is an important insight as we think about knowing God. He tells us from the outset that he will not tell us everything about himself, but also that we can rely on him to be consistent. There will be gaps in our knowledge, but there are no gaps in his. A fully written systematic theology of God would be infinite in content and take an eternity to read. But God guarantees us that our partial, finite understanding is still valid, to the extent that it is based on the Scriptures, which are completely reliable and fully adequate for our needs. Here is something we need to have for the dark times when life seems to turn to ash and God seems to have gone: it is possible to know God truly without knowing him completely. That the Bible does not answer all our questions does not mean that God has no answers, and about some of them we might even begin to make a biblically informed suggestion. Nor does it give us licence to think of the Bible as only one route to knowing God, or a flawed, human construct that is impossible to interpret reliably. God, in his infinite wisdom, is quite capable of making a finite book speak with complete truth about him.

So why then do I suggest the Bible is not a book about God? Compare it with those excellent dictionaries, encyclopedias, systematics and monographs. They give information, but that is all they do. They are designed to clear my thinking, and replace woolly ideas with better ones. But that is all they do. Compare that again with Moses' summary: 'The secret things belong to the Lord our God, but the things revealed belong to us and to our children for ever, that we may follow all the words of this law.' God spoke to and through Moses to draw people into an obedient, covenant relationship. *The proper purpose of the Bible is not simply transferring truth about God from him to us, but that through those truths we meet him, know him, love him and obey him.*[2] The Bible makes claims upon me in a way a dictionary does not. I cannot claim I have ever mastered it, in the way I might have mastered any other book. The Bible masters us, for it is God's voice to his people, always drawing us into a deeper and more intimate relationship. I enjoy reading classic fiction, and I remember coming to the end of a series of novels that had taken me a couple of years to read through. I had an enormous sense of triumph as I closed the final back cover. At last! I had done it! They could go on the shelf as finished! But I can never, ever do that with the Bible. Although the back cover gets closed and it is put back on the shelf, it is always with the expectation that it will be reopened, and that God will take us on in knowing him.[3]

---

2. See Scott Hafemann, 'The Covenant Relationship', in Scott Hafemann and Paul House (eds.), *Central Themes in Biblical Theology: Mapping Unity in Diversity* (Nottingham: Apollos, 2007), pp. 20–65.

3. I therefore agree that Scripture is fundamentally covenantal; see Timothy Ward, *Words of Life: Scripture as the Living and Active Word of God* (Nottingham: Inter-Varsity Press, 2009).

The Bible is not only a book about God's establishing a relationship with his people; it is the daily means he uses to achieve that, as he draws us to trust in the person and work of Jesus Christ.

'The Bible is a book about me!'

There is therefore one (and only one) exception to this rule that the Bible is not a book about me, and it is a foundational one. Here is Jesus' first recorded sermon, from Luke's Gospel, and notice the emphases:

> He went to Nazareth, where he had been brought up, and on the Sabbath day he went into the synagogue, as was his custom. He stood up to read, and the scroll of the prophet Isaiah was handed to him. Unrolling it, he found the place where it is written:
>
> > 'The Spirit of the Lord is on *me*,
> >   because he has anointed *me*
> >   to proclaim good news to the poor.
> > He has sent *me* to proclaim freedom for the prisoners
> >   and recovery of sight for the blind,
> > to set the oppressed free,
> >   to proclaim the year of the Lord's favour.'
>
> Then he rolled up the scroll, gave it back to the attendant and sat down. The eyes of everyone in the synagogue were fastened on him. He began by saying to them, 'Today this scripture is fulfilled in your hearing.' (Luke 4:16–21)

And here is Jesus' final sermon, again from Luke's Gospel:

> He said to them, 'This is what I told you while I was still with you: everything must be fulfilled that is written about *me* in the Law of Moses, the prophets and the psalms.'
> Then he opened their minds so they could understand the Scriptures. He told them, 'This is what is written: the Messiah will suffer and rise from the dead on the third day, and repentance for the forgiveness of sins will be preached in his name to all nations, beginning in Jerusalem. You are witnesses of these things. I am going to send you what my Father has promised; but stay in the city until you have been clothed with power from on high.' (Luke 24:44–49)

On both occasions Jesus says that the entirety of the Scriptures is about him. He is the only person in human history who looks in an all-embracing way at the whole of God's revelation, in detail and in sweep, and says, 'The Bible is a book about *me*!'

When we encourage each other to study the Bible carefully, we often say, 'Pay attention to the context! Context is king!' I encourage my students to look more closely at the text with the words 'A text without a context is a con!' But what Jesus explains here is that if he is the centre of the Bible, then everything in it must be understood in relation to him. The most fundamental way to ignore the context is to ignore Christ, because he is the deepest context. To open and apply the Bible without mentioning Christ is to take the whole Bible out of context. The king is the context.

This is not an occasion for balance. This is a real and stark choice: either the Bible's storyline is fundamentally about the person and work of Jesus Christ, or it is fundamentally about me. As we saw in a previous chapter, either he, his ways, his glory are centre stage, or I am. Either Jesus is the hero of the story, or it is about me. There are lots of times in life to want a both/and approach that allows both sides to win and keep their dignity intact; this is not one of them. The first challenge when we open the Bible is to realize that there is a fight to the death between our will to run our life and God's demand that he does. As believers, our sin has been paid for and we have already determined to live for God's glory – but we must live in line with that commitment every moment, because our wriggling, selfish, sinful nature is taking a long time to die, and where it can it will want to ease God off his throne.

But having made the right choice at that point, another door wonderfully and lovingly opens. We have seen that the Bible is a book about God in relationship with his people, and we have seen that the hero of that story is Jesus. But because the purpose of his work was to bring us back into a right relationship with God, if we think rightly about him we must end up thinking rightly about ourselves as well.

One Sunday a few years ago my wife and I had an evening off and went to a well-known church in London; we wanted to hear some great teaching, sing to a good band and meet some new people. The preacher was speaking from the story of Jesus' transfiguration (Mark 9:2–13), where God unveiled his heavenly glory in the presence of Moses and Elijah, and the preacher's three points went something like this:

1. Jesus went aside to pray, and therefore we should go aside to pray.
2. Jesus heard God speak to him when he prayed, and therefore we should expect to hear God speak to us when we pray.
3. Jesus saw evil spirits defeated when he prayed, and therefore we should expect revival to come when we pray.

I turned to Sharon and muttered, 'Does that mean I should expect Moses and Elijah to turn up in my quiet time?' It was a snarky comment I admit, and every preacher has bad days, but I think my question is still valid: On that preacher's template of how to read the story, what is wrong with my expectation of Moses and Elijah's appearance?

In thinking again about the story, make Jesus the hero. It is actually quite hard to think of a story in the Gospels that is more God soaked than this one, and less about us. It is as though Jesus ceases to modify his glory, as he and his Father gaze at each other with the intensity of love that they have for eternity. People fade away and Jesus is centre stage.

And then God speaks. But not to Jesus. 'This is my Son, whom I love. Listen to him' (Mark 9:7). So suddenly the first disciples, and then each generation of readers of Mark's Gospel, come on stage again. What has this strange story to do with me? God tells me that it is to insist that I 'listen' to Jesus. But we can go further.

About what should I listen to Jesus? My car insurance? My boss? In the context Jesus and the disciples have been having an argument. This section of Mark's Gospel contains three clear predictions about Jesus' death and resurrection, one in each of chapters 8, 9 and 10. Each one erupts in a row about who is in charge (8:32–33; 9:33; 10:41). So in the transfiguration it is as though God is taking sides. Peter has begun to 'rebuke' Jesus, and Jesus has 'rebuked' Peter, and so God speaks with unmissable clarity: Jesus is right about his death and resurrection, and therefore we should pay attention to him about that. If we think Peter is right, God rebukes us too – and that's how we end up in the story.

Sophisticated people who want to turn Jesus into a moral religious teacher find themselves rebuked by God. Sensitive types who think the cross is too barbaric for a contemporary faith find themselves rebuked. Muslims who think Jesus was one of the greatest prophets but did not die on a cross find themselves rebuked. Scientific listeners who can accept the idea of death but not of resurrection find themselves rebuked. Pastors who lead churches by bullying and force of personality find themselves rebuked. Do you see how it works? Because the Bible is a book about God in relationship with his people, and because Jesus is the hero of the story, if we gaze at him we will find ourselves addressed and the Bible becomes the most relevant book there is.

That is actually a necessary consequence of those two sermons Jesus preached about himself. Look again at the first one, but with a different emphasis:

> The Spirit of the Lord is on me,
>> because he has anointed me
>> to proclaim *good news to the poor*.

He has sent me to proclaim *freedom for the prisoners*
   and *recovery of sight for the blind,*
to *set the oppressed free,*
   to proclaim the year of the Lord's favour.
(Luke 4:16–21)

Is it about God? Yes. Is the hero Jesus? Yes. And because he is the kind of generous God he is, his heroic action and loving speech have a direct consequence for us. Take Jesus' final sermon, again with a different emphasis:

> Then he opened their minds so they could understand the Scriptures. He told them, 'This is what is written: the Messiah will suffer and rise from the dead on the third day, and *repentance* for the *forgiveness of sins* will be preached in his name to all nations, beginning at Jerusalem. You are witnesses of these things. I am going to send you what my Father has promised; but stay in the city until you have been clothed with power from on high.' (Luke 24:45–49)

Once again, if we rightly put the Lord Jesus as the hero, we find that the story has a direct relevance for us.

It's about Christ, and therefore it's about us

Jesus' great summary title *Christ*, or *Messiah*, is notoriously ambiguous. To those in the flow of biblical knowledge it means 'anointed one', and we think of the coronations of the biblical kings or the anointing of the priests. To those without the biblical data it means 'smeared one', and fitted a man who ended his life daubed in blood, spit and sweat. But what we need to see is the corporate nature of the elements of this title.

Famously, three principal groups were anointed with oil: prophets (Ps. 105:15; 1 Chr. 16:22), priests (Lev. 4:3, 5, 16; 16:15) and kings (e.g. Saul, 1 Sam. 9 – 10; David, 1 Sam. 16:1–13; Solomon, 1 Chr. 29:22; Ps. 2:1–6). Other groups and individuals were occasionally anointed, but these three seem to cluster the title 'Messiah' or 'Anointed one' with particular clarity. What happens to the title as it transfers to Christ himself is that the highest expectations of all three are summarized in him as one individual.

But those titles are not individualistic. The title 'prophet' implies people to speak to, even if they ignore him. The title 'priest' implies a people to sacrifice and pray for, and who need his intercession. The title 'king' implies a people to rule over, even if they rebel. Each of those three titles therefore requires us to think corporately and relationally, because we cannot think biblically about the Messiah without thinking of the Messiah's people.

An example: a psalm that is about Christ, and therefore about us

If taking the Bible out of Christ is to take it out of context, then we need to understand how the Bible fits together so that we can take any part through Christ to us. We will look more closely at that later, but for the moment, and as an example, consider Psalm 18:1–3:

> *I* love you, O Lord, *my* strength.
> The Lord is *my* rock, *my* fortress and *my* deliverer,
>   *my* God is *my* rock, in whom *I* take refuge,
>   *my* shield and the horn of *my* salvation, *my* stronghold.
> *I* called to the Lord, who is worthy of praise,
>   and *I* have been saved from *my* enemies.

At first sight that is a good candidate for a passage to be about 'me': I have italicized the first person, and it reads like a song of thanks and praise that any of us could take on our lips. Apart from that troubling last clause. When was that true of me? And if I have lived the exciting kind of life where there are stories like that I could tell about me, the next few verses (4–5) knock that on the head:

> The cords of death entangled me;
>   the torrents of destruction overwhelmed me.
> The cords of the grave coiled around me;
>   the snares of death confronted me.

And verses 20–21 are the final nail in the coffin:

> The Lord has dealt with me according to my righteousness;
>   according to the cleanness of my hands he has rewarded me.
> For I have kept the ways of the Lord;
>   I am not guilty of turning from my God.

That has never been true of me. To force myself out of the picture I need only to have glanced at the introduction: 'For the director of music. Of David the servant of the Lord. He sang to the Lord the words of this song when the

LORD delivered him from the hand of all his enemies and from the hand of Saul.' So this is King David reflecting on his experiences and seeing God's faithful hand keeping him safe. King David. Because the point here is that this is one of a number of such psalms that have a similar shape of the king in peril, possibly dying, and being rescued by God. And the New Testament consistently takes such psalms as anticipating Jesus in his role as king. So we are to catch the echo of this in the climax of Psalm 18. Imagine Jesus singing this (vv. 43–50):

> You have delivered me from the attacks of the people;
>> you have made me the head of nations.
> People I did not know now serve me,
>> foreigners cower before me;
>> as soon as they hear of me, they obey me.
> They all lose heart;
>> they come trembling from their strongholds.
>
> The LORD lives! Praise be to my Rock!
>> Exalted be God my Saviour!
> He is the God who avenges me,
>> who subdues nations under me,
>> who saves me from my enemies.
> You exalted me above my foes;
>> from a violent man you rescued me.
> Therefore I will praise you, LORD, among the nations;
>> I will sing the praises of your name.
>
> He gives his king great victories;
>> he shows unfailing love to his anointed,
>> to David and to his descendants for ever.

If the Bible is about me, I shake my head in puzzlement over passages like that. But instead, Jesus takes the book and says, 'No, it's all about *me*. Do you not see the story of how God rescued me from the enemies? Do you not see how he rewarded me for my righteousness? Do you not see the story of how God has installed me as his beloved anointed king for eternity?'

But we cannot leave it there, wonderful as that is. Because Jesus would then point out that I am in there too. I am one of the rebellious nations who now *serve* and *obey* him (v. 44). He would take me to his cross, where he was attacked and died, and show me how his righteousness answers my rebellion; he would take me to his throne and show how his empty tomb reveals God's vindication of him and therefore he is the eternal king for me. And he would encourage me to sing, carefully, and knowing I was taking his words on my lips:

The LORD lives! Praise be to my Rock!
Exalted be God my Saviour!

Sometimes biblical theology can become so dazzling as we discover Christ everywhere in the book about him that we forget why he is there. Some preachers even become uneasy about talking about us at all. Surely, they say, Christ and Christ alone must be the subject of our preaching. We must not preach about Elijah or David, Peter or Paul. It is hard to disagree with them, but we must in order to get our preaching fully biblical. Good biblical theology is not an alternative to applying the Bible. Graeme Goldsworthy is right to stress that *'There is no aspect of reality that is not involved in the person and work of Christ.'*[4] The glory of Christ is to lead us, as our prophet, priest and king, into a right relationship with our Father. It is hard to get this right, but in order for Christ to have his true glory we cannot leave ourselves out of the story. We have to show him as our saviour. Geerhardus Vos, one of the pioneers of good biblical theology once wrote that the 'all embracing slogan of the Reformed faith is this: the work of grace in the sinner as a mirror for the glory of God'.[5] Vos rightly calls this a 'Reformed' view because it goes back to Calvin. In his classic description of the offices of Christ as prophet, priest and king, Calvin carefully applies each one in turn, individually and corporately: 'Such is the nature of his rule, that he shares with us all that he has received from the Father. Now he arms and equips us with his power, adorns us with his beauty and magnificence, and enriches us with his wealth.'[6]

So it is rather alarming to discover that biblical theology can also become trite. The reason, typically, is that a younger preacher is given some tools that suddenly turn the vast mass of the biblical data into a coherent whole, and the excitement that follows means that every Old Testament sermon has the same

---

4. Graeme Goldsworthy, *Christ-Centred Biblical Theology* (Nottingham: Apollos, 2012), p. 186, italics his.
5. Geerhardus Vos, 'The Doctrine of the Covenant in Reformed Theology', in *Redemptive History and Biblical Interpretation: The Shorter Writings of Geerhardus Vos* (Phillipsburg: P&R, 1980), pp. 241–242.
6. J. Calvin, *Institutes of the Christian Religion*, tr. Ford Lewis Battles (Philadelphia: Westminster, 1975), vol. 1, p. 499.

shape as our young friend helicopters out of the dangers of a particular passage into the safety of the known framework. The inevitable result shrivels the biblical richness down into a short formula or pattern. What we need as an alternative is a biblical theology that is not only coherent and capable of being simplified, but encourages us to stay longer in the detail of the text to allow each verse to speak with its own contribution.

So the Bible is about us, after all

We saw earlier that the Bible deals in ultimates, and the ultimate ultimate is the glory of God. Everything is to be done for his glory. But unless we are wary, ultimates suck the oxygen from the air for everything else. So we must be careful to describe those ultimates properly. It would be possible, for instance, to describe God's passion for his own glory in a way that made him a selfish tyrant. That would not do, so we then redefine his glory in a way that is consistent with his generous and sacrificial love. That allows him to create a spectacular universe for us to live in and enjoy, for his glory.

The universe in that case is not an ultimate. If we studied it for its own sake without reference to God, it would become an alternative to him. But it is possible to study the universe for God's sake, and the word for the universe in that case is 'proximate' – something that is not ultimate, but is important in a sequence. And because the Bible talks about the universe, it talks about proximates as well as ultimates.

My next-door neighbour happens to be an astrophysicist and a Christian. I do not pretend to understand what his area of research is, although I know it is complex. He once mentioned that getting a human being to the moon was relatively straightforward, 'not rocket science' was his innocent phrase. Peter is a fascinating man, but I imagine that it would not be hard to make him feel guilty by confusing ultimates with proximates. 'Why are you wasting your time staring up that telescope?' I might say. 'Come inside and enjoy a Bible study on God's glory. That's much more important.' Of course it is more important, but God's glory has resulted in the stars and planets Peter sees, and that the Bible also actively encourages him to admire and understand. There is a time for Peter to gaze up his telescope. Something that is proximate can also be enjoyed, once we know what it is for.

Bible study is a good thing. The psalms describe God's Word as a precious, delightful thing to be adored and explored. Psalm 119, the longest psalm, is an extended exploration of the goodness of God's Word, and at one point it uses an unusual metaphor of sugary intensity (vv. 103–104):

How sweet are your words to my taste,
    sweeter than honey to my mouth!
I gain understanding from your precepts;
    therefore I hate every wrong path.

If you have ever been in a really good Bible study, heard a wonderful sermon or just had a deep private quiet time, you will understand what the writer means. There is a gorgeousness about God's Word that is hard to put into words, but it is just so wonderfully, self-evidently true that it is sweet. Several times God said directly to his spokesmen to 'eat' his words:

When your words came, I ate them;
    they were my joy and my heart's delight,
for I bear your name,
    Lord God Almighty.
(Jer. 15:16)

Then he said to me, 'Son of man, eat this scroll I am giving you and fill your stomach with it.' So I ate it, and it tasted as sweet as honey in my mouth. (Ezek. 3:3)

So I went to the angel and asked him to give me the little scroll. He said to me, 'Take it and eat it. It will turn your stomach sour, but "in your mouth it will be as sweet as honey."' (Rev. 10:9)[7]

Studying God's Word is good, sweet and delightful. It is enjoyable. But it is not the ultimate – God himself is. Ultimates have ends in themselves, but it is not the point of the Bible that we know the Bible better. Now obviously we tread carefully here, because the Bible is God's Word, and we treat it as his speech, but I was talking about studying God's Word: sermons, books, and so on. It is not the point of the Bible that we spend our lives in permanent Bible study. For me to keep neglecting being a husband and dad because I am reading the Bible is to miss the point of why I should be reading the Bible. I would be dazzled by a proximate. Look again at Psalm 119:104:

I gain understanding from your precepts;
    therefore I hate every wrong path.

---

7. It is striking that both Ezekiel and John eat messages of bitterness and judgment, but these still taste good to them because God's Word comes from a good God.

The goal of reading God's Word is that I might gain understanding of what God wants from me; I am to understand his rules for life (here it is 'precepts', but the psalm uses dozens of similar words) so that I can tell right from wrong. The goal is to understand God's intentions for me as a Christ-centred husband and dad, and live accordingly, and in that way I bring him glory.

Lessons

So here are some lessons preachers need to take to heart, and that we will need to take further.

First, Jesus is the hero of the Bible story, and he will not allow us to displace him. He is the saviour of every saint throughout covenant history. But our unnatural sinful selfishness will constantly want to find another prophet, priest or king, and often we will try to meet our own idolatrous cravings in this regard. Sermons that give ten points on how to improve your marriage, but do not relate them to Christ, have not preached Christ and therefore have not preached the gospel. We will need to return to this.

Secondly, the gospel relates to every area of life, not just to itself in a narrow sense. I cannot meet Christ in his Word without his making some claim on me, and because he is Lord of the cosmos his claims must cover every area of my life. That means it is quite legitimate for a church to hear a sermon that contains ten points on how to improve our marriages, because the way we relate as husband and wife is an explicit visual expression of the gospel of Christ (Eph. 5:22–33). Ten points that relate the self-sacrificial love of Christ to my roles at home are profoundly relevant and Christ-exalting. I become more like Christ as I seek to apply such a sermon to myself. We do not need to choose.

Thirdly, because such preaching always relates the grit of life to the gospel, it will always be relevant to both Christians and non-Christians, seekers and found. Christians never get beyond the need to hear the gospel, because we never get beyond our ability to forget it when this suits us. Non-Christians need the gospel, but they do not think they do. Sometimes it is because of their sinful blindness, but often it is because we have wrapped it up in such a small space that they cannot see its relevance.

And fourthly, because God's Word always makes a claim upon us and never leaves us as it finds us, it follows that the gospel is always about change, and proper preaching must address the need for every Christian to grow in Christlikeness.

Questions for reflection and discussion

- Why might we be keen to think that the Bible is about us?
- Why might we be keen to think that the Bible is about God?
- What are the principal problems those assumptions might produce? Can you think of some examples of sermons you have heard, or preached, that fell into either error?
- What does Chris Green mean when he says, 'The most fundamental way to ignore the context is to ignore Christ'?
- Try to come up with a better sermon outline for the story of Jesus' transfiguration.
- What does Chris Green mean when he says, 'The Bible is about Christ, and therefore about us'?

PART 2

HOW IS THE BIBLE SUPPOSED
TO BE RELEVANT?

5. FALSE CHOICES

> I want you to recall the words spoken in the past by the holy prophets and the command given by our Lord and Saviour through your apostles.
>
> (2 Peter 3:2)

So the Bible is a book about God in relationship with his people; and because Jesus Christ is the hero of the story, if we gaze at him we will find ourselves addressed. Every biblical theme constantly encourages us to relate the grit of life to the gospel. But we need to develop a model to make sure that 'grit' and 'gospel' fit together properly, because history shows us how fatally easy it is to make a terrible mistake at this point, and for what are apparently good, God-honouring reasons. In particular, preachers become so passionate about one element that they start to dismiss the other. Consider two true examples.

Poisoning the well in the public square

The enormous church was packed every week, and the preacher was passionate. His sermons were relevant and life-changing, and they were reprinted and circulated around the world. Key people from business and politics backed him. He influenced a city, a nation and a generation. Dr Martin Luther King identified him as 'the greatest preacher of this century' because of the latter's influence in promoting the Civil Rights movement – so if we want to raise a question mark against this preacher, that only shows how difficult relating 'grit' to 'gospel' can be.[1]

The preacher's name was Harry Emerson Fosdick, and he preached a message to New York in the 1920s and 1930s that was radically different from orthodox Christianity. He has left us a poisonous legacy.

Fosdick was passionate about reaching the lost people of his day, both cultured and secular. He wanted to do so by talking about what was relevant to them, but his passion combined a message of social relevance on issues such as race and alcohol abuse with a new theological model for addressing them. It called itself the 'social gospel', and although Fosdick did not invent the title, he certainly popularized it.[2] Rather than use the language of classical theology, which Fosdick thought was both outdated and wrong, he head-lined 'The Kingdom of God' and 'Justice', and treated the Old Testament as virtually pagan. Instead, he was an early advocate of psychiatry and pastoral counselling for Christian preachers. He took on what we now call 'evangelicals' in a bitter battle, with a deliberate piece of targeted journalism, dressed up as a sermon called 'Shall the Fundamentalists Win?', and the resultant row led to his being built an even larger building, Riverside Church, to hold a growing congregation. Orthodoxy became something for him to oppose, in the name of relevance.

The dilemmas he faced are still with us – will today's non-Christians listen to, or even understand, us? Can we answer their questions and address their needs? Are there new models of ministry better suited to a new day? But in addressing the problems of his time, Fosdick tied his passion for relevance and his championing of justice (using biblical terms to describe them) to an unorthodox and unbiblical message, and so he poisoned the well. The funda-mentalists he despised quickly identified any form of political or social engagement as a social gospel, and therefore spiritually toxic. As if it were a landscape wasted by an industrial accident, most evangelicals fled the public debates and emptied the public square, with a residual fear that anyone who remained might be on the way to losing the gospel. And precisely because it was the most theologically orthodox who fled, it was the least orthodox, the ones most likely to cause the traditional gospel to be lost, who remained. It became a self-fulfilling prophecy.

---

1. Martin Luther King, *Papers Volume IV: Symbol of a Movement, January 1957–December 1958*, 2nd ed. (Berkeley: University of California Press, 2000), p. 536.

2. The formative theologian was Walter Rauschenbusch, in his *A Theology for the Social Gospel* (New York: Abingdon, 1917).

Only rarely, and with trembling, have evangelicals picked up the issue of social justice as one they should properly address.[3] In some circles the issues are still so polluted by the traces of Fosdick's theology that anyone who addresses the issues of 'justice', 'inclusiveness' or 'poverty' is automatically thought to be making a political statement based on an unbiblical theology.

Fosdick's irrelevant Bible

The fear of being a Fosdick is a right one, because he put his finger on a proper problem even though he reached a dangerously wrong conclusion. Fosdick famously mocked the irrelevance of much orthodox preaching, stating that people 'do not come to church with a burning interest in what happened to the Jebusites, but with their own questions and problems'.[4] And of course he is right. By and large, and however much we regret it, people do not come to church wanting to learn about the Jebusites. And their questions and problems, some trivial and some tragic, do dominate their thinking.

Fosdick understood the people, but he misunderstood the Bible. He had not understood that the Bible is the means God uses to address real people, to answer their questions and pose God's, and reorient their needs to what they should desire; and therefore God's words must be relevant. Consider those Jebusites Fosdick dismissed. They were one of the seven tribes who occupied the land God gave to Israel, and who were forcibly and bloodily engaged (Josh. 10:1–3), and whose continual presence in the land was a source of temptation for the new people of Israel (Josh. 15:63). In an aggressively secular context such as ours the Jebusites therefore raise questions of apologetics, morality and politics, such as the following:

- How can a good God condone ethnic cleansing?
- Are the moral values of the Bible tolerable?
- Is the Old Testament worthy of any ethical respect?
- Isn't this history written by the winners to justify their war?
- Does this justify the practices of the modern state of Israel?

---

3. See James Davis Hunter, *To Change the World: The Irony, Tragedy and Possibility of Christianity in the Late Modern World* (Oxford: Oxford University Press, 2010).

4. Harry Emerson Fosdick, 'What Is the Matter with Preaching?', *Harper's Magazine* 157.2 (July 1928), p. 135.

Put it like that, and Fosdick becomes clearly wrong. Those are questions almost continually raised in today's newspapers, websites and books, and will be troubling many thinking people in any congregation and its fringes. Such may not have learned how to find the answer; but, looked at this way, it is hard to think of a more dangerously relevant group than the Jebusites!

Our challenge, then, is to demonstrate the truthfulness and rightness of God's actions in the Bible, but answering those thoughtful questions will take us into issues of justice, law, ethics and politics today, the very areas where Fosdick's wrong theology had been thought to leave toxins in the air.

The irrelevant world

Across the Atlantic, and back in Europe, the opposite theological battle was being fought. Walter Rauschenbusch and Harry Fosdick had assumed the rightness of much nineteenth-century biblical scholarship, which had undermined academic respectability for theological orthodoxy and created a new form of theology, often calling itself 'liberal' theology. But the Swiss theologian Karl Barth had instead roared a defiant 'No!' at any such views, however innocent they appeared and created a passionate move for a new theological orthodoxy.

Barth's fundamental position is that God must be allowed to be God, on his own, ultimate terms, and Christian theology has as its only concern what God has said about himself. His work is enormous and elusive, and it is easy to become lost in a cascade of ideas that are often portrayed in ambiguous and antithetical ways. Yet because he resisted that liberal theology so fiercely, generations of theological students who found themselves facing those same theological dangers have reached for his massive certainties and shelter. But a closer examination shows that they are not as certain, nor as safe, as they look.

For our purposes we will focus only on his short book *Homiletics*, which is the fuller version of lectures he gave in various places on the issue of preaching.[5]

Barth was notoriously difficult to pin down on the exact nature of the Bible, and he certainly would not identify with any recognizable evangelical view of Scripture today.[6] That puts a significant, if hairline, crack between Barth's

---

5. Karl Barth, *Homiletics* (Louisville: Westminster/John Knox, 1991).

6. For a summary and response to Barth's position on Scripture, see Mark D. Thompson, 'Witness to the Word: On Barth's Doctrine of Scripture', in David Gibson and Daniel Strange (eds.), *Engaging with Barth: Contemporary Evangelical Critiques* (Nottingham: Apollos, 2008), pp. 168–197.

view and ours. But Barth's wider stand is firm, unequivocal and attractively the opposite of Fosdick's: according to Barth, all we do is point to the Bible. 'Two things call for emphasis. First, God is the one who works, and secondly, we humans must try to point to what is said in scripture. There is no third thing.'[7]

What might be 'a third thing'? Well, here Barth is talking about the implications of a Bible passage for a congregation, and seems to deny even the possibility of relevant application:

> It is dangerous even to address a specific congregational situation or experience in terms of a specific text. In such situations we must bring the Bible as a whole to bear. Then God might perhaps legitimately speak to the situation and work a miracle. But we may not count on this. The pastor might easily become the pope of his congregation, presenting his own idea instead of God's Word.[8]

Again, can we seek biblical wisdom on particular issues facing us? No, it 'is not good church practice to single out special church events or commemorations'.[9]

He addresses whether we should try to make connections with the culture:

> What does it mean to 'apply' a text? What does it mean to *witness* to people today on the basis of a text? At all events it does not mean adducing quotations from the newspaper with more or less relevant contents, or merely alluding to them with the aid of catchwords ... Association with external thoughts of this kind often results in the listeners wandering off on thoughts of their own. Especially unhelpful is the method of seasoning a sermon with all kinds of illustrations. In no circumstances should we hunt around for these![10]

Now Barth does not mean that we simply declare our message into dead space. We are supposed to expect what he calls 'a responsive echo' in the believer.[11] But such is Barth's fear that we or the world set an agenda rather than God's doing so, that he puts the contrast in the most extreme terms. Consider this:

---

7. Barth, *Homiletics*, p. 45.
8. Ibid., p. 50.
9. Ibid., p. 95.
10. Ibid., p. 117.
11. Ibid., p. 111.

In my parish work in Switzerland I often fell into this danger of misunderstanding how preaching is to be congregational. In 1912, when the sinking of the *Titanic* shocked the world, the next Sunday I had to make this disaster the major theme of my sermon, and a monster of a full-scale *Titanic* sermon resulted. Again in 1914, when the outbreak of war left the whole world breathless, I felt obliged to let this war rage on in all my sermons until finally a woman came up to me and begged for once to talk about something else and not constantly about this terrible conflict. She was right! I had disgracefully forgotten the importance of submission to the text.[12]

Well, if he were preaching about the war every week I suppose she had a point. But could he really have meant that he regretted ever mentioning it, or the sinking of the *Titanic*?

In his life outside the pulpit Barth took quite a different approach. He bravely resisted both world wars, and was a fierce opponent of Hitler. That, surely, should have been addressed before and to the church, weekly if necessary.[13] Much later in life he advised preachers to read both the Bible and a newspaper, but to read the news in the light of God's Word.[14] Perhaps he modified over time.

From the opposite side to Fosdick, Barth has also raised a good question but given the wrong answer. Of course God is the Lord, and his concerns and questions alone have the right to set the terms of what we preach. No one holds God to account or finds him wanting.

But when we listen to what he says, we find it speaks into and about our world, under his lordship. It affects whether I should be a member of the Nazi party, or whether the church could display a swastika. Or tolerate racism, pornography or financial exploitation. If Fosdick makes the Bible irrelevant, Barth makes the world irrelevant. In the next section we will see how evangelicals have tried to find a third way through the dilemma of identifying proper relevance.

Questions for reflection and discussion

- Have you seen examples of preaching that make God's world seem irrelevant? Why do you think that happens for apparently good reasons?
- Can you identify any traces of that in your own preaching?

---

12. Ibid., p. 118.

13. See Daniel Doriani, *Putting the Truth to Work: The Theory and Practice of Biblical Application* (Phillipsburg: P&R, 2001), p. 264, n. 7.

14. 'Barth in Retirement', *Time*, 31 May 1963, pp. 35–36.

- Have you seen examples of preaching that make God's Word seem irrelevant? Why do you think that happens for apparently good reasons?
- Can you identify any traces of that in your own preaching?
- Why do you think Barth regretted preaching on the sinking of the *Titanic*? Was he right to do it, or to regret it?

6. THE DANGER OF BALANCE

Paul's letters contain some things that are hard to understand, which ignorant and unstable people distort, as they do the other Scriptures, to their own destruction.

(2 Peter 3:16)

Perhaps the pre-eminent evangelical preacher and scholar of the last century was John Stott. Both in his example, and in his writing about his method, he laid out what has become the standard pattern for biblical exposition in significant parts of the church in the twenty-first century. One book in particular, published in the UK as *I Believe in Preaching* and elsewhere as *Between Two Worlds*, has become such a widely used handbook that his way of describing the challenge of biblical preaching has become the norm.

Stott recounts a seminal conversation with some bright undergraduate students while he was conducting a university mission:

'What we want to know,' they went on, 'is not whether Christianity is true, but whether it's relevant. And frankly we don't see how it can be. Christianity was born two millennia ago in a first-century Palestinian culture. What can the ancient religion of the Middle East say to us who live in the exciting, kaleidoscopic world of the end of the twentieth century?'[1]

For Stott that conversation crystallized the problem. He writes, 'The chasm is the deep rift between the biblical world and the modern world.'[2]

---

1. John R. W. Stott, *I Believe in Preaching* (London: Hodder & Stoughton, 1982), p. 138.
2. Ibid., p. 138.

Given this chasm, our task is daunting but clear: 'It is across this broad and deep divide of two thousand years of changing culture (more still in the case of the Old Testament) that Christian communicators have to throw bridges.'[3] We must learn to live in two worlds, and to speak two languages,[4] being both biblical and contemporary.

Since Stott wrote those words the issue is even more pressing. The inroads of cultural postmodernity mean that it is probably truer to talk of exciting, kaleidoscopic *worlds* (in the plural). There is a dazzling series of mutually inter-locking subcultures in the media marketplace. On the other hand, where Stott regrets that questions of relevance had eased out questions of truth, my evangelist and apologist friends tell me that the truth questions are strongly back in currency again, and without displacing personal relevance.

Continuing with the image of a bridge across a chasm, Stott describes a long history of bridge-building preachers, and then comes to the contemporary world. There are, he says, dangers associated with living at only one end of the bridge. 'On the one hand, conservatives are biblical but not contemporary, while on the other liberals and radicals are contemporary but not biblical.'[5] So the preacher's task is to walk across the bridge, addressing contemporary concerns with biblical truth, and bringing biblical truth to a contemporary expression. The preacher moves between the Word and the world.

We need to tease this out, because while I find it is stimulatingly helpful in a number of ways, the idea is also potentially, but subtly, damaging.

Stott is quite clear about the danger of the dominance of the contemporary side of the bridge, which is that 'we may find ourselves the servants rather of fashion than of God'.[6] Starting only with our questions will mean that God's questions, which are much more important, are rarely heard.

Stott is also quite clear on the danger for preachers in assuming the automatic understandability of the gospel message in a contemporary context. That is, he warns us not to lock ourselves in on the biblical side. One of the previous bridge builders Stott admires is Spurgeon, who says this:

> For instance, the great problems of sublapsarianism and supralapsarianism, the trenchant debates concerning the eternal filiation, the earnest dispute concerning the double procession, and the pre- and post-millenarian schemes, however important

---

3. Ibid.
4. Ibid., p. 149.
5. Ibid., p. 144.
6. Ibid., p. 139.

some deem them, are practically of very little concern to that godly woman, with seven children to support by her needle, who wants far more to hear of the loving-kindness of the God of providence than of these mysteries profound. I know a minister who is great upon the ten toes of the beast, the four faces of the cherubim, the mystical meaning of badgers' skins, and the typical bearings of the staves of the ark, and the windows of Solomon's temple: but the sins of business men, the temptations of the times, and the needs of the age, he scarcely ever touches upon.[7]

It would be a hard-hearted preacher who did not echo Spurgeon's concern. The need of the lost for the gospel, and our responsibility to get it to them, is a fire in our bellies. So the irrelevance of much of our Christian in-house chatter drives us to speak yet more freshly. Yet this desire for relevance has been a constant problem for evangelicals, because there is a justifiable concern that preachers who start to desire to be contemporary end up ceasing to be biblical.

The middle of the bridge?

Here is the dilemma – how can we agree with Spurgeon without agreeing with Fosdick? How can we be relevantly biblical, but avoid irrelevant biblicism? Perhaps a little voice in our heads even starts to point out that it might just be name calling. I am a biblically faithful contemporary preacher, while the person on my right is an irrelevant biblicist and the person on my left is an unbiblical liberal. I must be right. I am standing at the middle point of the bridge.

And perhaps we may even wonder about travelling too far with Spurgeon. In today's theological climate, thinking about the trinitarian relationships between the Father and the Son (that is what he refers to by 'eternal filiation' and so on) have a direct relevance to questions of church order and ministry, and are the subject of major debate.[8]

Before I make some critical observations, let me underline one point from Stott that must be affirmed most strongly. He writes:

7. Charles Spurgeon, *Lectures to My Students*, first series (London: Passmore & Alabaster, 1885; repr. Grand Rapids: Baker, 1977), p. 78.

8. Compare, for instance, K. Giles, *The Trinity and Subordinationism: The Doctrine of God and the Contemporary Gender Debate* (Downers Grove: InterVarsity Press, 2002), and Stephen R. Holmes, *The Quest for the Trinity: The Doctrine of God in Scripture, History and Modernity* (Downers Grove: IVP Academic, 2012).

> Our bridges . . . must be firmly anchored on both sides of the chasm, by refusing
> either to compromise the divine content of the message or to ignore the human
> context in which it has to be spoken. We have to plunge fearlessly into both worlds,
> ancient and modern, biblical and contemporary, and to listen attentively to both.[9]

Indeed so. And the dangers of remaining locked on one side of the bridge
remain as real.

Stott is therefore right to insist that we do not fool ourselves about the difficulty of the communication challenge, because it is dangerously easy to do so.
Writing more about counselling than preaching, Michael Emlet notices that
sometimes that gap feels like a ditch, sometimes a chasm – and we gravitate
towards ditch passages:

> Did you ever wonder why publishers sell the New Testament packaged together with
> Psalms and Proverbs? Why not sell the New Testament with Leviticus and Esther?
> Or the New Testament with 1 and 2 Kings and the Minor Prophets? A value
> judgement is being made. The New Testament, Psalms and Proverbs are deemed
> more relevant for contemporary life. The New Testament is included because it's
> about Jesus and the church. Proverbs makes the grade because of all that pithy,
> helpful, concrete advice. And the Psalms are important because of the emotions
> they evoke and because of their use in worship.[10]

Because we will always be tempted to cross the easy ditches, we must make sure
we have an approach that will face the chasms and cross them properly.

The biblical end of the bridge

But look for a moment at what Stott calls the biblical end of the bridge: for
there are actually two places to stand there, not one, and it is important to
distinguish them.

There are near where I live a number of historical re-enactment societies.
They have great fun dressing up as Roman centurions or Cromwellian foot
soldiers, and replaying significant battles of the past. The Wars of the Roses
are fought and refought in today's world. Now military strategists and soldiers

---

9. Stott, *Preaching*, p. 145.

10. Michael R. Emlet, *CrossTalk: Where Life and Scripture Meet* (Greensboro: New
   Growth, 2009), pp. 16–17.

in training need to study the battles of the past because it helps them to understand tactics, terrain and resources. There are always lessons to be learned. But
there is a considerable difference between on the one hand fighting an old battle
for the fun of it or because we prefer the sixteenth century, and on the other
hand learning from the past in order to combat tomorrow's terrorist.

What Spurgeon is mocking is the historical re-enactment approach to
preaching: that in our admiration for our heroes of the past we act as if we are
their contemporaries, as if their battles are the only ones worth preaching about,
and anyone who does not like historical re-enactment is not worthy in the pulpit.
Or in the pew. In fact, unless you engage in historical re-enactment you are not
really preaching at all.

That is self-indulgent and foolish. There is great wisdom from the Christian
past, and there are resources there for many of today's issues. Spurgeon himself
repeatedly raided the libraries of the past for his sermons. But the past is not all
relevant. Preaching has an urgency about it that historical fancy dress undercuts.
Although our secular friends confuse being biblical with being antiquarian, we
know that the two are not the same. We need to find another place to stand.

Suspended between two worlds

Let me highlight what I find most unhelpful about the bridge image. If we read
Stott carelessly, we may think that he means we are suspended between two
worlds – although he is careful to guard against that. He draws on the doctrine
of the incarnation to say that just as Jesus is neither exclusively divine nor
exclusively human but is God incarnate, so our preaching task is 'earthing the
Word in the world'.[11]

Nevertheless, something in that word 'between' troubles me. I do not live
between two worlds, or at the place where two worlds fleetingly meet. I live in
creation where Jesus is the risen king, and where he commands civilizations to
repent before him. He is not king of one world and not of the other; he is not
even king of both. There is one world, of which he is king.

The incarnation is an illuminating parallel at this point, but in a different
direction. Stott's position seems to be that just as Christ was incarnate at a
particular cultural time and place, so we must freshly re-present him today. I
think I know what he means, but there is a missing element. The culture in
which Christ was incarnate was uniquely prepared for him, as a result of God's

11. Stott, *Preaching*, p. 145.

unfolding covenant plan in history. His teachings and titles might have been misunderstood, but the raw data was there so that after his resurrection it became luminously clear that his coming was the high point in the unfolding plan. His biblical content and explanations were in the context of a people and language made ready for the coming of the Messiah by two thousand years of covenant history.

That is a critical point to assert if we wish to guard against Jesus' being portrayed as a man of his time, with teachings relevant only to his culture. Instead, we have to affirm that God created that particular culture of Israel precisely so that Jesus' words and works would be universal in extent.

There is a point where Stott comes close to saying this, or at least to following through on its implications. In describing the two errors he sees on either side of the bridge, he says:

> previously both my theory and my practice were to expound the biblical text and leave the application largely to the Holy Spirit. Moreover, this method is by no means as ineffective as it may sound, for two reasons. First, the biblical text is itself amazingly contemporary, and secondly, the Holy Spirit does use it to bring the hearers to conviction of sin, faith in Christ, and growth in holiness.[12]

Consider the phrase 'the biblical text is itself amazingly contemporary'. What Stott is emphasizing, but what the 'bridge' diagram does not account for, is the common experience of preachers that *it is precisely as we become more biblical that we become more contemporary, and the closer we look at the text, the clearer we see our world.* This is the other place to stand at the biblical end of the bridge.

Double listening?

Taking further the image of the bridge between two worlds, Stott alludes to Barth's image of the preacher being someone with the newspaper in one hand and the Bible in the other.

It is an appealing image, both biblical and contemporary, and understandably can serve as useful shorthand for the person who is familiar with both. We are to engage in 'double listening'.

But what do we mean by being 'familiar' with both? Once again, Stott's 'double' language can confuse us unless we also notice the differences. Because

---

12. Ibid., p. 141.

those two texts, the Bible and the newspaper, have different origins, authority and purpose, we read them in different ways and for different reasons. With the newspaper I check the weather forecast, disagree with the leading article, laugh at the clever cartoon, read about the match I watched last night and plan a grumpy letter to the editor. The only part of it that is of relevance to me, in the sense of making a change to my day, is the weather forecast. I do not read the Bible like that. It is the living, active word of God – life itself. Which is why it is always so contemporary to be biblical.

It is striking that this most fair-minded of thinkers does not have an equivalent road travelling in the opposite direction. There is no sense that being more contemporary makes us more biblical.

Questions for reflection and discussion

- Have you seen examples of what Chris Green calls 'historical re-enactment' preaching?
- Can you identify traces of that in your preaching?
- Can you identify with the idea that the more biblical you become, the more relevant you become?
- What are the differences between the two 'biblical' ends of the bridge?
- What are the strengths and weaknesses of 'double listening'?

7. TIMELESS PRINCIPLES

> They are not just idle words for you – they are your life. By them you will live
> long in the land you are crossing the Jordan to possess.
>
> (Deut. 32:47)

Two writers who have developed Stott's model further into a clear textbook form
are J. Scott Duvall and J. Daniel Hays. In both *Grasping God's Word* and *Preaching
God's Word* they have provided an admirably lucid model of how classic evangelical hermeneutics has come to understand how we cross Stott's bridge.[1] Their
image for the gap is a river,[2] with a town on one bank called Bible town, and
several on the other side, as our towns today. In between, the river is made up
of various elements that separate the Bible from Christians today, and make it
difficult to understand and apply today. I should emphasize that I am not taking
Duvall and Hays as a bad example, but precisely because they are so clear and
well thought-through, and I have used their book as a classroom text.

They name the bridge over the river 'Principlizing Bridge'. The method they
model is that we should go deep into the text on the Bible side to discover the
undergirding principle we should bring across the river to today.

---

1. J. Scott Duvall and J. Daniel Hays, *Grasping God's Word: A Hands-on Approach to
   Reading, Interpreting, and Applying the Bible*, 2nd ed. (Grand Rapids: Zondervan, 2005);
   Terry G. Carter, J. Scott Duvall and J. Daniel Hays, *Preaching God's Word: A Hands-on
   Approach to Preparing, Developing, and Delivering the Sermon* (Grand Rapids: Zondervan,
   2005).
2. Duvall and Hays, *Grasping*, p. 24.

Haddon Robinson makes a similar point when he says that we need to climb up 'the ladder of abstraction', to God, the truths about fallen humanity and the wonder of salvation.[3] Sometimes the bridge is broken down into a series of steps. Rick Warren attributes this version to David Veerman, the senior editor of the Life Application Bible:[4]

```
                        PRINCIPLES
                POINT            PRESENT
          PLOT                          PARALLELS
      PLACE                                  PRIORITIES
PEOPLE                                              PLAN
```

And Warren says that each of those nine represents a helpful question:

PEOPLE: Who are the people in this passage and how are they like us today?

PLACE: What is the setting and what are the similarities to our world?

PLOT: What is happening, is there any conflict or tension, and how would I have felt or acted in that situation?

POINT: What was the intended message for that audience? What is the purpose of the passage? What does God want them to learn or feel or do?

PRINCIPLES: What are the timeless truths?

PRESENT: How is this relevant to our world today?

PARALLELS: Where does this truth apply to my life?

PERSONAL:[5] What needs to change in me?

PLAN: What will be my first step of action?

What the above three models have in common is the way they describe the highest point of the bridge or ladder, the point furthest away from both the ends. Duvall and Hays call it 'principlizing'; Robinson calls it 'abstraction'; Warren calls it 'principles' or 'timeless truths'. There is, in the 'timely word' of Scripture, a 'timeless principle'.

This is put most clearly in the standard introduction to the New International Version Application Commentary series. Each section of a commentary includes

---

3. Haddon Robinson, 'The Heresy of Application', in Haddon Robinson and Craig Brian Larson, *The Art and Craft of Biblical Preaching* (Grand Rapids: Zondervan, 2005), p. 30.

4. Handbook to Rick Warren's *Purpose-Driven Preaching* conference (http://www.pastors.com: Foothill Ranch, California, 1999), p. 18.

5. Warren changes that from PRIORITIES in the pyramid diagram.

what is called 'bridging contexts', and the standard introduction to each of the series explains it like this:

Bridging Contexts
THIS SECTION BUILDS A BRIDGE between the world of the Bible and the world of today, between the original context and the contemporary context, by focusing on both the timely and timeless aspects of the text.

God's Word is *timely*. The authors of Scripture spoke to specific situations, problems, and questions. The author of Joshua encouraged the faith of his original readers by narrating the destruction of Jericho, a seemingly impregnable city, at the hands of an angry warrior God (Josh. 6). Paul warned the Galatians about the consequences of circumcision and the dangers of trying to be justified by law (Gal. 5:25). The author of Hebrews tried to convince his readers that Christ is superior to Moses, the Aaronic priests, and the Old Testament sacrifices. John urged his readers to 'test the spirits' of those who taught a form of incipient Gnosticism (1 John 4:1–6). In each of these cases, the timely nature of Scripture enables us to hear God's Word in situations that were concrete rather than abstract.

Yet the timely nature of Scripture also creates problems. Our situations, difficulties, and questions are not always directly related to those faced by the people in the Bible. Therefore, God's Word to them does not always seem relevant to us. For example, when was the last time someone urged you to be circumcised, claiming that it was a necessary part of justification? . . .

Fortunately, Scripture is not only timely but *timeless*. Just as God spoke to the original audience, so he still speaks to us through the pages of Scripture. Because we share a common humanity with the people of the Bible, we discover a *universal dimension* in the problems they faced and the solutions God gave them. The timeless nature of Scripture enables it to speak with power in every time and in every culture.[6]

Timeless and timely

Because this is a widely used model, there is much senior consensus about it and it has been produced with good intentions to address a profound difficulty, so I am cautious about criticizing it. Nevertheless, as it stands I suggest it needs some work to improve it.

---

6. Series introduction to the NIVAC, italics original. The page number varies by volume, but these are the introductory few pages to each volume.

The first problem to notice is that it invites us to use the Bible in a way that the Bible does not use itself. Graeme Goldsworthy rightly says that the theology within the Bible 'is never in the form of timeless abstraction. It is given within the historical processes of God acting within history to bring about his purposes.'[7] And I would join him in asserting that that holds even for such apparently timeless thoughts as we find in Proverbs. They too must be taken in the overarching context of the covenant that reaches its fulfilment in the arrival of Christ, the one wiser than Solomon, and whose death displays God's wisdom.

Goldsworthy takes it further, to say that biblical revelation 'without some framework of salvation history would, I believe, be reduced to timeless religious ideals'.[8] Philosophers and religions deal with such claimed timeless truths, but every aspect of biblical revelation is given in the context of God's covenant that unfurls in time: there are no timeless truths. Even such apparently timeless truths such as God's love are explained by his acts of history. Even God's nature as the eternal Trinity of love is not a timeless principle in the sense of a mere religious idea.

If we have ideas that do not engage with history and culture, then we may be asserting that we know things about God that make no claim upon us.

Let me underline that with a second point. If I reduce an Old Testament text to a timeless principle that then arcs across to us, but makes no proper attempt to explain how that issue is related to Christ and his death, then I have produced, under the guise of an evangelical method, Christless Christianity.

Muzzling the ox

The objection might come at this point that I am being too absolute. Haddon Robinson argues that this method I am criticizing is precisely the one Paul uses in relation to the Old Testament.[9] In 1 Corinthians 9:7–12 Paul asserts the rights of Christian workers to a salary on the basis of Deuteronomy 25:4:

> Who serves as a soldier at his own expense? Who plants a vineyard and does
> not eat its grapes? Who tends a flock and does not drink the milk? Do I say this

---

7. Graeme Goldsworthy, *Christ-Centred Biblical Theology* (Nottingham: Apollos, 2012), p. 48.
8. Ibid., p. 74.
9. Robinson, 'Heresy', p. 308.

merely on human authority? Doesn't the Law say the same thing? For it is written in the Law of Moses: 'Do not muzzle an ox while it is treading out the grain.' Is it about oxen that God is concerned? Surely he says this for us, doesn't he? Yes, this was written for us, because whoever ploughs and threshes should be able to do so in the hope of sharing in the harvest. If we have sown spiritual seed among you, is it too much if we reap a material harvest from you? If others have this right of support from you, shouldn't we have it all the more?

How is it that Paul moves from a verse about oxen to a truth about Christian workers? Does he not move up the ladder of abstraction?

The reason why I do not think this example proves that Paul himself looked for timeless principles in the Old Testament is that it does not notice the unique way those laws were constructed and were to be used. Our legal systems produce laws of enormous length and complexity, moderated by demo-cratically elected leaders, and interpreted by the courts. The published material on any legal matter in such a system is vast. By contrast, the Old Testament law works on the basis of giving one distilling example that then serves to safeguard the idea. Old Testament law, within its own architecture, models that its users extract a principle from an example and apply it elsewhere. But that only demonstrates how the legal material was to function within Israel. It does not prove that this is generally how all Old Testament material functioned.

So Paul is not using this method thoughtlessly, or without regard for original context. The original context of legal material endorses the extraction of a principle.

Moreover, Paul is not describing a general religious truth, which I have described as Christless Christianity. He identifies this as 'the Law of Moses', which locates it in a specific time in gospel history. A few sentences later he explicitly uses Jesus' own teaching to endorse his conclusion: 'In the same way, the Lord has commanded that those who preach the gospel should receive their living from the gospel' (1 Cor. 9:14). Paul is using this verse in its covenantal context.

I would agree that by this instance Paul shows that the correct use of Old Testament law was always the extraction of a principle and its reapplication in a different context. But I do not think that this proves that the method is therefore the one to be used across all types of Old Testament literature, nor does it prove the existence of timeless principles. Paul shows how case law worked. He also insists that we must relate any Old Testament text to Christ. The king is the context.

Who decides?

There is a second, and to my mind much more serious, set of problems with the principlizing method.

I once heard the famously radical Episcopalian bishop John Spong defend the possibility of gay marriage as a biblically valid concept. His explanation was that in the Bible there are timeless principles embedded in time-bound words. There were cultural expressions of heterosexual marriage that contained within them the timeless principles of love, faithfulness and sexual expression. What we must do, he said, is extract the timeless principle from its historical expression, and then re-embed it today in a new cultural context.

Do you see what he just did? In order to justify gay marriage, he used an impeccable evangelical interpretative method. What he did, though, was to start to change labels. I would look at the biblical teaching on marriage and say that one timeless principle is its heterosexual nature; but Spong identified that as merely a timely word. The timeless principle he extracted was faithfulness in marriage, whether heterosexual or homosexual. This method turns out to be fundamentally subjective, because one person's timeless principle can just as easily be another person's timeless word.

We need to slow this down. John Stott himself observed the problem with regard to attempts to rewrite Christian doctrine: 'What is sad and reprehensible about liberals is that in discarding the ancient formulations they tend also to discard the truth formulated, and so to throw out the baby with the bathwater.'[10] I suspect that Stott operated with such a clear distinction in his mind between the categories of 'timeless' and 'timely' that he did not see that other people, while sharing that language, were either not so clear, or meant other things by it. Like Fosdick before them, the liberals also thought they were only throwing out more bathwater and that the baby was safe. In particular, Stott did not anticipate the day that Spong would support a liberal position by using the same methodology.

Somebody might suggest that Spong 'misused' rather than 'used' the method, but I am being careful. Built into the method are two *shared assumptions* that are usually hidden. First, there is the assumption that any biblical text has the probability of elements that do not apply to Christians today. Readers on the 'conservative' or 'cautious' end of the spectrum might interpret the word 'probability' to mean 'possibility' (i.e. they are open to the idea that there might not be a simple 1:1 correspondence between Bible times and ours, but it is an unlikely

---

10. John R. W. Stott, *I Believe in Preaching* (London: Hodder & Stoughton, 1982), p. 144.

idea that would need to be proved). Readers on the more 'radical' end of the spectrum would more likely interpret the word 'probability' to mean 'working assumption' (i.e. they are not open to the idea that there might be a simple 1:1 correspondence between Bible times and ours). Both positions are built on other views about the nature of God's revelation within and after Scripture. But both share a suspicion of an assumed 'simplistic' 1:1 application.

The second assumption is that the difference between the 'timeless' and 'timely' is discoverable, but for that discovery to be made the decision must be based on criteria outside the text in question. So someone who agrees with Stott would probably defend a traditional view of marriage not so much on a single text but on a raft of them, and on a narrative that ends with the marriage of the Lamb in Revelation 21. Similarly, someone who agrees with Spong would appeal to an arc of biblical texts that speak about equality, which ends in Galatians 3:28. Both explain an individual text in the light of a biblical theology.

There are strong disagreements to be built in as well, of course: readers on the radical end would be open to the idea that the biblical writers might be wrong on something. In theory (although one rarely hears it expressed) they would be open to the idea that Jesus was a man of his time and wrong in some of his teaching; in reality that debate happens over the less explosive question of whether Paul might have been wrong. A reader on the conservative end, like Stott, might operate with such a high view of the inspiration, authority and sufficiency of Scripture that the idea of any biblical writer being 'wrong' is unthinkable. A radical might be open to subsequent truth being unveiled through the discoveries of science, whereas a conservative might not be – and so on.

And the two views confront each other. A radical observes that the conservative view is built of individual texts, each of which can be deconstructed in the same way, and the arc collapses. A conservative replies that when she 'interprets' a passage, she is trying to get as close to the author's mind as possible, but that the radical 'interprets' the original author's words like a jazz musician might use a theme as a basis for improvisation. Those are differences that are strong enough to say that we are not dealing with a continuum here: the two views are fundamentally different.

But for all the differing assumptions, it is the shared assumptions in the common model that ultimately, to my mind, make it unstable. Both use the idea of a timely principle and a timely word. And so the question always remains: Who decides, and on what basis, which is which? Which means it is always a model that, even in conservative hands, is capable of producing dangerously radical conclusions.

A river runs through it

Let us revisit the 'bridge and river' model from Duvall and Hays, because there is a third set of fundamental problems to notice: in their diagram the river flows between the Bible and us, *but in many cases the river actually flows within the Bible itself.* The rural culture of Abraham's day was massively different from the urban thrust of first-century Rome. He would have been as bewildered by his experience of that context as he would by twenty-first-century Rome. Would the cultured converts of Corinth have understood the Hebrew and Aramaic of the Old Testament? We see the similarities across the biblical texts perhaps because we romanticize them, and perhaps because we assume that the leaps caused by the invention of the printing press, the Industrial Revolution and the Web are so great that nothing before them could have had any equivalent significance. But that is naive.

Furthermore, Duvall and Hays put as one element of the river the word 'covenant'. Now that aspect of the river does need to be clearly demarcated, but once we identify it, it messes with the diagram. Because while every Old Testament believer is on the far side of that part of the river, every New Testament believer from John the Baptist onwards lives on our side of the river. *Covenant is a point of dissimilarity within the Scriptures, but of commonality between the New Testament Scriptures and us.* And the gap between the twenty-first century and the first is as nothing compared to the gap between BC and AD. One is merely cultural, whereas the other is theological.

In fact, the NIVAC introduction unwittingly affirms this. It gives four examples of a problem caused by God's Word being *timely* and given in a concrete context: the destruction of Jericho at the invasion of the Promised Land; Paul's warning the Galatians about the dangers of trying to be justified by law; Hebrews' teaching that Christ is superior to Moses, the Aaronic priests and the Old Testament sacrifices; and John's warning of incipient heresy about Christ. But each of these is actually a variation of the question of where we stand in relation to the covenant, now that Christ has come. In each case the river runs through the Bible itself.

A self-inflicted wound

We need to find a way to resolve this with some urgency, because if I am right that the standard way for evangelicals to read the Bible shares significant similarities to a radical way, then we are not equipping people to be plausible apologists for orthodox Christianity. Instead, we will produce Christians who are orthodox by instinct, culture and background, but who are unable to derive that orthodoxy convincingly from the Scriptures. And when they discuss their views with a more radical friend, they will find that their arguments come apart in their hands, because they will discover that their friend, like John Spong, uses the same method, and all they are left with is an unprovable argument. If they are intelligent, and realize they can no longer use the Bible with any confidence, that will cause a crisis of faith, as their liberal hermeneutic collides with their conservative instincts; and, as Michael Emlet puts it, if 'the Bible becomes functionally irrelevant, people will turn elsewhere for guidance'.[11] That would be a self-inflicted wound.

Questions for reflection and discussion

- What are the strengths of the idea of 'timeless principles', and what are the weaknesses?
- Why does Chris Green say that this method can produce 'Christless Christianity'?
- What was wrong with the radical theologian's *method* (as opposed to his conclusions)?
- What does Chris Green mean by saying, 'the river runs through the Bible'?

11. Michael R. Emlet, *CrossTalk: Where Life and Scripture Meet* (Greensboro: New Growth, 2009), p. 18.

8. THE BUSY PREACHER'S LITTLE SECRET

They read from the Book of the Law of God, making it clear and giving the meaning so that the people understood what was being read.

(Neh. 8:8)

So it really is no wonder that this business of bringing the Bible to today is so notoriously difficult. Linger in the pages of the Bible, and we know we can become fascinated with it as a puzzle book rather than as a guide for life. Lift our eyes from it for too long, and we forget that it, and it alone, is our safe guide for life. We fear being in turn simplistic, superficial, moralistic, legalistic, tasteless, faddish, dry or even heretical. There is barely enough time in a minister's week to do exegesis and commentary work, let alone biblical and systematic theology. And a 20 minute sermon gives barely enough time for text and context. Haddon Robinson says, 'Sermon application is like peeling an onion. At first it seems easy, but as you go through layer after layer all you have is tears.'[1]

And so I suspect that by default we leave it to the listeners to work it out for themselves. That is the busy preacher's little secret. After all the hours we put into preparing a sermon, we allow the congregation a scant 20 minutes to listen, understand and grab some implications. Because doing the work of application ourselves is too hard.

It's rather as if I invited you round for a meal, and planned a delicious menu. I went shopping round the specialist shops that sell the spices I needed, spoke

---

1. Cited from class notes in Daniel Overdorf, *Applying the Sermon: How to Balance Biblical Integrity and Cultural Relevance* (Grand Rapids: Kregel, 2009), p. 13.

to the right butcher, even chose special coffee beans. But when you came round, I was happy to empty the shopping bags all over the table, and invite you to tuck in! You would rightly say that I hadn't made you a meal at all. Even if I put a saucepan on the table as well.

Isn't that your experience of some, or even many, sermons? All the ingredients are there, but they are uncooked. The preacher says, 'Here's the Greek exegesis, there's a paragraph I found in a book I read – help yourself.' The ideas haven't been given time to simmer, to break down and blend.

So at our imaginary evening together I put some music on for you, and grumble away in the kitchen. And in my largest pan I throw in together all the meat, all the cream, all the vegetables, coffee beans and spices, slam the lid on, turn the heat up, and half an hour later present you with your meal.

You might begin to wonder if I was your friend at all! You would certainly decide never to come round for a meal again.

And again, haven't you heard or preached sermons like that? Everything that's been discovered by research is thrown into the sermon, and thoughtlessly mixed in together, with little care or subtlety. Some people give up listening politely after a few moments because there is just too much 'stuff' on the plate; others struggle courageously to the end, but with indigestion.

The hearer's responsibility

To clear one objection out of the way, I don't think it's healthy for people in church to act as the guests at a meal, expecting to be served up a delicious meal and never having to work at it. Listening to God's Word together requires listening on our part, so we need to play our part too. We should expect to be sitting up, paying attention, Bibles open and phones closed. It is helpful for people to take notes of a sermon, even if they throw them away when they get home, because the mere act of being attentive enough to write down what is being said increases the chance of remembering and then using it. Is the sermon dull? Pray for the preacher to be enlivened. Is it difficult? Pray for the preacher's clarity, and for your understanding.[2]

Martyn Lloyd-Jones was right to highlight the responsibility of the listener in application:

---

2. See Christopher Ash, *Listen Up! A Practical Guide to Listening to Sermons* (London: Good Book, 2009).

It is one thing to believe the truth, it is a very different thing to apply it. We did listen, and apply the truth, initially, otherwise we would not be Christians at all. But it is possible for us . . . to go on, content with just listening to, or reading the truth, and never applying it to ourselves, or examining ourselves in the light of it. Is this not one of the most alarming possibilities in the Christian life?[3]

Nor is this an individual activity. Whether informally over coffee afterwards, or in a more structured way in a midweek group, we can help each other to process the ideas and bring them to bear on our lives.

The preacher's responsibility

But a niggling voice should stop us being happy with leaving it at that. I know my own sinful heart, and it is far too easy to blame others for not doing their work, while excusing my own sloth. Being theologically aware means that we can superficially justify our inaction by saying we are avoiding being legalists, or keeping people dependent, but deep down we know that will not do. Calvin Miller describes the experience of being a preacher in two minds well:

The riskiest single sentence that appears in a sermon is, 'Here's what to do with what I've just told you.' It sets the listener on edge and sometimes drives the preacher to the ledges of courage to bring up the issue of application. Why? Because it seems to the hearers that application is where the sermon ceases to be biblical and starts being meddlesome. It often seems that way to the preacher as well.

Yet application is the money on the game.[4]

And here are Bryan Chappell's wise words:

Recognize that the chief purpose of application is not simply to give people something to do. *Application gives ultimate meaning to the exposition.* Even if the explanation of a sermon were to define every Greek and Hebrew word for prayer, were to quote at length from Calvin, Luther, and E. M. Bounds of prayer's meaning, were to cite fifty passages that refer to prayer, and were to describe the prayer practices of David,

---

3. D. Martyn Lloyd-Jones, *Revival* (Westchester, Ill.: Crossway, 1987), p. 80.

4. Calvin Miller, *Preaching: The Art of Narrative Exposition* (Grand Rapids: Baker, 2006), p. 80.

Jeremiah, Daniel, Paul, and Jesus, would the listeners truly understand what prayer is? No. Until we engage in prayer we do not really understand it. Until we apply a truth, understanding of it remains incomplete. This means that until a preacher provides application, exposition remains incomplete.[5]

Indeed. The Bible is not a book simply to be heard or understood, but it has not done its work in us until we put it into practice (2 Thess. 1:8; 1 Peter 4:17).

Preaching that makes Jesus angry

We seem to be surrounded by pitfalls, and are dealing with a much more serious matter than simple technique or presentation. The question of what we do when we preach is a spiritual battleground that takes place in the heart of the preacher. So before we can find a way through the application maze, we must pay attention to our master. In Matthew 23:13–32 Jesus identifies and condemns seven types of dangerous preaching, and exposes the deepest roots of the problems we have seen so far, whether of triviality or stodge, irrelevance or unbiblical novelty. If you are a preacher, this is the point where I suggest you slow down, and expose your heart to Jesus' diagnosis and surgery:

1. Preaching that is godless (vv. 13–14): 'Woe to you, teachers of the law and Pharisees, you hypocrites! You shut the door of the kingdom of heaven in people's faces. You yourselves do not enter, nor will you let those enter who are trying to.'

Question: Have you heard or preached sermons that actually take people away from God?

2. Preaching that makes people worse hypocrites (v. 15): 'Woe to you, teachers of the law and Pharisees, you hypocrites! You travel over land and sea to win a single convert, and when you have succeeded, you make them twice as much a child of hell as you are.'

Question: Have you heard or preached sermons that are both passionate and persuasive, but not about the gospel?

---

5. Bryan Chappell, *Christ-Centered Preaching*, 2nd ed. (Grand Rapids: Baker, 2005), p. 203. italics his.

3. Preaching that trivializes God (vv. 16–22): 'Woe to you, blind guides! You say, "If anyone swears by the temple, it means nothing; but anyone who swears by the gold of the temple is bound by that oath." You blind fools! Which is greater: the gold, or the temple that makes the gold sacred? You also say, "If anyone swears by the altar, it means nothing; but anyone who swears by the gift on the altar is bound by that oath." You blind men! Which is greater: the gift, or the altar that makes the gift sacred? Therefore, anyone who swears by the altar swears by it and by everything on it. And anyone who swears by the temple swears by it and by the one who dwells in it. And anyone who swears by heaven swears by God's throne and by the one who sits on it.'

Question: Have you heard or preached sermons that downplay God's honour, his promises or demands?

4. Preaching that sounds biblical but ignores the Bible's centre (vv. 23–24): 'Woe to you, teachers of the law and Pharisees, you hypocrites! You give a tenth of your spices – mint, dill and cumin. But you have neglected the more important matters of the law – justice, mercy and faithfulness. You should have practised the latter, without neglecting the former. You blind guides! You strain out a gnat but swallow a camel.'

Question: Have you heard or preached sermons that were full of the Bible, but missed the core?

5. Preaching that addresses behaviour but not the heart (vv. 25–26): 'Woe to you, teachers of the law and Pharisees, you hypocrites! You clean the outside of the cup and dish, but inside they are full of greed and self-indulgence. Blind Pharisee! First clean the inside of the cup and dish, and then the outside also will be clean.'

Question: Have you heard or preached sermons that simply told people to try harder?

6. Preaching that is impressive but deadly (vv. 27–28): 'Woe to you, teachers of the law and Pharisees, you hypocrites! You are like whitewashed tombs, which look beautiful on the outside but on the inside are full of the bones of the dead and everything unclean. In the same way, on the outside you appear to people as righteous but on the inside you are full of hypocrisy and wickedness.'

Question: Have you heard or preached sermons designed to sound and look really impressive, but that you knew were untrue for the preacher?

7. Preaching that does not realize just how deep sin goes (vv. 29–32): 'Woe to you, teachers of the law and Pharisees, you hypocrites! You build tombs for the prophets and decorate the graves of the righteous. And you say, "If we had lived in the days of our ancestors, we would not have taken part with them in shedding the blood of the prophets." So you testify against yourselves that you are the descendants of those who murdered the prophets. Go ahead, then, and complete what your ancestors started!'

Question: Have you heard or preached sermons that make it appear that the preacher and hearers were better than the people outside the church, and not sinners needing a Saviour?

Did you notice the solemnly repeated 'Woe to you'? Jesus takes those kinds of preaching seriously, because of the spiritual damage they do.

And those are the teachers who are trying to teach truth! There was also the danger of preaching like a Sadducee, who trimmed the outdated supernatural parts out of the Bible. In Matthew's previous chapter Jesus was devastating even regarding their liberalism: 'You are in error because you do not know the Scriptures or the power of God' (Matt. 22:29).

Question: Have you heard or preached sermons that make it acceptable to question the Bible, or God himself?

So our dilemma is now clear: we need to present God's Word fully and faithfully, bravely and relevantly. Our personal bashfulness as preachers must not be allowed to enter the equation. In his kindness God has given us one New Testament book that presents a master class in how to do that, which gives us the 'why' as well as the 'how' of application.

Questions for reflection and discussion

- What does Chris Green identify as the hearer's responsibility in a sermon?
- What does he identify as the preacher's responsibility?
- Have you heard or preached sermons that actually take people away from God?

sermon must take people to God

- Have you heard or preached sermons that are both passionate and persuasive, but not about the gospel?
- Have you heard or preached sermons that downplay God's honour, his promises or demands?
- Have you heard or preached sermons that were full of the Bible, but missed the core?
- Have you heard or preached sermons that simply told people to try harder? *but not how*
- Have you heard or preached sermons designed to sound and look really impressive, but that you knew were untrue for the preacher?
- Have you heard or preached sermons that made it appear that the preacher and hearers were better than the people outside the church, and not sinners needing a Saviour?
- Have you heard or preached sermons that make it acceptable to question the Bible, or God himself?

9. THE GOOD LIFE

> Our people must learn to devote themselves to doing what is good.
>
> (Titus 3:14)

Knowledge is complicated

We have seen that true knowledge about God is a gift in the gospel, and we have seen that in order for it to be true knowledge it must be lived as well as believed. Knowledge that is not lived out gives a church spiritual indigestion. As Paul wrote to the famously knowledgeable but bloated church in Corinth, 'Now about food sacrificed to idols: we know that "We all possess knowledge." But knowledge puffs up while love builds up' (1 Cor. 8:1).

Paul knew that the danger of being 'puffed up' applied to him as much as to anyone, and earlier in that letter he described his relationship to the knowledge he had in this way: 'This, then, is how you ought to regard us: as servants of Christ and as those entrusted with the mysteries God has revealed. Now it is required that those who have been given a trust must prove faithful' (1 Cor. 4:1–2). Someone who is entrusted with something is not its owner. I am a trustee of a charity, but I am not the owner of its assets. I am forbidden by law from gaining any financial advantage from the trust. Its money and property are not mine to give away as I choose. Instead, I and my fellow trustees are bound by the trust deeds, and can do with the assets only what the founders intended.

So it was for Paul and the gospel, and so it is for us. We do not 'own' the knowledge we have of God, or the content of the Bible. The knowledge we have is for the benefit and blessing of the rest of the church, and indeed of non-Christians. We are accountable to Christ for the gospel – not just for maintaining its content securely and faithfully for ourselves, but also for its faithful transmission and spread, and its faithfully being lived out in the church. We are supposed to do with the gospel what its master intends.

So are we being good trustees? Willow Creek Community Church, a large church on the outskirts of Chicago, has conducted a series of surveys on precisely this issue. Initially it was a piece of internal research, but they have made their results public even though it shows that they have had a serious problem, and it has now been rolled out into thousands of churches, where their findings have been replicated elsewhere. I have never been part of a church that has conducted this survey, but my hunch is that their findings are widely true.

Here is the good news. The survey covered multiple ways (fifty-six of them) in which Christians grow, and one feature occurred repeatedly, with a consistently higher significance than any other. From what helps a sceptical enquirer to what helps the most mature, there was one constant: 'the Bible is the most powerful catalyst for spiritual growth. The Bible's power to advance spiritual growth is unrivalled by anything else we've discovered.'[1] Reflecting later, and on more churches, the authors write, 'Truly, if a church could do only one thing to help people grow in their relationship with Christ, it would be to get them immersed and in love with God's Word.'[2] Interestingly, they discovered that this was particularly true when it came to personal Bible study, but that other forms of biblical teaching contributed too. Their summary is clear: 'Nothing beats the Bible.'[3]

We could respond to that in a superficial way by saying that we already knew this, because the Bible already told us that, and it would still be true even if the data pointed in a different direction. That is right, but the reason that seems a superficial response to me is the level of detail the survey goes into about the various ways in which the Bible is used in Christian maturity, and their respective contributions, and also about the gap between expectations and reality.

Here is the bad news, which is repeatedly about our preaching, the four responses with the greatest gap between expectation and reality:

---

1. G. L. Hawkins and C. Parkinson, *Follow Me* (Barrington: Willow Creek Resources, 2008), p. 116.
2. G. L. Hawkins and C. Parkinson, *Move*, Willow Creek Resources (Grand Rapids: Zondervan, 2011), p. 223.
3. Hawkins and Parkinson, *Follow*, p. 117.

1. *The preaching incorporates relevant biblical teaching to help me with everyday life*: 87% of evangelical church members said it was important, but only 32% said that it happened. That is a gap of 55%. Over half the people who want life-changing Bible teaching, and who sit under weekly Bible teaching in order to get it, don't get it.

2. *The preaching is challenging or thought-provoking*: 84% said it was important, but only 30% said that it happened. We are boring 54% of our keen Christians.

3. *The preaching incorporates frequent use of scripture*: This should be an easy one to pass, you would think. 84% of church members surveyed said they really think it is important that we use the Bible a lot, but only 41% reckon we do it. 40% of our churches would like us to use the Bible more. They would also like us to give them more to chew on.

4. *The preaching provides in-depth study of the Bible*: Nearly three quarters of the people in front of us want it (72%), but only 19% say we are giving it to them. That is a gap of 53%.[4]

So are we being good trustees of the gospel? Perhaps this applies only to megachurches in North America. Perhaps this merely proves what you've always thought about churches like that. Perhaps you are confident that your church massively bucks this trend. Perhaps, if these statistics were true of your church, you would think that they merely prove that people don't know good teaching when you give it to them. Perhaps.

Doing what is good: Titus

One New Testament letter that directly addresses these kinds of issues is Paul's letter to Titus. We do not know the circumstances of Paul's visit to the island of Crete, but his stay had evidently been shorter than he would have liked, so Titus had been deployed to make good the problem. This letter seems to have been Titus' covering authorization, and he had the responsibility of appointing 'elders in every town' (1:5). That seems to have been Paul's general practice anyway, but there was a set of problems on the island that gave the task a sharpness that speaks straight into our concern. The issue on Crete lay at the interface between belief and life change.

On the surface of Titus lies the issue of good works. There is a repeated signature phrase:

---

4. Ibid., p. 38.

In everything set them an example by doing what is good. (2:7)

eager to do what is good. (2:14)

ready to do whatever is good. (3:1)

And I want you to stress these things, so that those who have trusted in God may be careful to devote themselves to doing what is good. (3:8)

That is underlined by the summary clause of the letter: 'Our people must learn to devote themselves to doing what is good, in order to provide for urgent needs and not live unproductive lives' (3:14).

Once that repeated phrase of 'what is good' has been noticed, an alert reader sees that this is a strong current running through the whole.

Also on the surface is a plague of false teachers with a false gospel. And the description of them, by contrast with the previous verses, is quite marked: 'They are detestable, disobedient and unfit for doing anything good' (Titus 1:16). There is an explicit contrast with 'unfit for doing anything good', but the word 'disobedient' shows the wider nature of the problem.

Paul's consistent applicatory stress throughout the letter lies on the characteristics either of being obedient, or of being the kind of person worth obeying:

An elder must be . . . a man whose children believe and are not open to the charge of being wild and disobedient. (1:6)

Teach the older men to be . . . worthy of respect. (2:2)

Likewise, teach the older women to be reverent in the way they live . . . Then they can urge the younger women . . . to be subject to their husbands. (2:2–5)

Teach slaves to be subject to their masters in everything. (2:9)

Encourage and rebuke with all authority. Do not let anyone despise you. (2:15)

Remind the people to be subject to rulers and authorities, to be obedient, to be ready to do whatever is good, to slander no one, to be peaceable and considerate, and always to be gentle towards everyone. (3:1–2)

We might have questions about how to apply Paul's teaching today, but there was no question about how it applied then. The issues of good works and obedience were directly in contrast to disobedient false teachers unfit for good works. And the Christians were to be called back into line.

Paul opens by describing himself as 'a servant of God and an apostle of Jesus Christ to further the faith of God's elect and their knowledge of the truth that leads to godliness' (Titus 1:1), and the key connection is to see that sequence of 'the truth that leads to godliness'. The good works and obedience Paul wants are not the product of nagging, or self-improvement, or a moral crusade. They arise from the gospel. This emerges more explicitly again towards the close:

> When the kindness and love of God our Saviour appeared, he saved us, not because of righteous things we had done, but because of his mercy. He saved us through the washing of rebirth and renewal by the Holy Spirit, whom he poured out on us generously through Jesus Christ our Saviour, so that, having been justified by his grace, we might become heirs having the hope of eternal life. This is a trustworthy saying. And I want you to stress these things, so that those who have trusted in God may be careful to devote themselves to doing what is good. (3:4–8)

The gospel results in Christians 'doing what is good', and a false gospel results in its adherents being 'unfit for any good work'.

So the elders Titus appoints have a number of characteristics to reflect these interlocking ideas.

- *Truth*: the elder must personally believe the message (1:9).
- *Change*: the elder must have a lifestyle that shows the gospel has done its work (1:7–9).
- *Encouragement*: the elder must be willing to encourage right belief and good conduct among the church members (1:9).
- *Refutation*: the elder must be willing to tackle the error that produces evil behaviour at its root (1:9).

This is a classic, logical 'square of opposition'. The gospel produces good fruit, and the error produces bad fruit; the gospel cannot produce bad fruit, and the error cannot produce good fruit; therefore the gospel minister must promote the gospel and its fruit, and resist the error and its fruit; and the errorists will distort and malign the gospel in order to justify their wicked crop. People who do good things will confront, and be confronted by, people who do wicked things. This alignment between gospel truth and doing what is good is based on the God 'who does not lie' (1:2).

We can put the network of relationships in diagrams (see below).

1. What is the fruit, and how is it produced?

2. So what cannot be the fruit of each position?

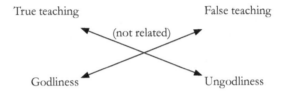

3. So what are the inevitable opponents?

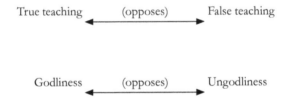

4. The square of opposition:

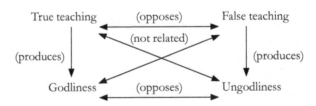

If this is correct, and there is a line between the gospel and good works that is traced through obedience, it may explain two sections in Titus, as follows.

Disobedient children

One qualification of an elder I did not mention in that list is 'a man whose
children believe and are not open to the charge of being wild and disobedient'
(1:6). I have sometimes wondered in a rather flippant way whether our family's
behaviour over the breakfast table rules me out from being an elder. I have even
wondered in a paranoid way whether my children have read Titus, and misbehave
over the cereal precisely to stop that happening. But more seriously, I remember
one mature and gifted man having long conversations with me about whether
the atheism of his adult children was a bar to his ordination.

The critical issue is context. Titus' elders must not be those who believe in
or tolerate the error and its consequences. But one whose children are 'disobedient' (remember the centrality of that phrase in Titus) shows that he can
tolerate the Cretan error and its consequences under his own roof. He can live
with it, even though it is known that the false teachers 'are disrupting whole
households by teaching things they ought not to teach' (1:11). He makes it a
second-order issue for the sake of keeping the family together. Such a person
cannot be the kind of elder Titus needs to appoint. That person has already
shown that he will not 'refute' (1:9). No promises or good references can hide
from Titus the evidence of spinelessness. So I reassured my mature friend that
this issue was not a matter of what his adult children got up to in their own
homes and lives, but whether he would have allowed them to propagate and
live out a false gospel at home.

Lying Cretans

The second section we may be able to cast light on is the famous Cretan
'paradox': 'One of Crete's own prophets has said it: "Cretans are always liars,
evil brutes, lazy gluttons"' (Titus 1:12), and a cocky logic-chopper will point out
that if such a prophet was indeed a Cretan, he would therefore by his own
admission be a liar, and therefore we could not believe his statement that all
Cretans are liars.

Why does Paul get himself into this convoluted position? Or if the commentators are right, and Paul is possibly quoting the Cretan poet Epimenides,
why is that relevant to his argument? Is it just local colour?

We need to translate more carefully. All English versions have to supply Paul's
sentence with a noun to make it clear, because what he says, more literally, is
'one of them, a prophet of their own, has said'. And every translator has to
answer the question 'One of *whose* own prophets?' Even the ESV, which normally

tries to avoid inserting ideas that are not in the text, translates it, 'One of the Cretans, a prophet of their own'. But that word 'Cretan' is not in the text.

Let me suggest an alternative: that the phrase 'their own' refers back to the previously named group, 'the insubordinate, empty talkers and deceivers' of 1:10, who are three times referred to in verse 11 ('They . . . they . . . they') and once again in verse 13 ('Rebuke them sharply'). In that case the word 'prophet' is not a reference to a Greek poet with a prophetic gift, but to one of the teachers and leaders of the errorist group on Crete. He is the one who, to justify the wild disobedience of his followers, quotes them a Cretan proverb, to the effect that Cretans are naturally wild, disobedient, and so on. In other words, if you believe his gospel, there is no need to change your behaviour. That, says Paul, is the shocking nature of what he has heard is being said. So, he continues, 'This saying is true. Therefore rebuke them [the same group] sharply.'

Is it hard for us to imagine a Mediterranean island full of alcohol and excess, where young people indulge themselves and the older ones tolerate it, saying it is only natural?

Why religion doesn't work

Yet other people on Crete were quite serious about wanting to change, and wanting others to change, and this brings us to a second Cretan danger we will need to keep before us.

We pick up the thread at the point where Titus is to rebuke that error:

> This saying is true. Therefore rebuke them sharply, so that they will be sound in the faith and will pay no attention to Jewish myths or to the merely human commands of those who reject the truth. To the pure, all things are pure, but to those who are corrupted and do not believe, nothing is pure. In fact, both their minds and consciences are corrupted. They claim to know God, but by their actions they deny him. They are detestable, disobedient and unfit for doing anything good. (1:13–16)

Reading this carefully shows that there are two impulses: the 'rebellious' one Paul has been describing so far, and a second: 'rebuke them [the rebellious ones] sharply, so that they will be sound in the faith and will pay no attention to Jewish myths or to the merely human commands of those who reject the truth'. Paul diagnoses that at some point the issue of rebellion and licence as a Christian lurches into its apparent opposite, of religion, commands and rule. Paul had consistent problems with Jewish groups who in various ways tried to impose religious rules on his new converts, and it is clear they operated in Crete too:

'But avoid foolish controversies and genealogies and arguments and quarrels *about the law*, because these are unprofitable and useless' (3:9). Titus is fighting on two connected fronts: rebellion and religion.

It is impossible for us to get into the minds of those Cretans from this distance, to know whether they came from a Jewish or Gentile background, and we can only wonder why they were so open to the imposition of a system of ascetic rule-keeping. But the square of opposition still applies. Notice Paul's fundamental diagnosis in 1:14: these religious teachers 'reject the truth'; they 'do not believe' (1:15). Therefore they cannot produce good works:

> To the pure, all things are pure, but to those who are corrupted and do not believe, nothing is pure. In fact, both their minds and consciences are corrupted. They claim to know God, but by their actions they deny him. They are detestable, disobedient and unfit for doing anything good. (1:15–16)

This is a counterintuitive thought but one that is critical to preaching faithfully: religious rules based on a denial of the gospel cannot produce good fruit.

The twenty-first-century West is a mirror of first-century Crete. It is an increasingly secular and self-indulgent society, and we Christians face temptation on a daily basis that our grandparents would have found shockingly decadent. Those of us with children face the responsibility of ensuring they do not grow up 'wild and disobedient' by our refusal to rebuke the mores of our time (1:6). Simultaneously, we Christians find ourselves placed together with other socially conservative (which normally means sexually conservative) religious groups in a culturally resistant ghetto. We find ourselves as co-belligerents of people with whom in the past we may have had little contact, or whom we saw in exclusively hostile or alien terms. And if a secular society can put us in a neat box like that, then we are explained, contained and implausible.

There are two classic Cretan responses to sinful desires, which we either indulge or inhibit: licence or law, rebellion or religion. I do my children harm by not pointing out to them the dangers of indulgence, licence and rebellion. But I do my Jewish and Muslim friends harm by not pointing out to them the dangers of inhibition, law and religion. Being socially conservative is not the gospel; changing the law does not change the heart; and the square of opposition applies as much to the religious right as it does to the rebellious left.

How the gospel teaches

What a contrast between the Cretan patterns and the pattern of the gospel. In

chapter 1 Paul explores 'the truth that leads to godliness' (Titus 1:1), and shows
the link between the gospel and doing what is good:

> For the grace of God has appeared that offers salvation to all people. It teaches us to
> say 'No' to ungodliness and worldly passions, and to live self-controlled, upright and
> godly lives in this present age, while we wait for the blessed hope – the appearing of
> the glory of our great God and Saviour, Jesus Christ, who gave himself for us to
> redeem us from all wickedness and to purify for himself a people that are his very
> own, eager to do what is good. (2:11–14)

So 'grace . . . teaches us'. How? It cannot be by holding out the carrot of heaven
if we are good, because salvation has already appeared and we have 'hope'. It
cannot be beating us with the stick of hell if we fail, because Jesus' death was
'to redeem us from all wickedness and to purify for himself a people that are
his very own'. But somehow it teaches us 'to say "No" to ungodliness and
worldly passions' and to be 'eager to do what is good'. Timothy Keller explains
it this way:

> Only the grace of God, Titus says, 'teaches us' to say no. It argues with us: 'You are
> not living as though you are loved! As his child! It is not because he will abandon
> you that you should be holy, but because at inestimable cost he has said he won't ever
> abandon you! How can you live in the very sin that he was ripped to pieces to deliver
> you from?'[5]

That is put even more strongly in Titus 3. For a long time it has been normal,
outside more evangelical scholarship, to argue that the three so-called 'Pastoral
Epistles', 1 and 2 Timothy and Titus, were not written by Paul but by someone
else, whether a close student or a distant admirer. They are dismissed as at best
a ragbag of Pauline fragments and second-generation churchiness. The result is
that the Pastorals are frequently omitted by overarching studies of Paul's theology.

But Titus contains one of the most intense summaries of what presents
itself as Paul's theology in the New Testament. Key themes appear: salvation,
justification, works of righteousness being unable to save, adoption, renewal,
the work of the Spirit, hope, and they all lead to the place of an obedient Christian life:

---

5. Timothy Keller, 'Preaching Morality in an Amoral Age', in Haddon Robinson and
   Craig Brian Larson, *The Art and Craft of Biblical Preaching* (Grand Rapids: Zondervan,
   2005), p. 169.

At one time we too were foolish, disobedient, deceived and enslaved by all kinds of passions and pleasures. We lived in malice and envy, being hated and hating one another. But when the kindness and love of God our Saviour appeared, he saved us, not because of righteous things we had done, but because of his mercy. He saved us through the washing of rebirth and renewal by the Holy Spirit, whom he poured out on us generously through Jesus Christ our Saviour, so that, having been justified by his grace, we might become heirs having the hope of eternal life. This is a trustworthy saying. And I want you to stress these things, *so that* those who have trusted in God may be careful to devote themselves to doing what is good. (3:3–8)

How Titus is to teach

Titus' role on Crete is therefore critical. He has a direct responsibility to deal with the various errors, but also has to model to the new elders how they are to do their job:

In everything set them an example by doing what is good. In your teaching show integrity, seriousness and soundness of speech that cannot be condemned, so that those who oppose you may be ashamed because they have nothing bad to say about us. (2:7–8)

Titus 2 is where that happens. We have already seen the engine that drives the chapter, in 2:11–14, but we need to see why it is there. What comes before it is a sequence of instructions to older and younger men and women, free and slave. Each is given a lifestyle application of the gospel, shaped around the threat of the false teaching. But the instructions to Titus as he teaches are our focus.

Paul begins the chapter, 'You, however, must teach what is appropriate to sound doctrine' (2:1). Not 'sound doctrine' alone, because the gospel is 'the truth that leads to godliness' (1:1). But what is 'appropriate' to sound doctrine? It must be the case studies in life change that follow. At the end of the chapter he concludes, after the engine of 2:11–14 and the necessary link between grace and doing good, 'These, then, are the things you should teach. Encourage and rebuke with all authority. Do not let anyone despise you' (2:15). What should he teach? That grace leads to these good works. The next section begins with another life change: 'Remind the people to be subject to rulers and authorities, to be obedient, to be ready to do whatever is good' (3:1), and at the risk of quoting the closing verses too much, 'And I want you to stress these things, so that those who have trusted in God may be careful to devote themselves to doing what is good' (3:8).

Turn your eyes

There was a song we used to sing at church when I was growing up:

> Turn your eyes upon Jesus,
> Look full on his wonderful face –
> And the things of earth will grow strangely dim
> In the light of his glory and grace.[6]

It is the chorus of a hymn urging discouraged and exhausted Christians to fix their eyes on Jesus rather than on their dispiriting circumstances, and to draw strength for the race and the battle. It is a great, grand chorus.

But if we took it in the wrong way, we might start to think that the purpose of the gospel was to distract us from real life. If we focus on Jesus, then the things of earth become irrelevant, or illusory: all the real battles are fought in the spiritual realm, and it is there, not here, where we must fix our gaze. I doubt if Helen Lemme had any such intention: she would have urged us to fix our eyes on Jesus to get energy for the fight, not so that we might think the battle was unimportant.

Preachers, however, may be tempted to take it the wrong way. In fact, when we are tempted to think we must talk about Jesus *rather than* the battles of life, then we have fallen into a trap. Paul's message to Titus, of course, goes in the opposite direction. Rather than teach the gospel as an alternative to gritty obedience, Titus must become so deeply personal in his application that there is no escape from it.

I have sometimes wondered about a different, additional chorus:

> Turn your eyes upon Jesus,
> Look full on his wonderful face –
> And the things of earth will grow *bright and clear*
> In the light of his glory and grace.

When I have properly understood the gospel and all that Christ has done for us, then issues of my obedience necessarily become central. I understand how I must behave in that meeting, or respond to the cold shoulder of my colleague.

---

6. 'Turn Your Eyes upon Jesus', Helen H. Lemme (1922). Public domain.

We are not alone

Older generations of preachers understood this well. It is not difficult to find a list of quotations from great preachers on the issue, and, as usual, Spurgeon put it most bluntly: 'Where the application begins, there the sermon begins.'[7] But more surprising perhaps are the views of John Calvin, who is often stereotyped as a dauntingly dry and intellectual preacher:

> I always make this my rule: That those who hear me may profit from the teaching I put forward. If I do not have that affection, and do not procure the edification of those who hear me, I am a sacrilege, profaning God's Word.[8]
>
> To be good theologians we must lead a holy life. The Word of God is not to teach us to prattle, not to make us eloquent and subtle and I know not what. It is to reform our life, so that it is known that we desire to serve God, to give ourselves entirely to him and to conform ourselves to his good will.[9]
>
> It is not enough, says St Paul, to preach what is good and useful. For if men were well-disposed and received what God set before them, and were so teachable that they could put their minds and hearts into line with it, to subject themselves to what is good, it would be enough to have said, 'This is what God declares to us.' But since men are malicious, are ungrateful, are perverse, ask only for lies in place of the truth, readily go astray, and after they have known God turn again and distance themselves from him – for this reason it is necessary, says St Paul, for us to be held as it were forcibly, and for God, having faithfully taught us, to exhort us to persist in obedience to his Word.[10]
>
> What advantage would there be if we were to stay here a day and I were to expound half a book without considering you or your profit and edification? . . . we must take into consideration those persons to whom the teaching is addressed . . . For this reason let us note well that they who have this charge to teach, when they speak to a people, are to decide that teaching will be good and profitable so that they will be able to disseminate it faithfully and with discretion to the usefulness of everyone individually.[11]

---

7. Spurgeon as quoted by John A. Broadus, *A Treatise on the Preparation and Delivery of Sermons*, 27th ed. (New York: Hodder & Stoughton, 1893), p. 245.

8. Quoted in T. H. L. Parker, *Calvin's Preaching* (Edinburgh: T&T Clark, 1992), pp. 11–12.

9. Ibid., p. 15.

10. Ibid., pp. 114–115.

11. Quoted in Peter Adam, *Speaking God's Words* (Leicester: Inter-Varsity Press, 1996), pp. 132–133.

If we leave it to men's choice to follow that which is taught them, they will never move one foot. Therefore, the doctrine of itself can profit nothing at all.[12]

A generation later the Westminster Directory of Public Worship urged preachers, 'The preacher is not to rest in general doctrine, although never so much cleared and confirmed, but is to bring it home to special use by application to his hearers.'[13]

So there is good historical precedent for a concern with application, which means our predecessors may have much to teach us by their example, as well as their persuasion. But the principal problem we encounter today is one they hardly considered: How do we construct that bridge across the river?

Questions for reflection and discussion

- Do the findings of the Willow Creek survey ring true in your context? What might be the implications for the way you preach?
- Take some time to read Paul's letter to Titus, and then think through the following.
- How does the letter show that true teaching produces godliness, and false teaching produces ungodliness?
- How does the letter show that true teaching cannot be related to ungodliness, and false teaching cannot be related to godliness?
- How does the letter show that true and false teaching are inevitably opposed?
- How does the letter show that godliness and ungodliness are inevitably opposed?
- Why does Chris Green say that 'religion doesn't work'?
- How does the gospel teach us to change?

12. John Calvin, *Sermons on the Epistles to Timothy and Titus* (Edinburgh: Banner of Truth, 1983), sermon on 2 Tim. 4:1–2.

13. Quoted in E. Alexander, *What Is Biblical Preaching?* (Phillipsburg: P&R, 2008), p. 29; 'What are we to believe, and what is our duty?' (Westminster Shorter Catechism Question 3).

10. BRIDGING THE GAP

These things happened to them as examples and were written down as warnings for us.

(1 Cor. 10:11)

Evangelism

People who give frequent evangelistic talks often conclude in a straightforward and similar way. I usually end with something like the following.

'When I give these kinds of talks, hearers respond in various ways, but basically there are only four. I call them A, B, C and D, and they match the letters at the bottom of the handout today. If I describe them, you may find yourself in the list.

'"A" means, "Absolutely! Agreed with every word of it." If that is you, thank you for coming, and thank for staying, even though you have heard it before. And thank you, if you have brought a guest here today – perhaps you can even think of someone you might invite next time.

'"D" means, "Don't believe a word of it!" If that is you, again: thank you for coming, and thank for staying, even though you think I'm wrong. Of course in a short talk like today's I've been able to scratch only the surface of what Jesus said, and I hope you don't dismiss him simply because I've not put things very well. I think there are serious, credible reasons to believe that there is a God, and that what the historical figure of Jesus said and did gives unique information about him. If you're staying for a coffee, head for the bookstall and look for this book [I wave a sample of the book I want to plug and explain why it's good].

'"C" means, "Considering it – I'm curious." If that is you, we have a couple of things to help you. The book I mentioned just now might be really helpful to you as well, so you could find that on the bookstall. But often the best way to get your head clear is through a series of talks and discussions [here I would give details about the next evangelistic course the church would be running].

'"B" means, "Beginning tonight!" As we have thought together tonight the penny has dropped and you realize you know who Jesus is, why he came and what it means to follow him. You're ready to put your life on the line for him, right now. In that case, I'm going to pray a prayer, and I invite you to join me, quietly echoing the words in your heart . . .' Then I would lead them in a prayer and might point them to where they could talk to someone, or where they might pick up a gospel, or a CD with a couple of talks on it they might find helpful.

I am not saying it is a perfect ending. Far from it. But because it will be similar to the endings of many evangelistic talks you have heard, and perhaps that you have given, take it as an example for the moment and consider what I have just offered:

- I identified four different responses, giving a chance for everybody present to identify in part with what I was saying at the end.
- There were clear steps forward for each of those four groups.
- There were resources to help three of those four groups.
- And for the last group there was support for their decision *right now*.

I would imagine that any evangelistic talk you give or hear does several of those, and perhaps all four. Now compare that in your mind with the sermon you heard last Sunday. Did that sermon identify some possible different responses? Did it make resources available? Did it offer encouragement to change specific-ally right now, or to take it further on your own? Did it make clear what you could or should do?

What makes the difference? Why are we so willing to make repentance and faith quite clear for non-Christians, yet become reluctant to do it for Christians?

The most obvious reason is that it would be boring for a preacher to be that identical and predictable every week. Passages differ in style and content, and their implications will vary in intensity and necessity.

But that is avoiding the question. I did not ask whether the previous Sunday's sermon ended in the same way as an evangelistic talk – I asked, in effect, whether the implications were equally clear, and was what the hearers were expected to do laid out for them so that they could not miss it?

But before we can answer that we have to ask whether we have any confidence in our words to communicate truth and response at all. How confident can we be that God speaks?

Can God speak?

The philosophical question of hermeneutics has become the principal dilemma for legitimate interpretation of any text by any reader, and is a notoriously pressing question for preachers. If you are not aware of it, the question goes something like this: Given my subjectivity as a writer, and given yours as a reader, how is it possible for you to come to an interpretation of this paragraph that is close to mine? The greater the cultural distance between you and me, the harder we have to work to understand each other. And in contemporary Western culture thoughtful readers frequently doubt whether they will be able to come to any coherent interpretation of the text, let alone what the author intended by what he wrote. More radical readers will question whether that matters, because the imposition of the author's intention on the reader is an exercise of power. There has come to be a wide gap between the writer and the reader.

The issue is a curious one, and not one that affects everyone equally. Manufacturers of fire extinguishers and writers of computer manuals have to assume a fairly high degree of correspondence between what they write and what we read. Nor is there a division between the arts and the sciences. I recently watched a performance of Shakespeare's *Richard II*, and interviews with the actors afterwards showed how hard they were working to get inside the text Shakespeare gave them so that they could give a coherent performance. Nor were the musicians who played the specially written score at liberty to break into 'Bohemian Rhapsody' if they felt like it. Both the playwright and the composer had communicated clearly, and with authority.

But of course the gap in those examples is quite narrow. The music had been written in notation that both composer and players shared, and there was a possibility of a conversation over any obscure notes. Shakespeare's English may be five hundred years old, but it is still recognizably English, and any playgoer will know the feeling that after taking 10 minutes to get 'your ear in', it becomes quite easy to follow along.

Three examples

The argument goes that the problem of interpretation is much more complex with the Bible. Despite appearances, this is not one book by one author, but sixty-six books written by dozens of people. It comes from not one but several cultures, and was written in languages unknown to most of us. But because many Christians are familiar with some parts of it, and read other parts selectively and without proper regard to their cultural setting, we have become dulled us to how difficult the Bible is to read. Three widely used examples show us the dimensions of the problem.

Consider the Old Testament laws. They instruct readers three times, without any explanation, 'Do not cook a young goat in its mother's milk' (Exod. 23:19; 34:26; Deut. 14:21). What are we to do with that? Is it something Christian cooks today should observe, or are we free to modify it somehow, or even ignore it? Many readers today would gloss over that sentence, as something that applied only to Old Testament believers.

We must not rush over this issue: many of our battles within churches over issues of morality will include debating the extent to which any of the Old Testament laws are mandatory for Christians.

A second kind of problem is where the Bible refers to something that is simply not an issue for me. The Council of Jerusalem, in Acts 15, wrote to all the churches, and summarized their advice:

> You are to abstain from food sacrificed to idols, from blood, from the meat of strangled animals and from sexual immorality. You will do well to avoid these things. Farewell. (Acts 15:29)

James later repeats it:

> As for the Gentile believers, we have written to them our decision that they should abstain from food sacrificed to idols, from blood, from the meat of strangled animals and from sexual immorality. (Acts 21:25)

The issue of whether Christians could eat meat sacrificed to idols became a live one in Corinth, and Paul devoted a lengthy section in 1 Corinthians to the issue, theologically, relationally and practically (1 Cor. 8). The issue here is the relevance of an apparently irrelevant instruction.

The third example is perhaps the most pressing of all, that when the New Testament instruction violates our cultural norms, and is therefore not so much irrelevant as implausible, or even offensive. Take, for instance, the example of Paul's instructions over head coverings for women, again a matter of lengthy discussion in 1 Corinthians (1 Cor. 11:11–16).

It would be quite easy to say that Paul was wrong, and that is a route many have found attractive and simple. Or we could adopt a more nuanced position, suggesting that Paul had an overall gospel trajectory that was gender blind, but that occasionally his thoughts betrayed ideas that had not fully been worked through, and this is one such example. He would say, 'I used to impose food laws, but now I see the gospel teaches me otherwise,' so does that mean we can say, 'Paul used to impose gender laws, but now we see the gospel teaches us otherwise'? In that way we apparently rescue Paul from himself.

But assume a standard evangelical position: that this is God's inspired Word for his church throughout time, and it is without error in all that it teaches. What, exactly, does Paul teach here?

There are undeniably complex issues of translations: Paul makes some interplay between physical 'heads' and spiritual 'heads'; it is hard to catch every nuance of every statement. But assume that we can clarify those issues.

Much more significantly, there is the issue of cultural distance. The question is, does obedience for us today lie in the direct obedience of Paul's instructions, for example requiring women today to wear hats and forbidding men to grow their hair long, or does it embed a deeper principle of that which is the cultural expression, and requires a different kind of obedience? How do such gender markers work in a culture where the gender markers change?

Imagine we were missionaries in a culture where having a bald head was a sign of extreme femininity, and the most masculine thing you could do was to wear a hat over a bushy head of hair. Would we as missionaries wear our hair long or short, would we be hatted or bare headed? Does obeying Paul mean we do what he says, or in that culture do the reverse of what he says?

Consider again the quotation at the beginning of this chapter: 'These things happened to them as examples and were written down as warnings for us' (1 Cor. 10:11). Paul applied the story of the temptations of the Israelites during their desert wanderings (*them*) to himself and his Corinthian readers (*us*). Where do we, as twenty-first-century believers fit into that move? Are we an identical group to the Corinthians, or do we need to make a further jump, to say that Paul's warnings to the Corinthians need to be rethought for *us*? Or are there other options? The way we answer that question defines how we read the New Testament.

Those three examples – the Old Testament law, an apparently irrelevant New Testament command and a difficult New Testament command – show the parameters of the problem we face whenever we open the Bible and try to apply it.

I do not intend to solve the complex issues of 1 Corinthians here! I do, though, want to look at one standard way of solving the problem, because it needs careful re-examining. It is the reason why I suggest the problem of hermeneutics may be largely self-inflicted. We need to think again about what it means to know a *God* who can *speak*.

Questions for reflection and discussion

- Do you notice any difference between the four elements of the way Chris Green concluded his evangelistic talk with the way you tend to end your sermons?
- Do you think we need to take the instructions to the Corinthians as if they were directly written to us, or do they need to be reinterpreted for today? Are there any other options?

11. GOD HAS HAD US IN MIND ALL THE TIME

I make known the end from the beginning,
from ancient times, what is still to come.

(Isa. 46:10)

Let us start in a different place.

The nineteenth-century philosopher Immanuel Kant taught that there are basically two levels to our existence, like a two-storey house. On the lower level are the mundane, everyday realities of things, and on the upper level are ideas and ideals, truths and values. To Kant's mind both existed, but there was no connection between the two: it was a two-storey house without a staircase.

That is an unforgivable simplification – except that it is a simplification people from that time to today have taken as the proper view of reality. It assumes that we cannot work out from the lower storey the things in the upper storey, and therefore for practical purposes they are irrelevant. It, God, or what we call God (or gods), or spiritual realities or truths have no functional reality for us, and any guesses we may have about what lives upstairs are never more than unprovable guesses. Moreover, the long wars of the twentieth century were put in train by various attempts to impose upper-storey values violently, by both the extreme left and the extreme right, which has taught us that any claim to truth is inherently a claim potentially to abusive power.

So since we cannot get rules for downstairs from upstairs, we must produce our own. Such rules cannot really express what is 'right' or 'wrong' because those are 'upper storey' words we cannot properly access, which is why one of the problems for contemporary ethics is how we express universal values, such as not murdering civilians during a war, when there is no deep answer to the question 'Why is that wrong?' Instead, avoiding divisive questions, we have to maintain a common way of life on the basis of what most people will agree to, or agree to tolerate, to keep society functioning. It is democratic self-regulation, and will keep changing as the public mood changes.

Once a Christian starts to believe that model, applying the Bible becomes impossible. If there is no staircase between the storeys, then either the Bible is a human construct that has only as much authority as we choose to give it, or it is a sacred text of no practical value. Which then means that our non-Christian friends will either accuse us of complete irrelevance, because no one can really know what God is like or thinks, or accuse us of being hypocrites, because we know we are only pretending to be speaking for God. Internally, we can start to suspect that too.

But the Bible claims to be an upper-storey derived text, of the God who not only lives upstairs but who speaks so that we can hear and understand him, and who even moved downstairs with us so that he would not be misunderstood.

Living downstairs

Take an example that is so obvious it is almost a cliché, but is such a presenting issue that we have to deal with it. How can we apply the Bible to a Christian who feels same-sex erotic attractions?

Our cultural milieu now has no problem with that attraction. Such a person could be an icon, 'out and proud', and the culture not only would affirm and encourage him or her in that, but would take self-pride in that affirmation. The general consensus is to express the greatest possible tolerance of each other's values. Which means that while the culture has no problem with that same-sex attraction, it has a great problem with anyone who has a problem with it. That means any Christian has to work out how to handle the Bible.

There are two culturally 'safe' options. One is to affirm the Bible is an upper-storey text of no provable universal value, so it has nothing to say about the realities of life. The other is to say it is a lower-storey construct that is of possible interest for the historically curious, but has no inherent authority. However, an evangelical would claim that this is a book that has built a staircase between the storeys.

The traditional Christian view has been that those who experience attractions towards such acts are experiencing what Christian pastoral care describes as a temptation. All Christians experience temptation and every Christian is sexually fallen, in heart and mind and imagination, even if not physically. Furthermore, at various times in Christian history different temptations have been easier or harder to resist: a hundred years ago I could have been sinfully racist and it would not have raised an eyebrow; today I could be sinfully blasphemous in the press and no one could complain. Swap the sins over, and I would have been arrested on both counts.

A 'tempted-to-same-sex Christian' lives in a time when there is enormous public encouragement to give in to the temptation – in fact, to refuse to identify it as a temptation at all. He or she will also be told that a traditional evangelical understanding of the Bible on this issue is a homophobic and hypocritical power play, at best a finger-wagging irrelevance and probably masking the fact that the preacher is a secret consumer of gay websites and consumed by self-loathing.

If we sit down and gently, constantly, lovingly encourage the Christian norms of resistance to temptation, and to embrace constant forgiveness, we will be described by all those names, and worse. But if we are right that the correct word for this attraction is 'temptation', and one that God describes as serious, then it is necessary for us to run that risk. It will be costly to do it, but eternally cruel to refuse. But do we have the courage to apply the Bible? And do we have plausible tools to apply it?

The God of the gap

The first step in gaining, or regaining, our confidence in applying the Bible is to bring our doctrine of Scripture into line with our doctrine of God.

We would not know God unless he had made himself known. He 'lives in unapproachable light, whom no one has seen or can see' (1 Tim. 6:16), and unless he had revealed himself, our created status as finite beings, and now our status as fallen, finite beings, means that we would be in absolute ignorance. But in his kindness, and in various forms, he has made himself known as a holy and real creator-judge. Even in sin we should know our status as creatures, and as morally accountable and guilty (Rom. 1:18–25).

God has made himself known in a way that brings salvation in three, inter-locked ways. First, there are his acts in covenant history; secondly, in sending his Son as our saviour, which is not merely one among many acts in covenant history but the one that brings all others their validity; and thirdly, in his speech, the means by which his covenant is promised and fulfilled throughout history up until the new creation.

That speech, his self-revelation in his explanation of his acts, is Scripture; and when he addresses it in his Word, he brings us into and maintains us in a loving covenant relationship.

In Scripture he repeatedly reveals three truths about himself that we need to bring to the foreground. First, God knows everything. He is omniscient. Secondly, therefore, God knows everything in advance, since the future as much as the past or present is open to an eternally omniscient God. On that basis he can foretell the future. Thirdly, God is unchallengeably powerful to achieve what he wants. On those three bases he can promise, because he not only knows what will happen, but can guarantee in words that his plans will achieve their end.

Those themes of God's omniscience and omnipotence intertwine as he foretells the future through Isaiah, comparing himself to idols that cannot speak truthfully about the present, foretell accurately the future or act decisively in either:

> Remember this, keep it in mind,
>   take it to heart, you rebels.
> Remember the former things, those of long ago;
>   I am God, and there is no other;
>   I am God, and there is none like me.
> I make known the end from the beginning,
>   from ancient times, what is still to come.
> I say, 'My purpose will stand,
>   and I will do all that I please.'
> From the east I summon a bird of prey;
>   from a far-off land, a man to fulfil my purpose.
> What I have said, that I will bring about;
>   what I have planned, that I will do.
> (Isa. 46:8–11)

God's knowledge, speech and power together produced the Bible, but they also guarantee its unchanging authority. God's knowledge means that he knew from eternity what would be in Isaiah 46. His omniscience means that even as he inspired Isaiah to write that prophecy, he had the full context of final Scripture in mind as Isaiah wrote. His omniscience means that he had every occasion that Isaiah 46 would ever be looked at in mind as he wrote. His omniscience means that from eternity he planned that you would be reading Isaiah 46 today, and his power means that he was able, from eternity, to guarantee that Isaiah 46 would be his living Word for us, today.

The deepest problem I have with the language of gaps, chasms or rivers is that they all seem to require not only that the Bible be on one side of the gulf, but that in some way God be too; further, if one of the components of the gap is time, then either side of that gulf must be moving further apart with each increasing day. God's actions and words are increasingly remote from us. If he still speaks through the Scriptures, it is from the other side of an increasingly wide canyon.

But consider the wonderful consequences if our current contexts were already taken into account by God in the way he inspired Scripture. God knew when human beings would invent the steam engine, discover the Higgs boson particle, and when we will first step on Mars. God's Word was designed to be adequate to deal with each of those events, and the billions of life events, trivial and traumatic, that have affected you and others today. Nothing that happens ever takes God by surprise; he wrote the Bible with all of them in mind.

Responsible interpretation

Not far from where I live in London is a famous missionary training college, All Nations, and a friend of mine was admissions tutor there. She would interview potential students, and ask them why they felt God was directing them to the college. All too often she had this conversation:

I'm applying because God told me to come.
Really? How do you know?
Well in my quiet time I read, Matthew 28, 'Go to *all nations*' – and here I am.

Responsible interpretation rightly insists that such short circuits cannot be allowed. Such a reading has distorted the text. We must use all the responsible tools of translation and exegesis, and we need diligent scholars to work hard at this, and we preachers rely on their faithful studies. When I start preparing a sermon, I must clear away all thoughts of that sermon, this church and the twenty-first century. I must immerse myself in the biblical world. There is absolutely no possibility that when God inspired Matthew to write the Greek words *panta ta ethnē* he meant 'All Nations Christian College'. He meant, 'all nations'.

But the omniscience of our speaking God guarantees that the biblical texts *still mean* what they meant; those words still mean 'all nations'. So although those potential students needed to take a basic course in Bible interpretation, their hearts were in the right place because God's intentions were and are to reach the lost through his obedient people, and to shape them into Christ's mature disciples. His Word achieves his purpose.

For us

Even within the Bible we can see the move that occurs, as New Testament writers appropriate Old Testament scriptures, and say, effectively, 'These apply to us, now. You will not be able to understand them without Christ, because God always intended them to be read by us Christians.'

Paul says as a general truth, 'For everything that was written in the past was written to teach us, so that through the endurance taught in the Scriptures and the encouragement they provide we might have hope' (Rom. 15:4). The word 'us' is key to his appropriation of all the Old Testament: '*everything . . . was written to teach us*'. To expand what we have seen before, the Old Testament was written with the coming of Christ as its centre, with the intention that it would only properly be read by Christians in the light of his resurrection and reign: to interpret it without him is to misinterpret the Scriptures.

- Narrative was written for us: Romans 4:23–24; 1 Corinthians 10:6–11.
- Law was written for us: 1 Corinthians 9:7–11.
- Psalms was written for us: Hebrews 4:1–11 (3:7–8).
- Proverbs (wisdom literature) was written for us: Hebrews 12:4–6.

Us

There is no equivalent move from the New Testament to us. The Old Testament contains mysteries that revealed the coming of Christ, and the New Testament alludes to mysteries that will be revealed at his return. But there are no further unrolling mysteries throughout Christian history. God has made himself transparent.

For instance, it is widely agreed that in the eighteenth century it became blindingly clear that slavery was a wicked blight that had to be erased, and that evangelical Christians were in the vanguard in driving the abolition movement. It is also widely agreed that evangelical Christians were on both sides of the argument. Today slavery is almost the standard example of how Christians have changed their minds on an ethical matter, and how they may do so again. Where Scripture seemed to be lacking, centuries of reflection have given clarity to an issue.

But the critical issue is that abolishing the slave trade was not a new thought. It reads right off the pages of the New Testament. Here is Paul:

> We know that the law is good if one uses it properly. We also know that the law is made not for the righteous but for lawbreakers and rebels, the ungodly and sinful, the unholy and irreligious, for those who kill their fathers or mothers, for murderers, for the sexually immoral, for those practising homosexuality, *for slave traders* and liars and perjurers – and for whatever else is contrary to the sound doctrine that conforms

to the gospel concerning the glory of the blessed God, which he entrusted to me.
(1 Tim. 1:8–11)

The Authorised Version translates the phrase 'slave traders' as 'men stealers', which is both accurate and would have been unmissably clear in the eighteenth century when the debate was raging.

And this is the announcement of judgment on Babylon, followed by the reasons, from Revelation:

> 'Woe! Woe to you, great city,
>   you mighty city of Babylon!
> In one hour your doom has come!'

> The merchants of the earth will weep and mourn over her because no one buys their cargoes any more – cargoes of gold, silver, precious stones and pearls; fine linen, purple, silk and scarlet cloth; every sort of citron wood, and articles of every kind made of ivory, costly wood, bronze, iron and marble; cargoes of cinnamon and spice, of incense, myrrh and frankincense, of wine and olive oil, of fine flour and wheat; cattle and sheep; horses and carriages; *and human beings sold as slaves.* (Rev. 18:10–13)

There was no excuse for the slave trade: the issue was not the clarity of the Bible, nor the need for some new revelation, but the willingness of people who had read the Bible to do what it said.

Idol meat

I was in India, the guest of a mission agency, having been asked to help its trainees with their skills in understanding and communicating the Bible. Over a weekend my hosts treated me with great warmth and friendliness, taking me around the various sights and getting enjoyably lost. At one point we came across a row of butchers' stalls against the walls of a local temple, and my hosts explained that they were there because the temple used them to sell off the meat they had left over after their sacrifices. And a little light bulb went on in my brain.

During the week, I had spent some time trying to explain to the trainees about the Bible's hermeneutical gap and the need to build bridges across. Trying to do that while being simultaneously translated into seven different languages was a lesson in communication in itself, but that is not what struck me that afternoon in the Indian street. It was this: I had often read the section in Paul's letter to the

Corinthians on eating or not eating meat sacrificed to idols (1 Cor. 8), and I had assumed that there was an enormous gap that contemporary readers need to navigate across – but for my Indian friends, living in a large contemporary city, there was no gap at all at that point. They would simply have read the section and taken it as what they were supposed to do. And they were right.

There is no one, insurmountable hermeneutical gap. There are times, and my experience is that this is overwhelmingly the case, that reading and applying the New Testament material presents no new problem at all, for any of us, other than our own willingness to obey. The work is normally easier than we might expect. With the Old Testament there is the added complication of taking into account our place in covenant history, but the similarities of being part of God's people normally dwarf the differences.

Later on I will develop the categories of being hearers or overhearers of a particular text, but it is useful to flag it here. My Indian friends' context was so close to urban, multicultural Corinth that the differences between then and now became irrelevant at that point: God's Word to the Corinthians was God's Word to the Indians, and they became, effectively, hearers.

I was an overhearer. I could see immediately the direct relevance of the message in their context, but I had to store it up and mull it over.

Fast forward a decade, and you find me in our local supermarket chain, buying some fresh lamb. I suddenly realized that the entire fresh meat section was advertised as Halal, and that the butchers were visibly preparing meat for me in strict compliance with Muslim tradition.

At that moment I became a hearer, facing on a food label the identical issue that both my Indian friends and the Corinthians faced. Does it matter to my guests and me if I know the meat is Halal meat?

What I learned at that moment was a second lesson: because God's Word is both living and sufficient, I do not need to strain too hard in fear of a hermeneutical gap, because any apparent gap that is open at one moment may close at any other.

The idea that the gap is much smaller than we fear and usually non-existent is quite a radical one, so for the sake of an example I want to try out a couple of suggestions from 1 Corinthians. Please take them as targets to be shot at, and think through their plausibility.

Baptism and the dead

Later in the letter, in a notoriously complex part of his argument for the necessity of a physical resurrection for Christians, Paul asks the Corinthians, 'Now if there is no resurrection, what will those do who are baptised for the dead? If the dead are not raised at all, why are people baptised for them?' (1 Cor. 15:29).

It is a classic example of a gap – we do not know what they were doing, commentators wrestle with it and it seems impossible to work out what possible benefit we are to gain from the verse. It is tempting to reduce it to the level of saying, 'Well the Corinthians were obviously doing something or other, maybe being baptized for a dead granny, maybe hosing down coffins; and without approving or disapproving, Paul simply says that their practice presupposes that they do believe in a physical resurrection.'

Such a problem would not be unique to us. We can imagine the Romans or the Ephesians hearing about this and saying, 'They are doing *what* exactly?' That is not a trivial point, because again it suggests that any misunderstanding is not necessarily to do with time or language or culture. If we do start to think in that way, we will assume that any text from the past or a different culture or language must come from the other side of the gap.

I suspect that is to give in too easily. The assumption that seems to be held in common by most possible solutions requires us to agree that the solution to the mystery lies in some practice of the Corinthians that lies outside the text and is inaccessible to us. But what if that assumption is wrong? It is an apparently necessary answer to our question 'What was baptism of the dead?', but that is not necessarily the only, or even the first, question. Here is the passage with its following context; and as you read it, ask yourself instead, 'Who are "the dead"?'

> Now if there is no resurrection, what will those do who are baptised for the dead?
> If the dead are not raised at all, why are people baptised for them? And as for us, why
> do we endanger ourselves every hour? I face death every day – yes, just as surely as I
> boast about you in Christ Jesus our Lord. (1 Cor. 15:29–31)

It looks as though Paul is putting himself, as a suffering apostle, in that company. His personal encounter with the likelihood of his death because of the gospel makes sense only if he believes in a physical resurrection.

There is also a translation issue: Paul's phrase is more literally 'baptism for the dead' (Greek: *hyper tōn nekrōn*), and that seems to need some kind of padding out for the sake of clarification. The latest NIV and ESV both take it in the direction of 'on behalf of'. The shape of this phrase (the preposition *hyper* combined with the genitive) can have a substitutionary sense, and often does in the New Testament with regard to Christ's death, which is why some argue here that it means the Corinthians were being baptized on behalf of dead and unconverted relatives. My hunch, and it is only a hunch, is that such a practice would have been so remote from Paul's practice that it would have called for some correction here. But *hyper* + genitive can also have a broader sense of 'with reference to', some to-be-specified means of identification between two parties.

We already know, from 1 Corinthians 1:14–17, that Paul's involvement in baptism was a live issue in Corinth. We know too from those verses that the Corinthians seemed to be taking pride in who baptized them, even claiming some kind of tribal loyalty from well-known Christians ('What I mean is this: one of you says, "I follow Paul"; another, "I follow Apollos"; another, "I follow Cephas"; still another, "I follow Christ"').

If we put those elements together, the context of Paul's death, the translation issue and the chapter 1 information, this verse might mean something like this: 'Why else are people in Corinth so willing to be identified by baptism with those messengers of a gospel who are being killed, unless they also believe in a physical resurrection?' It would be a powerful ad hominem argument in Corinth.

As I say, that is a suggestion – but it is one that searches for an explanation that is available within, not outside the text, and removes a worrying gap caused by culture, language, and so on. My Christian friends in India, facing both militant Islam and militant Hinduism, know the danger of death and the risks of being identified as a fellow Christian.

Because of the angels

Let us take a second example, this time from 1 Corinthians 11:2–16. This is again a complex passage, with translation and interpretative issues abounding.

Of all the New Testament this passage is one of a handful that if we could prove it lay on the other side of a hermeneutical gulf, we would be relieved to do so. The maintaining of gender distinctions, and restricting some aspects of church ministry on their basis, is one of our most implausible positions in the eyes of a watching world. So the reliability of our translation choices is critical, because while we might be willing to suffer for truth, it would be foolish to defend something where we have misunderstood Paul.

In 1 Corinthians 11:10 Paul says that the question of a woman's authority (and I am not tackling that issue) needs to be addressed in some way 'because of the angels'. It is a curious point because it comes out of the blue; elsewhere in this argument Paul has used evidence from Genesis, from the practice of the other churches, and from nature, or the natural order of things. But angels have not featured at all.

The ESV footnote points up another possibility: that the word means people sent to observe and report. Overwhelmingly, the word translated 'angels' in the New Testament means supernatural messengers, but there are at least five clear occasions where the word means a human messenger, a meaning the word can easily carry elsewhere (Matt. 11:10; Luke 7:24; 9:52; Gal. 4:14; Jas 2:25). What raises its plausibility as a translation for 1 Corinthians 11:10 to my mind is that chapter 16 explicitly deals with a series of people coming to and from Corinth, and that the other churches are explicitly mentioned in 11:16.

The reason I give these two tentative examples from 1 Corinthians may be obvious to you, but let me make it explicit: there remain significant translation issues within 1 Corinthians, and specifically within chapter 11, over the issue of what is meant by 'authority' and what is meant by 'head' in their various appearances. There also remain issues of what this passage means today.

The more 1 Corinthians remains a uniquely Corinthian letter, understandable only by addressing unique elements from within that culture, the wider the hermeneutical gap. It is not unthinkable that some interpreters might have a vested interest in making that gap look as wide as possible, by making the translation as difficult as possible, the interpretation complex and the application implausible.

I want to suggest that the sufficiency of Scripture should lead us to assume the narrowest of hermeneutical gaps, and that translation questions should be addressed from within the text first, as a matter of course. I am not absolutist here, because you will immediately think of places where external help has shed light on a difficult exegetical problem. Nor am I so cynical as to assume that the entire complex edifice of evangelical hermeneutical theory has been constructed in order to avoid women having to wear hats to church. Nevertheless, I do want to encourage you that God's sovereignty has foreseen all our current discussions in the churches, and guaranteed the relevance of his Word.

Such things

Going along with sufficiency we need to see too that some New Testament lists are not meant to be exhaustive, and they carry within them the principle that there may be other good or bad things than the authors considered, or mentioned. This is important if we are to address the issue of dilemmas or behaviours that the biblical writers could not have conceived. Rather than say that the Bible has fallen short in some way, or engaging in implausible exegesis to prove our point, we might do better to admit that there will be judgment calls we have to make for which the Bible gives the raw material, but we have to work an answer out.

Notice how Paul does this in Galatians:

> The acts of the flesh are obvious: sexual immorality, impurity and debauchery; idolatry
> and witchcraft; hatred, discord, jealousy, fits of rage, selfish ambition, dissensions,
> factions and envy; drunkenness, orgies, and the like. I warn you, as I did before, that
> those who live like this will not inherit the kingdom of God. But the fruit of the
> Spirit is love, joy, peace, forbearance, kindness, goodness, faithfulness, gentleness
> and self-control. Against such things there is no law. (Gal. 5:19–23)

The open-ended nature of such a list means that we can handle dilemmas not
written about in the Bible, with care, but also with confidence.

Questions for reflection and discussion

- What are the advantages or dangers of thinking of the Bible us an
  upper-, or lower-storey book? What might be the better alternative?
- Chris Green says we need to bring our doctrine of Scripture in line with
  our doctrine of God. What does he mean?
- Does the example of the slave trade show that Christians can change
  their minds on ethical issues?
- Chris Green gives three examples from 1 Corinthians: idol meat, baptism
  of the dead and the angels. Why does he raise them, and what is he
  trying to prove?
- Why is it helpful if some New Testament ethical lists are open-ended?

PART 3

HOW DOES THE BIBLE APPLY
THE BIBLE?

12. BIBLICAL MODELS

All Scripture is God-breathed and is useful for teaching, rebuking, correcting, and training in righteousness.

(2 Tim. 3:16)

So far I have tried to make two points: first, that the Bible teaches that the ultimate purpose of our preaching is to bring God glory by producing Christlikeness in our churches (see Rom. 12:2; Gal. 5:16; Eph. 4:20–24; Col. 1:9–11; 1 Peter 1:22–23), and secondly, that the means we have been given for doing that is the Bible itself, appropriated by the Spirit into the life of believers (see Eph. 3:14–20; 6:13–18; 1 Thess. 2:13; 2 Tim. 1:7–8; 3:16–17; 2 Peter 1:3–4).

I now want to make a third point: that the Bible itself gives us models for how to do this. The ones I will mention are not the only ones, and once you begin to see the ways the Bible teaches us to apply the Bible, you will collect many more yourself. What I have found helpful is to turn its statements into diagrams or grids, to make sure I am trying to do what the biblical writers encourage.

These diagrams are ones I use in preparing my preaching, and the two we will look at in this chapter are foundational. I have them in digital form, but I usually do a rough sketch version on a pad, and play with words until I find the best way to present the ideas. Is it more work? Yes, but just as doing sentence-flow diagrams helps me understand the flow and main ideas of the passage, so these ones force me to crystallize the application through the logic of the text. Like any new skill, it feels awkward and clumsy at first – but don't give up! Every world-class skier, golfer or Formula 1 racing driver had to learn the basics once – and, if they have good coaches, they keep relearning these skills too. So we too have to be taught by the Bible how to apply the Bible.

Why the Bible?

The first grid is 2 Timothy 3:16. It is a famous verse, often used to defend the inspiration of Scripture, but if we look at it more carefully we see that it is a purpose statement. Timothy, as a preacher in the line that goes back to Moses (which is what the phrase 'man of God' means), is to find the Bible a fully adequate resource for his work (Deut. 33:1; 1 Kgs 17:24; Neh. 12:36): 'All Scripture is God-breathed and is useful for teaching, rebuking, correcting and training in righteousness, so that the man of God may be thoroughly equipped for every good work' (2 Tim. 3:16–17).[1]

There are, then, four tasks Timothy is to engage in as he handles the Bible in his work:

- *Teaching*: Timothy is to produce better-informed believers, who understand the Scriptures and their implications in depth and with relevance (Rom. 15:4; 1 Tim. 4:13, 16).
- *Rebuking*: Timothy is to point out the negative implications as well, and to call to account people who teach wrong ideas. Some churches have a weird taste for pointing out other churches' faults, but that is not what Paul means. Most churches do not like the preacher being 'negative', so Timothy has to be encouraged to do it gently but clearly (2 Tim. 2:25).
- *Correcting* means taking people who are heading in the wrong direction and turning them round so they are facing the right way.
- *Training in righteousness* is modelled on a parent bringing up a child, and is part of every Christian's relationship with our heavenly father (Eph. 6:4; Heb. 12:5, 8).

These four tasks together are what Scripture does to make Timothy *competent* and to ensure he is *equipped*. But they are not randomly selected, nor are they

---

1. NIV – although from their footnote I have substituted the word 'man' for the word 'servant'. The title 'man of God' has a different set of Old Testament cross-references to 'servant of God'.

randomly sequenced. They are given in precise order: teach what is true, rebuke what is wrong, correct the mistakes and train people in righteousness.

Once we see this sequence, we can see how Paul uses it elsewhere. Here is his instruction from Ephesians 4:28 to converted burglars:

> Anyone who has been stealing [i.e. *teaching* on God's values – this is theft and we must not do it] must steal no longer [i.e. *rebuking* – stop it!], but must work, doing something useful with their own hands [i.e. *correcting* – this is the right way to go and will replace stealing in your life], that they may have something to share with those in need [i.e. *training in righteousness* – this is how you will be more like Christ].

This is set in the midst of an extended sequence of lifestyle changes that are the direct result of being gripped by the gospel:

> You were taught [i.e. *teaching* on God's values], with regard to your former way of life, to put off your old self, which is being corrupted by its deceitful desires [i.e. *rebuking* – stop it!]; to be made new in the attitude of your minds [i.e. *correcting* – this is the right way to go and will replace sin in your life]; and to put on the new self, created to be like God in true righteousness and holiness [i.e. *training in righteousness* – this is how you will be more like Christ]. (Eph. 4:22–24)

Once we have seen the full sequence like that, we see that Timothy's task is more developed than teaching the truth, as a mere exercise in giving people more information. Timothy is to make the implications of that truth unmissably clear in the thoughts and lives of his hearers. He is to do the work of working out the application.

Sermon series on that letter to the Ephesians often exemplify the problem. It is a short letter, but quite long for a single series. Since it falls naturally into two equal halves, it is common for preachers to take chapters 1–3, which are largely theological, in one series, and chapters 4–6, which are largely application, in a second one. All too often the inevitable result is one series of unapplied doctrine, and another of undoctrinal behaviours. But that is completely the opposite of what Paul intended! It is not even that we have to defend him by saying that doctrine is useful in itself. No, doctrine explodes into life. So the wise preacher, preaching through chapters 1–3 will always be showing their direct relevance from chapters 4 to 6; and preaching through chapters 4–6 will always be showing the gospel motivation for living from 1 to 3.

So the first and simplest grid is to lay out your thinking on a passage under these four headings, and work at the theological connections that drive the theology through.

What does this passage *teach*?	What does this passage *rebuke*?	How does this passage *correct*?	How does this passage *train in righteousness*?
Describe the beliefs and/or behaviour *commended* by the passage and its implications.	Describe the beliefs and/or behaviour *criticized* by the passage and its implications.	Describe how you intend to call on people to *change* in beliefs and/or behaviour.	How *specifically* will your hearers show they have changed their beliefs and/or behaviour? What help will they need to implement their new patterns?

The greatest commandments

A pair of grids emerges from Jesus' answer to the question 'Which is the greatest commandment?'

> 'The most important one,' answered Jesus, 'is this: "Hear, O Israel: the Lord our God, the Lord is one. Love the Lord your God with all your heart and with all your soul and with all your mind and with all your strength." The second is this: "Love your neighbour as yourself." There is no commandment greater than these.' (Mark 12:29–31; cf. Luke 10:27)

I doubt if Jesus was intending to give a detailed psychological map here: the biblical terms overlap too often in Scripture. In Matthew Jesus gives a three-way rather than a four-way summary (Matt. 22:37), and in any case the emphasis is on the totality of our response to God ('all . . . all . . . all . . . all'). Nevertheless, the four ideas are sufficiently distinguishable for us to ask some penetrating questions.[2] No passage will yield all of these every time, but they are a useful way of probing. (See the chart opposite.)

Loving God with all my heart: the heart is the seat of my spiritual life, my view of God, my attentiveness to his plans and commands – in a word, it is the seat of my *worship*.

---

2. See Craig A. Evans, *Mark 8:27–16:20*, Word Biblical Commentary (Nashville: Thomas Nelson, 2001), p. 264.

With all your *heart*: application to *faith*. What language does the writer use to describe what people should/should not *worship* in this section?		With all your *soul*: application to the *affections*. What language does the writer use to describe how people should/should not *feel* in this section?	
Idols and false faith	God and true faith	Negative affections	Positive affections
How does the writer say we move between the two? From idolatry to faith: From faith to idolatry:		How does the writer say we move between the two? From negative to positive: From positive to negative:	
With all your *mind*: application to the *understanding*. What language does the writer use to describe what people should/should not *believe* in this section?		With all your *strength*: application to the *will*. What language does the writer use to describe how people should/should not *behave* in this section?	
Negative: What is/ are the specific lie(s) to be exposed?	Positive: what is/ are the specific truth(s) to be embraced?	Negative: What is the specific action or attitude to be avoided?	Positive: What is the specific action or attitude to be adopted?
How does the writer say we move between the two? From lie to truth: From truth to lie:		How does the writer say we move between the two? From disobedience to devotion: From devotion to disobedience:	

So we could ask of any passage: What language does the biblical writer use to describe what people should or should not worship? What does he say about God, and right faith? What does he say about idols and false faith? How does he say we move between the two?

Loving God with all my soul: the soul is the seat of my emotional life, my feelings and desires, both voluntary and involuntary. Older writers called these my *affections*.

So we could ask of any passage: What language does the biblical writer use to describe what people should or should not feel? What does he say about God, and positive emotions? What does he say about idols and negative emotions? How does he say we move between the two?

Notice how in our culture we have switched the points of reference of those words: we would expect the heart to address emotions, and the soul, worship. Nothing hangs on that other than the need for us to make sure we read Scripture clearly.

Loving God with all my mind: there is no change here – the mind is the seat of my intellectual life, my thoughts, dreams and values. This is the realm of *truth*. It is also the seat of our creativity and imagination, and the storehouse of our intuitions, dreams and hunches. So loving God with *all* our minds will mean all those areas should be addressed.

So we could ask of any passage: What language does the biblical writer use to describe what people should or should not think? What are the specific truths to be embraced? What are the lies to be rejected? How does he say we move between the two?

Loving God with all my strength: the strength is the seat of my will, my ability to move between what I ought to do and what I should do. This is the realm of *behaviour*.

So we could ask of any passage: What language does the biblical writer use to describe what people should or should not do? What is the specific action or attitude to be avoided? What is the specific action or attitude to be embraced? How does he say we move between the two?

Those four areas effectively map out the totality of our interior life; the second contrasting command addresses our relational life: *Love your neighbour as yourself.* Here the meaning is clear and we therefore have to help people to see beyond their self-justifying attempts to limit the meaning of the text. So the question 'Who is my neighbour?' means we should be willing to probe the following:

- Home
- Neighbourhood
- Friendships

- Work
- Church
- People of other races or cultures who live near us
- People of other religions or none who live near us
- People who hate us and campaign against us
- National life
- International life

When Jesus was asked what the greatest commandment is, and he summarized it 'Love the Lord your God with all your heart and with all your soul and with all your mind and with all your strength' and 'Love your neighbour as yourself,' he gave them a central place, which would expand to fill all the other commandments. They make sense of everything else, and can serve as another foundational grid for any application.

Question for reflection and discussion

- Take the next passage you are preaching, leading a Bible study on, or, if none of those applies, one that you are reading in your Bible study group, and run it through the two grids. Then share your findings with others.

13. BIBLICAL PATTERNS[1]

> Follow my example, as I follow the example of Christ.
>
> (1 Cor. 11:1)

One of the easiest ways of putting some application into a sermon is the use of one of the great biblical heroes: Moses, David and Saul lived lives that can, in some respects, map onto contemporary Christians, and so we raid them. It is a route many great preachers have often used – Spurgeon, for example, jammed his sermons and lectures full of biblical character studies.

But we have now seen the great danger in this, because we could preach a 'be like so-and so' sermon without putting grace into the picture. We could draw helpful lines from Joseph's handling of sexual temptation in Genesis 39, which might meet approval in a synagogue or mosque. We should be troubled by that.

The case against: Christ the pattern

Let us begin by looking hard at the problem side of the dilemma.

There was a major debate in Dutch Reformed circles in the 1930s and 1940s,

---

1. A shorter version of part of this chapter appeared in a Festschrift for Dr Charles Anderson: Pete Myers (ed.), *Going Home: Essays, Articles and Stories in Honour of the Andersons* (London: Oak Hill College, 2012), and is reproduced and adapted with permission.

ably described and analysed by Sidney Greidanus.[2] On the one side were preachers and theologians who argued for a rich reading of Scripture that allowed them to preach on the minutiae of the inspired lives of biblical characters, and on the other were preachers and theologians who insisted on the proper historical context of the passage. Bear in mind that this is being played out in a theological context where the Biblical Theology movement was arising, a term that then meant getting behind the text to its original historical context, and also with the early Barth insisting on a Christocentric (I might even say, Christomonist – i.e. speaking only of Christ and not of the Father or the Spirit) approach to preaching.

The men who preached on minutiae were so confident of the inspiration of Scripture in detail, and so assured in the rich Reformed heritage of using the biblical characters as examples in sermons, that they would take apparently irrelevant details and from them construct lessons for life.

Greidanus lists a number of nuanced points of criticism against them, but three are of particular interest for us.

The first is: *Who is the proper subject of the sermon?* A sermon about Abraham is just that – a sermon about Abraham. We, however, preach Christ, and he is the proper subject of our sermons.

Someone might guard against that by saying, I am using Abraham as an example because of particular characteristics we know God honours from elsewhere in Scripture, which Abraham embodies here at a particular point. Greidanus's second criticism comes in here: *in preaching on the moral character of a biblical person because of other biblical texts, one is not actually preaching the historical text in question.* One is preaching on the other texts.

Thirdly, therefore, *if the moral lessons are derived from other biblical texts, then there is no need for the central subject to a biblical character at all.* One might as well, to use an example Greidanus uses on several occasions, be preaching from the life of Napoleon.[3]

In summary, the exemplarist preachers displaced Christ and distorted Scripture.

We will think about distorting Scripture shortly, but for the moment consider what is meant by displacing Christ. If that is a true charge, then it is a fatal blow to what those preachers were doing.

We need to make a careful distinction between Christ as the hero of the gospel and the hero of the Scriptures, and Christ as the only possible subject

---

2. *Sola Scriptura: Problems and Principles in Preaching Historical Texts* (Toronto: Wedge, 1970).
3. Ibid., p. 195.

of the sermon. I have already argued that anything in the sermon that is not integrally related to the gospel is out of context, but we must not be simplistic in how we describe that. For instance, the doctrine of the Holy Spirit is related to the gospel, and is understood only in relation to it – but that cannot mean we cannot talk about him and must talk about Jesus instead. What we need to do is ensure that our teaching on the Holy Spirit is properly aligned with the gospel.[4]

If that is true of God himself, then it is true of the human subjects of Scripture as well. It is not that Abraham is banned as the subject of a sermon, but that Abraham-unrelated-to-the-gospel is banned. In terms of our biblical theology that must mean it becomes sufficiently rich not only to put any given element of Scripture in line with any other, but that it does so in neither a trivial nor a predictable way. One criticism people have of our Old Testament sermons is that they are all the same after the first 10 minutes. We need to work harder.

Secondly, in terms of our systematic theology we must make sure that we see the increasing interdependence of doctrines, so that we can show how our understanding of prayer or marriage is related to the gospel. That will ensure we are not giving trivial 'top tips', but also enable us to continue talking about gospel-based prayer or gospel-based marriage without feeling guilty that we should be talking purely about the cross instead.

Thirdly, as a critical aspect of our doctrine, we must ensure that our Christology is rich enough that we can talk properly about its different aspects. It is theologically wrong to separate Christ's resurrection from his cross, but we need to be confident talking about the resurrection without feeling guilty that we should be talking about the cross instead.

Fundamentally, though, I want to restate my conviction that to talk about Christ is necessarily to talk about the believer, because Christ is what he wonderfully is, for us. That enables us to bridge from talking about him to talking about us, but also enables us to bridge talking about him and talking about Abraham, because Abraham was a believer too. No other character in the Bible can be directly mapped onto any Christian today, but Christ can, and because both we and the believers of old are related to Christ, through that the similarities emerge.

---

4. Graeme Goldsworthy is more nuanced than Greidanus at this point: 'I would stress again that the redemptive-historical does not exclude the exemplary, but rather provides the context that controls it' (*Christ-Centred Biblical Theology* [Nottingham: Apollos, 2012], p. 32).

The case for: biblical patterns

My difficulty with a strong argument that we should not use biblical characters as examples is that there are just too many to account for.

1. God: the deepest possible example to follow is God himself, and he repeatedly encourages us to be like him. As our creator he worked and rested: we are to be like him (Exod. 20:11). He is holy, and so are we to be (Lev. 11:44; 1 Peter 1:15–16). He is kind, loving and patient – in short, he is perfect, and so are we to be (Matt. 5:43–48).

2. The Son of God: therefore we are to be like Jesus. His humility, love, endurance, patience, forbearance, suffering and self-sacrifice are explicitly held out to us as templates for us to measure ourselves against (John 13:14–15, 34–35; Phil. 2:5–11; 1 Peter 2:20–23; 1 John 3:16; 4:9–11).

If we take any of those elements out of their proper gospel context, of course, we reduce Jesus to the worst kind of religious saint, an impossibly perfect person whom we try to copy to get into God's good books. But taking them in their proper gospel context does not mean that they therefore cease to be examples. John puts it like this, showing how the gospel work of the cross properly becomes an example:

> This is how we know what love is: Jesus Christ laid down his life for us. And we ought to lay down our lives for our brothers and sisters. If anyone has material possessions and sees a brother or sister in need but has no pity on them, how can the love of God be in that person? Dear children, let us not love with words or speech but with actions and in truth. (1 John 3:16–18).

This is no trivial point, because it begins to show how our fellow saints in the biblical context might serve as examples: in so far as they are like Christ, our common saviour, they function as examples, and in so far as they are not, they serve as warnings. The God who breathed out Scripture designed them in this way, which is why they function in a different way to a contemporary or historical Christian. We do not have God's infallible interpretation of Napoleon, nor was Napoleon part of the covenantal development; but both the covenantal context and the infallible interpretation are given as backgrounds for Abraham, as for all biblical characters we are to learn from.

A continuing quick list in biblical order shows how many more characters are drawn to our attention.

3. Cain: John warns us, 'Do not be like Cain, who belonged to the evil one and murdered his brother. And why did he murder him? Because his own actions were evil and his brother's were righteous' (1 John 3:12).

4. Sodom and Gomorrah: Jude says, 'In a similar way, Sodom and Gomorrah and the surrounding towns gave themselves up to sexual immorality and perversion. They serve as an example of those who suffer the punishment of eternal fire' (Jude 7).

5. Abraham: in Romans 4 Paul uses Abraham as an example of faith, and it is essential to his argument that Abraham is a functional model for us: he typifies the right response, which is why he is twice called 'our father', for both Jews and Gentiles. Paul concludes, 'The words "it was credited to him" were written not for him [Abraham] alone, but also for us, to whom God will credit righteousness – for us who believe in him who raised Jesus our Lord from the dead' (Rom. 4:23–24).

James also uses Abraham as an example, in his case of obedient faith:

> You foolish person, do you want evidence that faith without deeds is useless? Was not our father Abraham considered righteous for what he did when he offered his son Isaac on the altar? You see that his faith and his actions were working together, and his faith was made complete by what he did. And the Scripture was fulfilled that says, 'Abraham believed God, and it was credited to him as righteousness,' and he was called God's friend. You see that a person is considered righteous by what they do and not by faith alone.
> (Jas 2:20–24)

That final sentence extrapolates out from Abraham as an example of obedient faith.

6. Israel in the desert: Paul's use of the example of the wandering Israelites in 1 Corinthians 10 is perhaps the most famous example in this list. Repeatedly he insists that we must learn from (not just about) them:

> Now these things occurred as examples to keep us from setting our hearts on evil things as they did. (1 Cor. 10:6)

> These things happened to them as examples and were written down as warnings for us, on whom the culmination of the ages has come. (1 Cor. 10:11)

Some might suggest that there is something special about the Corinthians that Paul can show them themselves in Scripture, but Paul does not suggest that: he says these were examples 'to keep *us* from setting *our* hearts' (not 'to keep *you* from setting *your* hearts'); they were 'written down as warnings for *us* [all Christians] on whom the culmination of the ages has come'.

He deliberately draws four lines from Israel's behaviour to the Corinthians:

1. 'Do not be idolaters, as some of them were; as it is written: "The people sat down to eat and drink and got up to indulge in revelry."'
2. 'We should not commit sexual immorality, as some of them did – and in one day twenty-three thousand of them died.'
3. 'We should not test Christ, as some of them did – and were killed by snakes.'
4. 'And do not grumble, as some of them did – and were killed by the destroying angel.' (1 Cor. 10:7–10)

Nor is Paul the only New Testament author to use this story in this way. Hebrews 4:11 makes a similar point: 'Let us, therefore, make every effort to enter that rest, so that no one will perish by following their example of disobedience.'

These stories occur at a critical moment in covenant history, but neither Paul nor the author to the Hebrews uses that to make his point: these warnings might have made the Israelites more culpable in view of their occurring so soon after Exodus and Sinai, but their function here is as an 'example'. They work only if the experience is one that we and the Israelites share in common.

7. Elijah: Paul uses Elijah to illustrate the possibility of a faithful remnant of believing Israelites in a time of rejection:

> Don't you know what Scripture says in the passage about Elijah – how he appealed to God against Israel: 'Lord, they have killed your prophets and torn down your altars; I am the only one left, and they are trying to kill me'? And what was God's answer to him? 'I have reserved for myself seven thousand who have not bowed the knee to Baal.' So too, at the present time there is a remnant chosen by grace. (Rom. 11:1–5)

Elijah's experience, we notice, is not the explanation of Paul's experience in Jewish evangelism, but an illustration of a common problem.

James too uses Elijah, but for a different point:

> The prayer of a righteous person is powerful and effective.
>   Elijah was a human being, even as we are. He prayed earnestly that it would not rain, and it did not rain on the land for three and a half years. Again he prayed, and the heavens gave rain, and the earth produced its crops. (Jas 5:16–18)

In this case we are being given an example of prayerfulness, and the point of commonality is that 'Elijah was a human being, even as we are.'

8. Job: James also uses Job, this time as an example of patience:

> Brothers and sisters, as an example of patience in the face of suffering, take the prophets who spoke in the name of the Lord. As you know, we count as blessed

those who have persevered. You have heard of Job's perseverance and have seen
what the Lord finally brought about. (Jas 5:10–11)

If you look carefully in that verse, you will see that James has a number of
examples he encourages us to consider: 'as an example of patience in the face
of suffering, take the prophets'. Which prophets? He does not say. Isaiah,
Jeremiah, Ezekiel come easily to mind – but so do many of the others. James
sees the lives of the prophets, slim though that material is, to be a valid resource
for us as an example.

   9. The witnesses of Hebrews 11: the greatest single list of Old Testament examples,
of course, occurs in Hebrews 11, which runs through a chronology of characters, drawing out a variety of lessons.

   Is it a list of heroic examples? Some have expressed caution about taking the
list in this way. Graeme Goldsworthy, dealing with an apparent polarization
between biblical theology and application (one he is careful to nuance),[5] says this:
'The assertion . . . that Hebrews 11 establishes the exemplary connection between
the Testaments as primary is problematic. Hebrews 11:39 – 12:2a makes it clear
that there is something lacking in the exemplary nature of the saints of old.'[6]

   There are three observations I would make.

   First, I would agree that Hebrews is not attempting to 'establish' that connection, although it assumes there is some connection.

   Secondly, Goldsworthy is in a debate about what is 'primary', biblical theology
or exemplary exposition. He, rightly, deplores that false choice. 'My reply . . .
was that I did not think it was necessarily an either-or situation', and I fully agree.
But I am not sure I quite line up with how he completes that sentence: 'but that
the overwhelming evidence of the New Testament is that the testimony of the
Old Testament to Christ has priority over its testimony to the authentic Christian
life in today's world.'[7] If by 'priority' Goldsworthy means theological priority,
in that the purpose must be to lead us to Christ *first*, and then – and only then –
to us, of course I concur. But in a less elegant thinker than Goldsworthy,
the language of 'priority' might mean 'takes exclusive pre-eminence', and that
would be wrong. That would be the reverse of the false choice Goldsworthy

---

5. Goldsworthy identifies 'The pastoral application of biblical theology in the home
   and local church' as a necessity (ibid., p. 37), although exploring it lies outside the
   concerns of that book. I would also encourage application, even more broadly,
   to encompass work, politics, economics, the arts, and so on.

6. Ibid., p. 31.

7. Ibid., p. 30.

deplores. So the right kind of priority, the opposite of 'either–or' is 'first, and therefore second'. And while the 'overwhelming evidence' makes the case for Christ's theological priority, there is plenty remaining to make the case for exemplary theology as a necessary entailment.

My third observation is about Goldsworthy's phrase 'there is something lacking in the exemplary nature of the saints of old'. Again I am uneasy, because that is not quite how Hebrews 11 describes it. Here are the three summary statements from the chapter:

> Now faith is confidence in what we hope for and assurance about what we do not see. This is what the ancients were commended for. (vv. 1–2)

> All these people were still living by faith when they died. They did not receive the things promised; they only saw them and welcomed them from a distance, admitting that they were foreigners and strangers on earth. People who say such things show that they are looking for a country of their own. If they had been thinking of the country they had left, they would have had opportunity to return. Instead, they were longing for a better country – a heavenly one. Therefore God is not ashamed to be called their God, for he has prepared a city for them. (vv. 13–16)

> These were all commended for their faith, yet none of them received what had been promised, since God had planned something better for us so that only together with us would they be made perfect. (vv. 39–40)

What is 'lacking' in this scenario is that they had not received what had been promised – we have. But Hebrews is not cautious about them, because that is not the main point being stressed: these people were 'commended', presumably by God, on a point of similarity between them and us, not downplayed on a point of dissimilarity. True, we have received what they had only been promised, but that surely makes their example even more extraordinary than before. If, having not yet received what was promised they showed faith, how much more should their example stir us on now that Christ has come.

Goldsworthy suggests that when we move from chapter 11 to chapter 12, we discover that 'although faith was the operative principle throughout the old dispensation, it is incomplete without the principle that operates in the New Testament, that is faith in Christ; looking to Jesus and his gospel'.[8] But surely that word 'principle' is not quite right. The old dispensation believers did have

---

8. Ibid., pp. 31–32.

faith in Christ – they just did not know how, when, where, in what form, under what name, God's promises would be kept. The principle, believing God's promise that is fulfilled in Christ, *is precisely the same*; neither the faith nor the object of faith changes one whit – the knowledge that God has kept his promise and how he has done so is what has changed.

Indeed, when Goldsworthy moves from Hebrews 11 to chapter 12 he stops too short. Here is his complete citation:

> And all these, though commended through their faith, did not receive what had been promised, since God had provided something better for us, that apart from us they should not be made perfect. Therefore, since we are surrounded by so great cloud of witnesses, let us also lay aside every weight, and sin that clings so closely, and let us run with endurance the race that is set before us, looking to Jesus, the founder and perfecter of faith. (11:39 – 12:2a)[9]

Goldsworthy emphasizes that last phrase, rightly to emphasize that, all those Old Testament examples notwithstanding, the goal is Christ.

But notice what happens if we continue the paragraph:

> fixing our eyes on Jesus, the pioneer and perfecter of faith. For the joy that was set before him he endured the cross, scorning its shame, and sat down at the right hand of the throne of God. Consider him who endured such opposition from sinners, so that you will not grow weary and lose heart. In your struggle against sin, you have not yet resisted to the point of shedding your blood. (Heb. 12:2–4)

Hebrews' point is that *Jesus himself serves as an example of enduring faith* – in an utterly unique way because his death achieved what everyone else hoped for, but nonetheless at this point in the argument he is also an example, the ultimate one.

Let me put it another way: Hebrews pictures the Christian life, and Jesus as our goal, the object of our faith. But in that he showed how the Christian life is to be run, and as I face my battles with sin, opposition and temptation, I am to 'Consider him who endured such opposition from sinners, so that [I] will not grow weary and lose heart.' If I say that, and do not first say that Christ's death is penal and substitutionary, the sole means of justification and the sole saving object of faith, I have not preached the cross. But if I preach penal substitution and omit that here Christ's substitutionary death functions as an

---

9. Ibid., p. 31.

example and an encouragement, then I have not fully preached the cross, nor fully preached Hebrews 11 – 12.

10. Paul: once we move past Jesus' resurrection and into the new age he began, the next generation of leaders not only explicitly began to believe in him, but to follow or emulate him, and they then in turn use themselves as a template for the next generation. Because he wrote so much, Paul is the obvious example.

He makes it clear that there is a pattern to emulate, and then draws on it for their sake: 'For I am not seeking my own good but the good of many, so that they may be saved. Follow my example, as I follow the example of Christ' (1 Cor. 10:32 – 11:1). Christ's substitutionary death for the salvation of others can be mined as an example for our own self-sacrifice for the gospel. Earlier he had made the second point in the context of suffering: 'Therefore I urge you to imitate me' (1 Cor. 4:16).

Philippians plays the same tune in a different key. There, in chapter 2, Christ's substitutionary death becomes part example and part rebuke to the church's squabbling factions, but Paul's personal example is also laid out:

> Join together in following my example, brothers and sisters, and just as you have us as a model, keep your eyes on those who live as we do. (Phil. 3:17)

> Whatever you have learned or received or heard from me, or seen in me – put it into practice. And the God of peace will be with you. (Phil. 4:9)

And 2 Thessalonians spells it out in detail, with both negative and positive examples:

> In the name of the Lord Jesus Christ, we command you, brothers and sisters, to keep away from every believer who is idle and disruptive and does not live according to the teaching you received from us. For you yourselves know how you ought to follow our example. We were not idle when we were with you, nor did we eat anyone's food without paying for it. On the contrary, we worked night and day, labouring and toiling so that we would not be a burden to any of you. We did this, not because we do not have the right to such help, but in order to offer ourselves as a model for you to imitate. (2 Thess. 3:6–9)

We are to imitate Paul as he imitated Christ.

11. Other senior Christians: in holding himself up as a model, Paul was not giving himself a position of privilege. He wanted it to be natural for younger Christians to model themselves on the experience of older ones. We have already noticed the example motif in Philippians, and it emerges here as well. Timothy, Epaphroditus and Clement are all held up as implied models and contrasts, but it becomes explicit at one point:

> Join together in following my example, brothers and sisters, and just as you have us as a model, keep your eyes on those who live as we do. (Phil. 3:17; see 2:19–24, 25–30)

Nor is this unique to Paul. Hebrews, continuing its theme of examples, encourages us to remember

> your leaders, who spoke the word of God to you. Consider the outcome of their way of life and imitate their faith. (Heb. 13:7)

12. Set an example: it is therefore quite natural that the next generation of leaders should themselves be willing to serve as examples. Paul directly instructs them in this way. Timothy is told:

> Don't let anyone look down on you because you are young, but set an example for the believers in speech, in conduct, in love, in faith and in purity. (1 Tim. 4:12)

And Titus:

> Similarly, encourage the young men to be self-controlled. In everything set them an example by doing what is good. (Titus 2:6–7)

Paul also implies that both men are to look for this characteristic in future pastors (1 Tim. 3:1–13; Titus 1:5–9), and that is made explicit outside the Pauline material in 1 Peter:

> be shepherds of God's flock that is under your care, watching over them – not because you must, but because you are willing, as God wants you to be; not pursuing dishonest gain, but eager to serve; not lording it over those entrusted to you, but being examples to the flock. And when the Chief Shepherd appears, you will receive the crown of glory that will never fade away. (1 Peter 5:2–4)

We will come back to this idea when we think about applying the Bible to the church.

Patterns

I give this long list of examples, because they encourage us to be more comfortable with the idea of finding biblical patterns.

Some Old Testament offices have a unique role in being typologically focused: the role of prophet, priest and king, for instance. They are not the only types, of course: places such as the land, or Jerusalem, function in this way, as do objects such as the altar, and systems such as the sacrificial one. Even listing them like that, however, shows how intimately connected they are.

And although the offices are typological, not every occupant of those offices is so. There are corrupt priests, false prophets and rebellious kings. Their significance, I suspect, comes more from their place in biblical theology. Nevertheless, some humans are clearly identified typologically: Moses and Aaron, David and Solomon. By involvement in those narratives other characters also function typologically in a negative direction: Pharaoh and Saul would be obvious examples.

This crystallizes into three questions.

1. Once we have identified any typological or biblical-theological patterns, are there other legitimate ways of handling those characters? The danger in even posing the question like that is that because typology points us to the infinite wonder of Christ, and because biblical theology leads us to the glory of the Day of Glory, I might be thought to be dismissing God's precious gospel and looking for something else, or in addition. That would indeed worry me, but I think it is a caricature.

Let me give a parallel example, and one I alluded to earlier. The cross is where God's love, wisdom and power are displayed, and where his great victory was won. We must never move away from the cross. We must never tire of the cross. So, what would you think if I were to preach a series on the resurrection narratives? Would you be right in inferring from that that I had tired of or moved on from the cross? No, that would be a false inference.

Within our theology of the cross, penal substitution rightly holds the central place. This is not the place to defend that argument,[10] but I suspect the reason why it is central is that it, alone, is not a model of the atonement – it is the reality. We must never move away from penal substitution. We must never tire of penal substitution. So, what would you think if I preached a series on other biblical explanations of the cross, would you be right in inferring from that that I had

---

10. See Steve Jeffery, Mike Ovey and Andrew Sach, *Pierced for Our Transgressions: Rediscovering the Glory of Penal Substitution* (Leicester: Inter-Varsity Press, 2007).

tired of or moved on from penal substitution? That is a better example, in fact, because in the current theological climate among evangelicals you would be right to be suspicious. You would press me. But I hope, once you had identified that I have not moved on the central position, you would agree that it is valid to explore other biblical themes as well.

So it is, I suggest, with biblical theology and typology. They are the central, organizing way in which the biblical data points us to Christ and develops us in Christlikeness. Having established that centrality, I cannot see that it damages it to say that Christ, in his infinite goodness, has given us additional ways to learn from the biblical data. Indeed, it is the primacy of biblical theology that puts safeguards around the other lessons we may or may not learn.

2. Can we learn from other characters who are not typological? Again I put this cautiously, because there is a sense in that every biblical character is typological: since Israel is a type, every Israelite is; and since the nations react to Israel, they function in typological rebellion.

Again, though, once we have established that, is there more to learn? It is noticeable, for example, that the examples we just saw of Job or Elijah are not put in any biblical-theological schema at all: they are simply examples of patience and prayer. Or, take the Hebrews 11 list. The only biblical-theological frame I can see is that they lived BC and we live AD. That is critical for the argument; but if that exhausted the point Hebrews 11 was making, the writer would have needed only one example. The series, and the variety within that series, pushes us to explore some of the individual circumstances of those characters, and their individual examples of faith. There is one, repeated lesson that biblical theology gives us, but we should dive deeply into the text itself to see the subtle variations within that lesson.

3. Is this like learning from the life of Napoleon? It is a harsh charge; and if we treat the biblical text as little more than examples, we may be guilty.

But I do think there is something flat-footed about this question, and it has to do with the nature of narrative and how we read it. The commandment about not committing adultery is clear. Knowing that is one thing, but being caught up as we see the threat to the biblical promise line caused by the temptation of Joseph or the fall of David is quite another. Their prominence in the line means that their struggle to obey is more, not less, exemplary

On the other hand, consider Hebrews 13: by the end we do seem to be dealing with characters who are not on the main line through the biblical text:

> Some faced jeers and flogging, and even chains and imprisonment. They were put
> to death by stoning; they were sawn in two; they were killed by the sword. They went
> about in sheepskins and goatskins, destitute, persecuted and ill-treated – the world

was not worthy of them. They wandered in deserts and mountains, living in caves and in holes in the ground. (Heb. 11:36–38)

Again I want us to see that Hebrews' intention is not that we merely have a properly informed faith, but that we are motivated to suffer for that faith in Christ, cheered on by the 'great cloud of witnesses' who went that way before us (Heb. 12:1).

So the lesson is that we make the exemplary lessons trivial when we take them out of their biblical-theological place; but put them back in, even if it is quite a light context, and they are valid.

Being a pattern

There is one final consequence. The New Testament data we have reviewed has shown that we, as Christian leaders, are supposed to be examples to the churches. That is a challenge, but also an encouragement, and one to which we will need to return.

Questions for reflection and discussion

- What are the dangers of using Bible characters as examples?
- Does the New Testament fall into any of those traps? Were you persuaded that it does use examples? What safeguards does it have in place?
- How is biblical theology a particularly important safeguard?
- How would you answer the allegation that it is like learning a moral lesson from any significant historical figure, such as Napoleon?

PART 4

HOW DOES THE BIBLE ADDRESS
THE HEART?

14. CHANGING THE HEART

> If by the Spirit you put to death the misdeeds of the body, you will live.
>
> (Rom. 8:13–14)

So how does God's Word change us as we engage with it?

I find it helpful to make a diagram out of these processes, and to see the problem and solution in an overview, summary form. This diagram (see p. 152) has five boxes, and we need to take a particular route through them. There is also a 'No Through Road' we need to take care to avoid. This summary diagram should help you think through the application for any passage, and again you will find it helpful to trace it out for the next passage you are speaking on, or the last one, or even the passage from your quiet time. The diagram takes us behind the appearance of sin into the nature of sin itself, and the nature of the gospel.[1]

Let's slow the journey down.

Box 1: what you're doing wrong

The first encounter with God is a bruising one. In Matthew, Mark and Luke's Gospels, for instance, John the Baptist prepares the way for Jesus by preaching some version of 'Repent, for the kingdom of heaven has come near' (Matt. 3:2; Mark 1:4; Luke 3:3). And similarly, Jesus' first sermons are summarized by

---

1. My wife, Sharon, has therefore named this 'Presuppositional Application'.

Behaviour . . .	. . . and its supporting lie
1. The sin *Repent, for the kingdom of heaven has come near.* (Matt. 3:2) What are the specific actions, attitudes, etc. that must change from this passage? What are the reasons given?	**2. The lie** *They exchanged the truth about God for a lie, and worshipped and served created things rather than the Creator . . .* (Rom. 1:25) What are the lies that people must believe or the truths they must suppress in order to permit that behaviour? Why are those lies preferable to truth?

This is the dangerous 'box of snakes' so loved by those 'vipers' the Pharisees

NO THROUGH ROAD
Attempting to produce change without repentance and faith is moralism, and only increases sin and guilt

For no good tree bears bad fruit, nor again does a bad tree bear good fruit. (Luke 6:43)

3. Repentance
Do not conform to the pattern of this world, but be transformed by the renewing of your mind. (Rom. 12:2)

Are you crystal clear on where the change to belief and behaviour must happen?

5. The godly life *Produce fruit in keeping with repentance.* (Matt. 3:8) What is the pattern of behaviour that will demonstrate that someone has repented?	**4. The truth** *You will know the truth, and the truth will set you free.* (John 8:32) What is the new truth that people must believe in order to support their new behaviour?

Matthew and Mark as 'Repent, for the kingdom of heaven has come near' (Matt. 4:17), and 'The kingdom of God has come near. Repent and believe the good news!' (Mark 1:15).

'Good news' and 'repentance' sit uncomfortably together; but if we emphasize only one, we distort the message. So a church that emphasized the repentance motif would run the risk not only of smug finger-wagging, but of implying that if only someone behaved properly (by implication, like *we* do), then God would love them. But that is not the good news. Equally, a church that emphasized the good news motif would run the risk of implying that God finds us adorable just as we are, and there is no need to change, just to improve. That is not repentance.

It is good news that God loves us so much he has warned us of his coming judgment, and it is good news that he loves us so much he has told us what to do about it: repent.

The word 'repentance', like the Greek word behind it, means to think again, to change your mind, and it needs to be fought on the battlefield of the mind. But we dare not leave people with the idea that the gospel is an academic pursuit, an intellectual puzzle in that all we have to do is think the right thoughts. We need to ensure that people see that this is a whole-life enterprise, and that when they understand and believe in line with the truth of the gospel, then their lives will inevitably change.

Box 5: the right things to be doing

This fifth box, the end of the process, describes what life would look like if we fully believed this passage of the Bible, and leaned the whole weight of our lives on it. John the Baptist not only warned of the need to repent, but said, 'Produce fruit in keeping with repentance' (Matt. 3:8; Luke 3:8). That obviously needed expanding:

'What should we do then?' the crowd asked.

John answered, 'Anyone who has two shirts should share with the one who has none, and anyone who has food should do the same.'

Even tax collectors came to be baptised. 'Teacher,' they asked, 'what should we do?'

'Don't collect any more than you are required to,' he told them.

Then some soldiers asked him, 'And what should we do?'

He replied, 'Don't extort money and don't accuse people falsely – be content with your pay.'

The people were waiting expectantly and were all wondering in their hearts if John might possibly be the Messiah. John answered them all, 'I baptise you with water. But one who is more powerful than I will come, the straps of whose sandals I am not worthy to untie. He will baptise you with the Holy Spirit and fire. His winnowing fork is in his hand to clear his threshing-floor and to gather the wheat into his barn, but he will burn up the chaff with unquenchable fire.' And

with many other words John exhorted the people and proclaimed the good news
to them. (Luke 3:10–18)

All of those actions are specifically laid out as 'fruit in keeping with repentance',
but they make no gospel sense without the final one, which is about being
properly related to Jesus.

So the critical question is how we travel from Box 1 (repentance) to Box 5
(fruit in keeping with repentance) – and it is critical because there is one route
that is forbidden, because it is so tempting.

A box of snakes!

This deadly box is the route through which everyone who wants to be good
without God must travel. And the human heart wants to be good without God.
Even people who want God want to be good without him. Even Christians
have to be reminded they cannot be Christ-honouringly good without God.
John the Baptist called the Pharisees 'a brood of vipers' for trying to be good
enough for God (Matt. 3:7). An assertion

Travelling this way is the route of rules and self-improvement. It says, 'Stop
doing that and start doing this'; and it says, 'You can if you think you can.' It
tells us to clean ourselves up before we come into God's presence

We must keep on insisting that it is impossible for anyone to be good this
way. The law, even though it is God's law, is powerless to produce change because
of the effect of sin (Rom. 8:3–9; Heb. 7:18–19). The only function it can have
that has any spiritual advantage is to drive us to Christ in bondage (Rom. 3:20;
Gal. 3:24). So what about our wills, drive and ambition to change for the good?
'The flesh', says Jesus, 'counts for nothing' (John 6:63). 'The flesh' makes us
resist Christ-honouring change, and produces such things as guilt, anger and
fear before God.[2] 'The flesh' makes even our good intentions and actions unac-
ceptable to God. This box is a poisonous dead end. Henry Cloud and John
Townsend repeatedly insist, 'We cannot stop sin; we have to be saved from sin.'[3]
I want to add that we have to be saved from even our best intentions as well.
How does God see those best efforts?

---

2. Rom. 7:9–11; 8:1–4. On guilt, anger and fear, see Rom. 5:9–10, 20–21; 6:14; 8:1–2;
   1 John 4:18.

3. Henry Cloud and John Townsend, *How People Grow* (Grand Rapids: Zondervan,
   2001), p. 301.

All of us have become like one who is unclean,
     and *all our righteous acts are like filthy rags*;
we all shrivel up like a leaf,
     and like the wind our sins sweep us away.
(Isa. 64:6)

Our secular friends will resist this idea, with moving examples of heroism, altruism and compassion from an atheist world view. We need to push back in our turn. I am not saying that only a Christian can be kind – that would be insulting. It would be trivial to swap examples of heroism, like children trading cards. I would say that only a Christian can account for why we should be kind, to both friends and enemies, family and strangers alike, even to the point of self-sacrifice. But that is too shallow. I want to say that no one, no Christian, can be good. And only the Christian message can account for why we *cannot* be good. We need grace.

But human beings hate that message, and love this box of snakes! Modern-day Pharisees love application, because deep down it means they can get into God's presence by their own effort. They can get into God's presence by a little self-improvement, rather than dying daily, by being crucified with Christ. That is why getting application wrong is so spiritually dangerous.

And here's the problem. Churches that preach strongly against sin, but in the wrong way, can encourage people to enter into this box and stay here! They use fear of hell or pride in our achievements to motivate us to change, or tell each other there is no need to change, or that it is other people outside who need to change, or that the change is a little matter of self-improvement on a basically good effort. And if we start to teach and live by that message, we are building on sin, not removing it.

The Continental Reformers were accused of having such an emphasis on grace that they undermined the need for an obedient life. They countered this strongly: 'Therefore it is so far from being true that this justifying faith makes men remiss in a pious and holy life, that on the contrary without it they would never do anything out of love to God, but only out of self-love or fear of damnation.'[4]

That is a devastating insight. Our capacity for sinful self-delusion is so profound that we need God's Word to point this out to us: you can even repent

---

4. Belgic Confession, Article 24, 'Confessio Belgica. The Belgic Confession. A.D. 1561. Revised 1619', in Philip Schaff and David S. Schaff (eds.), *The Creeds of Christendom* (New York: Harper & Row, 1931; repr. Grand Rapids: Baker, 1996), vol. 3, pp. 410–411.

for selfish reasons. 'John said to the crowds coming out to be baptised by him, "You brood of vipers! Who warned you to flee from the coming wrath? Produce fruit in keeping with repentance"' (Luke 3:7). This box is a box of snakes. Telling people to repent because otherwise God will get them is to motivate them by fear of damnation. Notice, they have not been rescued from hell by God; they have been rescued from God by themselves. And telling people to repent because their lives will improve if they do and won't if they don't is to motivate them by pride in themselves. Neither is proper biblical repentance; rather, they are both sinful ways to avoid repenting.

Box 2: into the heart

What, then, is the proper route of repentance? Here is Jesus, on why the superficial but religious attitude of the Pharisees cannot do the deep work needed:

> Don't you see that whatever enters the mouth goes into the stomach and then out of the body? But the things that come out of a person's mouth come from the heart, and these defile them. For out of the heart come evil thoughts – murder, adultery, sexual immorality, theft, false testimony, slander. These are what defile a person; but eating with unwashed hands does not defile them. (Matt. 15:17–20)

On the surface lie the actions: Jesus lists murder, adultery, sexual immorality, theft, false testimony, slander. So here are violence, greed, corruption and sexual exploitation. They are things that many people, religious or otherwise, claim to be against, and that religious people in particular are known to be against because we say so repeatedly.

But the earlier item on Jesus' list is the hidden engine behind those actions: 'evil thoughts'. And as we know, although society can police actions to try to control people to behave, it is notoriously hard to police thoughts. Because thoughts do control actions, some people who are able to produce some change in thinking can change some behaviours, which is why some counselling contexts or support groups can be effective in a limited way.

The limitation is because of the even deeper engine on Jesus' list, the 'heart'. This is the rotten core, the sinful nature that corrupts at every point and is inaccessible to human ability to change. Pharisees address sin, which they may interpret seriously or lightly, but can interpret it only on its own terms. They can never address the problem that our sinful nature will not let us stop sinning.

We can put this in a different way: in failing to love God as we should, we love something in his place. Paul puts it this way in 2 Timothy 3, as he describes the destructive impact of false teaching in the church:

> People will be lovers of themselves, lovers of money, boastful, proud, abusive, disobedient to their parents, ungrateful, unholy, without love, unforgiving, slanderous, without self-control, brutal, not lovers of the good, treacherous, rash, conceited, lovers of pleasure rather than lovers of God – having a form of godliness but denying its power. (2 Tim. 3:2–5a)

Once again a veneer of religion ('having a form of godliness but denying its power') masks a vicious set of sinful values that are fuelled by a series of idolatrous loves 'rather' than being 'lovers of God'.

Paul Tripp puts it this way, in a series of diagnostic observations:

1. Our hearts are always being ruled by someone or something.
2. The most important question to ask when examining the heart is, 'What is functionally ruling this person's heart in this situation?'
3. Whatever controls my heart will control my responses to people and situations.
4. God changes us not just by teaching us to do different things, but by recapturing our hearts to serve him alone.
5. The deepest issues of the human struggle are not issues of pain and suffering, but the issue of worship, because what rules our heart will control the way we respond to both suffering and blessing.[5]

Box 3: the gospel changes the heart

God promised that his solution to the fallen condition would operate at the deepest level. The critical step in coming to know God is to realize that in his omniscience there are no secrets before him:

> I the LORD search the heart
>   and examine the mind,
>   to reward each person according to their conduct,
>   according to what their deeds deserve.
> (Jer. 17:10)

---

5. Paul David Tripp, *Instruments in the Redeemer's Hands: People in Need of Change Helping People in Need of Change* (Phillipsburg: P&R, 2002), p. 71.

Moreover, his consistent promise was that he would replace disobedient hearts with willing ones, stone ones with flesh, with his law written on them (Jer. 31:31–34; 32:18–40; Ezek. 36:25–32).

The work of Christ, applied to each of us by the Holy Spirit, is God's means for effecting that change:

> For what the law was powerless to do because it was weakened by the flesh, God did by sending his own Son in the likeness of sinful flesh to be a sin offering. And so he condemned sin in the flesh, in order that the righteous requirement of the law might be fully met in us, who do not live according to the flesh but according to the Spirit. (Rom. 8:3–4)

Here, then, is the turning point in application, as we realize that the gospel can achieve what religion cannot – the gospel can change us, and we ourselves are part of the outworking of that change:

> Therefore, brothers and sisters, we have an obligation – but it is not to the flesh, to live according to it. For if you live according to the flesh, you will die; but if by the Spirit you put to death the misdeeds of the body, you will live. (Rom. 8:12–13)

We can contrast those two messages like this:

- *The message of religion*: my fundamental goodness *plus* God's kindness when I blow it.
- *The message of the gospel*: my total sinfulness *entirely replaced by* Christ's righteousness.

So the heart of gospel repentance is not 'Do better' or 'try harder' – *but realizing that we cannot ever do that*. Instead, the gospel puts us right with God. That means we see sin for what it truly is, a destructive, death-dealing power that has been destroyed by the cross, and by the power of the Holy Spirit we are enabled to love and serve God as we should.

Box 4: the new heart

How, then, do we now obey?

One aspect is that our heart is captivated as we realize the extent of Christ's work for us. As we dwell on being in Christ, with Christ, under Christ, like Christ, so our desire to please him replaces, and causes us to want to replace, the desire to sin. We do this for Christ, knowing we live to Christ, and we know that this is an individual matter because of 'Christ in you, the hope of glory' (Col. 1:27). Here is how Paul expands the Ephesians' understanding of the gospel and then immediately brings it down to earth:

> For this reason I kneel before the Father, from whom every family in heaven and on earth derives its name. I pray that out of his glorious riches he may strengthen you with power through his Spirit in your inner being, so that Christ may dwell in your hearts through faith. And I pray that you, being rooted and established in love, may have power, together with all the Lord's holy people, to grasp how wide and long and high and deep is the love of Christ, and to know this love that surpasses knowledge – that you may be filled to the measure of all the fullness of God.
>
> Now to him who is able to do immeasurably more than all we ask or imagine, according to his power that is at work within us, to him be glory in the church and in Christ Jesus throughout all generations, for ever and ever! Amen.
>
> As a prisoner for the Lord, then, I urge you to *live a life worthy of the calling you have received*. (Eph. 3:14 – 4:1)

This is how grace changes our motivations, and how the Spirit equips us to want to please God.

Timothy Keller illustrates it like this:

> I lie most often to avoid others' disapproval. If I just try to stop lying it won't work because my need for others' approval overwhelms my good intentions. I allow other people, instead of Jesus, to determine my worth. If you want to stop lying, you have to find out what is motivating your sin – like my tendency to look to others for affirmation – and replace it with the security you can find in Jesus.[6]

This is why the Christian message on morals and lifestyle can never sit easily with other religious groups, no matter how similar our views on behaviour may seem to be to an outsider. Faced with social and family disorder we cannot simply say, 'Stop it!' We know that as the Bible is true, they *cannot* stop it until their hearts are gripped by grace. To use the Bible without Christ makes matters only worse.

---

6. Timothy Keller, 'Preaching Amid Pluralism', in Haddon Robinson and Craig Brian Larson, *The Art and Craft of Biblical Preaching* (Grand Rapids: Zondervan, 2005), p. 178.

Box 5 again: the new life

The gospel of free grace, rightly heard, therefore leads to change. The gospel breaks the power of sin, because it unmasks sin for what it truly is, discounts its penalty, replaces its superficial attractiveness with the deep attractiveness of Christ and gives us the Spirit-led desire to want to live in line with it:

> We are those who have died to sin; how can we live in it any longer? Or don't you know that all of us who were baptised into Christ Jesus were baptised into his death? We were therefore buried with him through baptism into death in order that, just as Christ was raised from the dead through the glory of the Father, we too may live a new life . . .
>
> In the same way, count yourselves dead to sin but alive to God in Christ Jesus. Therefore do not let sin reign in your mortal body so that you obey its evil desires. Do not offer any part of yourself to sin as an instrument of wickedness, but rather offer yourselves to God as those who have been brought from death to life; and offer every part of yourself to him as an instrument of righteousness. For sin shall no longer be your master, because you are not under the law, but under grace. (Rom. 6:2–4, 11–14)

Bryan Chappell puts it like this:

> There are many 'be' messages in Scripture, but they always reside in a redemptive context. Since we cannot be anything that God would approve apart from his sanctifying power, the source of that grace must permeate any exhortation for biblical behaviour. 'Be' messages are not wrong *in* themselves, they are wrong messages *by* themselves . . . Challenges to holiness must be accompanied by a Christ-focus or they promote only human centred, doomed-to-fail religion.[7]

I would add that such messages often reside in a corporate context, where fellowship, encouragement or discipline help us to obey God. The pronouns in Romans 6 are plural, not singular. Older writers called such helps 'the means of grace': they are God's kind gifts to make it easier for us to obey, and harder to justify disobedience.

---

7. Bryan Chappell, *Christ-Centered Preaching* (Grand Rapids: Baker, 1994), p. 285, italics mine.

Questions for reflection and discussion

- Summarize the essential meaning of each of the five boxes in the diagram.
- Why is the 'No Through Road' so tempting, but dangerous?
- Work through the diagram from the chapter for your next sermon, Bible study or passage you are reading privately.

15. HOW THE GOSPEL CHANGES US

> We wait for the blessed hope – the appearing of the glory of our great God and
> Saviour, Jesus Christ, who gave himself for us to redeem us from all wickedness
> and to purify for himself a people that are his very own, eager to do what is good.
>
> (Titus 2:13–14)

We all need the gospel, all of the time

There is a permanent danger that we treat 'gospel preaching' as a concept that
applies only to evangelistic preaching. We take it as a useful summary of a clear
and simple presentation of the cross, with an opportunity for people to come
to Christ for the first time.

The danger that expresses is that we leave 'the gospel' behind, as we might
leave an entrance gate, and act as if our growth as Christians is dependent on
something else. There are only two options for that – either we add to the gospel,
or God does.

What happens if we supplement the gospel

The most common way we supplement the gospel is by our efforts. In some
Christian traditions those efforts are religious (go to church more, read the Bible
more, pray more, evangelize more); in others they are more broadly based (don't
drink, don't smoke, certainly don't do drugs). Whether they are things we start
doing or stop doing, they can have only two outcomes.

Outcome 1 – we succeed: by force and concentration we manage to carve a notch
in our Bibles and say we did something more, or something less. In that case

we run the danger of thinking that we are partially responsible for our own salvation. We become smug. There is a part of our heart that God did not need to save. He cannot claim that as his own. He owes us.

Outcome 2 – we fail: our efforts let us down, and even if we succeeded for a while (that is all option 1 is, really), we have now failed. God is therefore now someone for us to be ashamed before, afraid of – and is possibly even our enemy. He makes us feel guilty.

So we are back with the box of snakes, the way of trying to produce good works without going the way of the gospel. Luther put it like this:

> there is not one in a thousand who does not put his confidence in the works, presume that by having done them he wins God's favor and lays claim to his grace. They turn the whole thing into a fairground. God cannot tolerate this: God has promised his grace freely, and he wills that we start by trusting that grace and perform all works in that grace, whatever those works may be.[1]

Here is the danger. Supplementing the gospel in this way by our obedience means that we need the gospel only when we fail. The consequences for our relationship with God are devastating, because we need him only when we are in the wrong with him; when we might be in the right with him, we arrived under our own steam.

We cannot go this route. Hear again the consequences of the gospel:

> Therefore, there is now no condemnation for those who are in Christ Jesus. (Rom. 8:1)

> Whoever believes in him is not condemned, but whoever does not believe stands condemned already because they have not believed in the name of God's one and only Son. (John 3:18)

> For by one sacrifice he has made perfect for ever those who are being made holy. (Heb. 10:14)

That position of 'no condemnation' and of being 'perfect' is given to us irrespective of our obedience. One reason for the importance of a wide and deep grasp of the gospel is that we become so captivated by the vastness of what

---

1. Martin Luther, 'A Treatise Concerning Good Works', sect. 11, in James Atkinson (ed.), *Luther's Works*, vol. 44: *Christian in Society I* (Augsburg: Fortress, 1966), pp. 32–33.

God has done that we never think of ourselves as teetering on the edge of the kingdom. We are completely in, for ever. It is not the preacher's job to make Christians guilty – there is only one judge, and he has declared the Christian righteous.

But our pride finds that very hard to live with. When things go well, secretly we still want the law to be operating a little bit so we can take some credit. What happens when things then go badly, as they will, is that we find that the law still contains its toxins; the guilt it produces is too hard to bear and so we run away from God. The law is a dangerous addiction for Christians – one small lick tastes so good, but has you hooked and trapped. It cannot kill you anymore, but it can make you both crave and fear its destructive power.

Henry Cloud and John Townsend see it in their experience as Christian counsellors:

> Too often Christians who fail think of God as being mad at them and view him as someone they need to avoid instead of being the One they need to turn to. They are still 'under the law' at a deep emotional level. Christians who fail also avoid other Christians, especially when they are feeling bad and guilty in the midst of failure. It is sad to see this dynamic of the law happen in the church and then see the opposite happen in Twelve Steps groups. In these recovery groups, people are taught that the very first thing to do when you fail is to call someone in the group and get to a meeting. They are taught to 'run to grace' as it were, to turn immediately to their higher power and their support system. The sad part is that this theology is more biblical than what is practised in many Christian environments, where people in failure run from instead of to God and the people they need.[2]

So because Christians are prone to alternating between pride and despair, we all need the gospel, all of the time.

The quest for the magic bullet

If we do not add to the gospel, we want God to – and that also leads to pride and despair. Christian history has seen a steady stream of people wanting, or promising, some definitive Christian event that marks the decisive 'second step'

---

2. Henry Cloud and John Townsend, *How People Grow* (Grand Rapids: Zondervan, 2001), p. 170.

in our growth. Different times have given that quest different names, but what they all share is a quite understandable but wrong desire for a 'magic bullet'. They want to get out of the tensions caused by living as a believer who still struggles with sin. It is quite understandable, because any believer who has seen the price Jesus paid for us learns to hate sin. I struggle with sin – but sin does not control my destiny. That is what the cross does, and sin has lost. It is the search for something in addition to what the cross has achieved that is the search for a silver bullet.

In some Christian circles the magic bullet is an experience of God's power. The impression is given that the cross gets us part of the way, but a particular experience of God takes us to the next level of knowing him. The promise is that this experience will make the struggle against sin go away, by the sheer infusion of new power. I am the last person to want a Christian to stop seeking God, and I firmly believe in the power of the Holy Spirit to transform our lives, but this 'magic bullet' approach is not the way God has laid out for us. The right response to such a desire must be to help people so see the magnificent breadth, length, depth and height of God's love in Christ that it would never occur to them to look for something else on top.

There is another, more recent, magic bullet. This one looks at the struggle against sin, and makes it go away by saying that there is no sin to struggle against. This has a particular force in our current debates over sexuality, so we need to be aware of it. The way it works is to say that, for example, a homosexual desire, which was traditionally thought of as a temptation to sin, is not sinful. The magic bullet effect makes someone say, 'So that is a good and natural desire after all? And I don't need to fight it? What wonderfully liberating good news! I now feel much freer to serve God without guilt. What wicked people some Christians are for making me feel guilty about such natural instincts.'

I think this is a more dangerous magic bullet, and arguably a more wicked one, because it is usually offered by theologically sophisticated people who know how much some of us want to find it, and to be rid of a burden of temptation.

However, the way to be rid of the burden of temptation and guilt is not to deny the nature of sin or its effects, but to submit to the gospel. There is no burden of guilt for a Christian, not because I have no sin, but because the One who had no sin paid the price for mine. He did not magically remove it, nor does he relabel a bad thing as good, but he takes away its power to send me to hell. And when I face temptation, I find his arm around my shoulder saying, 'I was tempted in every way, just as you are, but I did not sin. No temptation has come to you that I did not fight first. Come to me for grace, forgiveness and power for the next day's fight.' The gospel is the key to growth.

Who am I?

I remember hearing a man describe the devastation that alcoholism had caused in his life and marriage. He had come to Christ, and his pastor had pointed him to the resources of Alcoholics Anonymous.

He described one seminal meeting of AA, where the group had begun, as normal, with people giving their names and admitting their problem. He heard his mouth say the words 'My name is John, and I am an alcoholic,' and simultaneously had a different thought: 'My name is John, and I am a believer in the Lord Jesus Christ who struggles with obedience in the area of alcohol. Why am I defining myself by my sin?'

That was a profound and most true thought. He refused all the magic bullets: he could not effect the change he wanted, God was not magically going to remove his sin, nor was drunkenness going to cease to be sin. Instead, he clung to the gospel, where he was defined by his identity in Christ.

If there were magic bullets, it would be cruel to hide them. But there are not. And the cruelty lies with those who pretend to sell them.

The sign in the pulpit

The theological term for the kind of position we have been discussing is semi-Pelagianism. Pelagius (c. AD 354–440) was the British monk who argued against the doctrine of original sin. Instead of the entirety of humanity being included in the fall, Pelagius argued that Adam's fall affected him only, and merely gave us a bad example. Pelagius' views were condemned as heretical in 418 at the Council of Carthage.

Semi-Pelagianism is subtly different. It says that the fall has affected but not ruined my capacity for free will; details vary, but the general shape of this view is that God and Christians cooperate, either in their conversion or their maturity. I do not want to be too precise about the historical definition here, because the general shape is what we need: we do what we should and God makes up the deficit. He is the one who helps us to do what we need to do. He is the God of the gaps.

An experienced pastor once observed to me that when we get into a pulpit, everyone facing us is a semi-Pelagian. We need to have a sign nailed in the pulpit, 'You're looking at semi-Pelagians!' My only observation is to wonder why he left the preacher out of it. Our sinful pride longs for some kind of semi-Pelagianism to be true. We want God to owe us.

At the Reformation Luther's principal charge against Rome was lined up on this issue. And, as we know, one of his main weapons was the letter to the Galatians. Now, it would of course be anachronistic to assume Paul was writing against Pelagianism or semi-Pelagianism, nor am I requiring us to agree with Luther's exegesis in detail. My point is simply this: Galatians, with its gospel of free, justifying grace still contains instructions on how to live. *Just because someone is semi-Pelagian doesn't mean you don't tell them what to do.*

The place of works in the life of the believer

So here are two truths we need to affirm.

First, the gospel is all free grace, not works. The law could not save us, and cannot change us. My favourite example, because it is the first, and so clear, is the thief on the cross:

> One of the criminals who hung there hurled insults at him: 'Aren't you the Messiah? Save yourself and us!'
>
> But the other criminal rebuked him. 'Don't you fear God,' he said, 'since you are under the same sentence? We are punished justly, for we are getting what our deeds deserve. But this man has done nothing wrong.'
>
> Then he said, 'Jesus, remember me when you come into your kingdom.'
>
> Jesus answered him, 'Truly I tell you, today you will be with me in paradise.'
> (Luke 23:39–43)

The criminal was guilty, and knew it. Jesus was innocent, and the criminal knew that too. Jesus was going to be a king coming into his kingdom very shortly, and the criminal asked Jesus to remember him when he was enthroned. And – this is remarkable – Jesus, a man not far from from death, makes the criminal a promise.

So picture the scene shortly after, when the criminal bangs on the gates of paradise, and God says, 'Why should I let you into my heaven? Have you lived a good life?'

'No, I lived a wicked one. But Jesus said I could come in.'

'But what about your good works after your conversion? Baptism? Lord's Supper? The work of the Spirit? You have heard that justification is on the basis of the life lived?'

'Alas,' says our criminal, 'I lived no life after my conversion. If justification is on the basis of the life lived, I cannot come in. But if it is on the basis of the death died, and that not mine but his, he promised me I could come in.'

And the man did. Salvation is all, and only, grace.

But our second truth is that obedience is necessary for a believer:

> Just as you used to offer yourselves as slaves to impurity and to ever-increasing wickedness, so now offer yourselves as slaves to righteousness leading to holiness. (Rom. 6:19)

> Do not conform to the pattern of this world, but be transformed by the renewing of your mind. (Rom. 12:2)

Moreover, some of that is described in terms of change:

> And we all, who with unveiled faces contemplate the Lord's glory, are being transformed into his image with ever-increasing glory, which comes from the Lord, who is the Spirit. (2 Cor. 3:18)

> Like newborn babies, crave pure spiritual milk, so that by it you may grow up in your salvation. (1 Peter 2:2)

Sometimes that is described in pointedly clear ways. Notice how the speakers move from general to particular in their call to repentance:

> This is what the Sovereign LORD says: repent! Turn from your idols and renounce all your detestable practices! (Ezek. 14:6)

> Wash and make yourselves clean.
>   Take your evil deeds out of my sight;
>   stop doing wrong.
> Learn to do right; seek justice.
>   Defend the oppressed.
> Take up the cause of the fatherless;
>   plead the case of the widow.
> (Isa. 1:16–17)

> This is what the LORD Almighty said: 'Administer true justice; show mercy and compassion to one another. Do not oppress the widow or the fatherless, the foreigner or the poor. Do not plot evil against each other.' (Zech. 7:9–10)

'What should we do then?' the crowd asked.

John [the Baptist] answered, 'Anyone who has two shirts should share with the one who has none, and anyone who has food should do the same.'

Even tax collectors came to be baptised. 'Teacher,' they asked, 'what should we do?'

'Don't collect any more than you are required to,' he told them.

Then some soldiers asked him, 'And what should we do?'

He replied, 'Don't extort money and don't accuse people falsely – be content with your pay.' (Luke 3:11–14)

Now, because God is not at war with himself, his two truths will cohere. None of God's commands exist in tension, even though they may appear so to fallen, finite minds like ours. One piece of evidence that they cohere is the way a truth is revealed in order to produce a result. Notice the purpose behind Scripture in each of these statements:

Jesus performed many other signs in the presence of his disciples, which are not recorded in this book. But these are written *that* you may believe that Jesus is the Messiah, the Son of God, *and that* by believing you may have life in his name. (John 20:30–31)

For everything that was written in the past was written to teach us, *so that* through the endurance taught in the Scriptures and the encouragement they provide we might have hope. (Rom. 15:4)

So Christ himself gave the apostles, the prophets, the evangelists, the pastors and teachers, to equip his people for works of service, *so that* the body of Christ may be built up until we all reach unity in the faith and in the knowledge of the Son of God and become mature, attaining to the whole measure of the fullness of Christ.

Then we will no longer be infants, tossed back and forth by the waves, and blown here and there by every wind of teaching and by the cunning and craftiness of people in their deceitful scheming. Instead, speaking the truth in love, we will grow to become in every respect the mature body of him who is the head, that is, Christ. (Eph. 4:11–15)

[Christ] is the one we proclaim, admonishing and teaching everyone with all wisdom, *so that* we may present everyone fully mature in Christ. To this end I strenuously contend with all the energy Christ so powerfully works in me. (Col. 1:28–29)

All Scripture is God-breathed and is useful for teaching, rebuking, correcting and training in righteousness, *so that* the [man] of God may be thoroughly equipped for every good work. (2 Tim. 3:16–17)[3]

His divine power has given us everything we need for a godly life through our knowledge of him who called us by his own glory and goodness. Through these he has given us his very great and precious promises, *so that* through them you may participate in the divine nature, having escaped the corruption in the world caused by evil desires. (2 Peter 1:2–4)

I write these things to you who believe in the name of the Son of God *so that* you may know that you have eternal life. (1 John 5:13)

Scripture is written to achieve an end.

Indicative and imperative?

It is not hard to give biblical texts that demonstrate that there is an inherent connection between God's actions and ours. The pattern is the foundation for the Ten Commandments:

I am the LORD your God, who brought you out of Egypt, out of the land of slavery. You shall have no other gods before me. (Exod. 20:2–3)

And it runs through the gospel too:

As a prisoner for the Lord, then, I urge you to live a life worthy of the calling you have received. (Eph. 4:1)

Quite often they cluster around clear logical connections:

It is for freedom that Christ has set us free. Stand firm, *then*, and do not let yourselves be burdened again by a yoke of slavery. (Gal. 5:1; see Col. 3:1; 1 Thess. 3:1)

For you died, and your life is now hidden with Christ in God.
When Christ, who is your life, appears, then you also will appear with him in glory.

---

3. My alteration, as I have explained above.

> Put to death, *therefore*, whatever belongs to your earthly nature: sexual
> immorality, impurity, lust, evil desires and greed, which is idolatry. (Col. 3:3–5;
> see Phil. 2:1)

Often that connection is described as moving from indicatives (what God has
done) through to imperatives (what we must do). My problem with that description is that it is too narrow, at both ends. 'What God has done' easily morphs
into just looking at the past; but biblical motivation is just as much to do with
the present and the future. Both are a working out of what he 'has done' in the
past, of course, but we must make explicit our present experience and future
hope. Otherwise, that narrow description can leave me uninvolved, like someone
being told a story about someone else.

At the other end of the formula, 'what we must do' focuses on simply one
part of our response, and the language of command. Not everything in the
Bible requires us to 'do' something – sometimes the right response is to 'know',
or 'understand', or 'love', or 'adore'.

I have similar problems with some of the alternative shorthands: 'Covenant
precedes command' and 'Relationship precedes rules'[4] are both better on the
first side of the equation, but to my mind still fail on the second.

No longer, now and not yet

I want to replace the narrow idea of 'indicative' with the rich narrative of biblical
theology. Graeme Goldsworthy has helpfully summarized the three elements
of biblical theology as God's people in God's place under God's rule, and argues
that if we address those three areas at any point of the biblical timeline, we can
unearth the unfolding riches of God's salvation plan.[5] I would alter two of
those words to 'God's people in God's presence under God's promise': partly
because I like the three P's, but more seriously because the idea of God's *place*
could be thought to be external and physical, but we have been drawn into a
relationship in his *presence* that is only partly expressed in spatial metaphors. If
we took the language of place to its climax of being 'in Christ', and 'the new
heavens and the new earth', I would be content with *place*, but Christians have

---

4. Both cited in Michael R. Emlet, *CrossTalk: Where Life and Scripture Meet* (Greensboro:
   New Growth, 2009), p. 187.

5. Most accessibly, see Graeme Goldsworthy, *The Goldsworthy Trilogy* (Carlisle:
   Paternoster, 2000).

had a terrible tendency to idolize buildings and lands. In a similar way God's *rule* could be misread as a static, human Christendom exercised through political means, and Christians have placed way too much emphasis on kings and their kingdoms. *Promise* drives us onwards to Christ's return, connecting with the foundation idea of covenant.

Having placed those three elements on the biblical timeline, we also need to understand our own story. I don't mean an individual's testimony or dramatic conversion account – not every Christian has the latter. But there is a biblical story about each of us that the Scriptures use. It is the way the biblical story redescribes reality for us. There are three phases, which we can call *no longer, now* and *not yet*.

When I come to Christ, some things are *no longer* true about me. I am no longer solely 'in Adam', because I am also 'in Christ'. And the two are not equal: although I still sin and will die, I am no longer under the rule of sin and death because they no longer determine my eternal destiny. I am no longer under God's judgment and wrath.[6]

Instead, there are things that are true *now*. In Christ I am forgiven and free. Born again and made new, adopted, holy, chosen and loved. I am a new creation and an alien in the old one. I know God's future plans, and I experience the work of the Spirit (2 Cor. 5:17; Eph. 2:10; Phil. 2:1–4; Col. 3:1–10). But, to underline the issue, I still sin and fall sick – those are also *now* experiences.

So there are some things that are *not yet* true – I am not yet immortal or sinless. I am not yet what I will be. I am not yet *like* Christ, although I am *in Christ*.

Theological discussions often focus on the second and third boxes: what is true now and what is not yet true. The technical language of 'inaugurated eschatology' has given us the concept of the two time zones or realms, although theologians disagree about their relative content.

But when we talk about the first area, *no longer*, we often think in personal conversion terms; and if someone has a dramatic story, we use it in church. The script is often fairly similar: 'I had problem X (debt, illness, bad marriage) – but now that I have become a Christian it has gone away. God is faithful and kind.' Those stories, when true, are wonderful, and I am not seeking to demean them. But I am not arguing for externally dramatic stories – rather, I am arguing for one that is true of every Christian, and it is not getting that story clearly in our minds that causes us problems.

If we highlight externally dramatic stories, we cause doubt or envy in the minds of people who have not had them. We start to think that the gospel

---

6. See David Peterson, *Possessed by God: A New Testament Theology of Sanctification and Holiness* (Leicester: Apollos, 1995), p. 107.

benefits lie in those dramatic stories. We start to long for some dramatic experience ourselves. But if we give people the bigger biblical-theology picture, then we all have a dramatic story, the most dramatic of all, and the newest and oldest Christians share it: 'I had problem X (debt, illness, bad marriage), and since I have become a Christian I still have it. But I also had a far deeper one, in sin, and God has taken that away. And every day, as I deal with problem X in the power of his forgiving grace, I discover that God is faithful and kind.'

We can diagram it as below.

Christ's story				
God's plan from eternity.	Creation and fall.	Christ's redemption and resurrection.	Christ's reign.	Christ's return, and God's plan for eternity.
			The Christian, *now* in Christ.	What is *not yet* true of the Christian.
		Our story		
		What is *no longer* true of the Christian.		

The range of response

And to repeat what we have seen before, what is *now true* embraces the full-orbed response contained in the four ideas of 'heart, soul, mind and strength'.

The grace that teaches

To start to put this together, let us revisit Titus 2:11–14:

> For the grace of God has appeared that offers salvation to all people. It teaches us to say 'No' to ungodliness and worldly passions, and to live self-controlled, upright and godly lives in this present age, while we wait for the blessed hope – the appearing of the glory of our great God and Saviour, Jesus Christ, who gave himself for us to

redeem us from all wickedness and to purify for himself a people that are his very own, eager to do what is good.

We can see the various elements all in play here. There is the level of biblical theology where salvation has been won 'in Jesus Christ, who gave himself for us to redeem us from all wickedness'. He 'has appeared', and the final event in the biblical-theology drama will be 'the appearing of the glory of our great God and Saviour, Jesus Christ'; we live between the two appearings. This is clearly the dominant story.

But there is also the level of our story, God's grace 'teaches us to say "No" to ungodliness and worldly passions' (i.e. the *no longer*) 'and to live self-controlled, upright and godly lives in this present age' (i.e. the *now*), 'while we wait for the blessed hope' (i.e. the *not yet*).

Moreover, if I am being taught, as an individual Christian, to say 'No' to certain things and to live in a different way, then there is a clear expectation of individual life change on the basis of the universally true gospel. That is what the gospel does. That is how the two levels of the story engage. David Powlison puts it like this: 'The distinction between "biblical truth" and "practical application" is artificial. In the Bible, truth arrives in action. Paul teaches by applying biblical truth to himself and others.'[7]

If I see biblical theology as something that is true for me, then appropriating it for my personal life will not be an alien, indicative command, but a matter of understanding what has been done for me and therefore its consequence.

Here is a second example, this time from Ephesians 2. Notice how this time Paul explicitly interweaves the two narratives of biblical theology and our story, only this time the foreground story is ours. Christ's is the more important story, and the language of 'with Christ' and 'in Christ' is the key to understanding it, but our personal appropriation of it is where Paul is driving throughout, that is why the personal pronouns (we, us, our) run right through the biblical theology:

> As for *you*, *you* were dead in *your* transgressions and sins, in which *you* used to live when *you* followed the ways of this world and of the ruler of the kingdom of the air, the spirit who is now at work in those who are disobedient. All of *us* also lived among them at one time, gratifying the cravings of *our* flesh and following its desires and thoughts. Like the rest, *we* were by nature deserving of wrath. But because of his great love for *us*, God, who is rich in mercy, made *us* alive with Christ even when *we* were dead in transgressions – it is by grace *you* have been saved. And God raised *us* up with

---

7. David Powlison, *Seeing with New Eyes* (Phillipsburg: P&R, 2003), p. 18.

Christ and seated *us* with him in the heavenly realms in Christ Jesus, in order that in the coming ages he might show the incomparable riches of his grace, expressed in his kindness to *us* in Christ Jesus. (Eph. 2:1–7)

Paul's logic is that because we are in Christ and with Christ, our life story is to be interpreted in terms of biblical theology. And again it therefore has a direct, individual applicatory force. He continues:

For it is by grace you have been saved, through faith – and this is not from yourselves, it is the gift of God – not by works, so that no one can boast. For we are God's handiwork, created in Christ Jesus to do good works, which God prepared in advance for us to do. (Eph. 2:8–10)

Biblical theology, then, does three things: it shows us what is objectively true in the biblical narrative, it ensures that I know I am part of that narrative and it points out the implications of that. Let us think through what that looks like in practice with some of the central turning points of the gospel.

Sin

We have just seen Paul do that with sin. Sin makes people 'disobedient', 'deserving of [or children of] wrath', imitators of 'the ways of this world' and captives of 'the ruler of the kingdom of the air'. Such people are 'dead in transgressions'.

But he will not allow his hearers to turn into self-justifying, Pharisee mode. Those personal pronouns grind deep into each of us until we understand that the objective biblical theology is simultaneously therefore my story, and in this case he has given the implication throughout.

This move of bringing biblical theology to earth in our Christian experience is true elsewhere.

The cross

1 John deals with the cross in this way. 'This is love: not that we loved God, but that he loved us and sent his Son as an atoning sacrifice for our sins' (i.e. the biblical theology, and again the personal pronouns show that we are involved in it). 'Dear friends, since God so loved us, we also ought to love one another' (i.e. our story) (1 John 4:10–11).

Or, earlier in the same letter, he writes:

Everyone who sins breaks the law; in fact, sin is lawlessness. But you know that he appeared so that he might take away our sins. And in him is no sin. No one who lives in him keeps on sinning. No one who continues to sin has either seen him or known him. (1 John 3:4–6)

The turning point is again when we are taken into the biblical theology: 'No one who lives in him keeps on sinning.'

The resurrection

In 1 Corinthians 15 Paul first shows the biblical theology of Christ's resurrection (15:1–4), and then shows the disastrous implications for our story if that story is not true (15:5–58a). But even that chapter, which is so concerned with the future and our resurrection, still explodes in present-day life change: 'Therefore, my dear brothers and sisters, stand firm. Let nothing move you. Always give yourselves fully to the work of the Lord, because you know that your labour in the Lord is not in vain' (1 Cor. 15:58).

The future

1 John 3 shows the impact of the future on us now, in terms of hope:

> See what great love the Father has lavished on us, that we should be called children of God! And that is what we are! The reason the world does not know us is that it did not know him. Dear friends, now we are children of God, and what we will be has not yet been made known. But we know that when Christ appears, we shall be like him, for we shall see him as he is. All who have this hope in him purify themselves, just as he is pure. (1 John 3:1–3)

In Colossians 3 Paul shows all of this together. In 3:1–4 he takes Christ's death, resurrection and return, makes all of them our story and then shows how that necessarily produces change. And then in 3:1–10 he starts with our story (*no longer, now, not yet*) and shows how life change is produced by the gospel:

> Since, then, you have been raised with Christ, set your hearts on things above, where Christ is, seated at the right hand of God. Set your minds on things above, not on earthly things. For you died, and your life is now hidden with Christ in God. When Christ, who is your life, appears, then you also will appear with him in glory.
>
> Put to death, therefore, whatever belongs to your earthly nature: sexual immorality, impurity, lust, evil desires and greed, which is idolatry. Because of these, the wrath of God is coming. You used to walk in these ways, in the life you once lived. But now you must also rid yourselves of all such things as these: anger, rage, malice, slander, and filthy language from your lips. Do not lie to each other, since you have taken off your old self with its practices

and have put on the new self, which is being renewed in knowledge in the image of its Creator.

Peter argues in exactly the same way in 1 Peter 1, and, as he spreads out the magnificence of the biblical drama, notice how he presses each of us into it (*no longer, now, not yet*) and points out the consequences:

> Therefore, with minds that are alert and fully sober, set your hope on the grace to be brought to you when Jesus Christ is revealed at his coming. As obedient children, do not conform to the evil desires you had when you lived in ignorance. But just as he who called you is holy, so be holy in all you do; for it is written: 'Be holy, because I am holy.'
>
> Since you call on a Father who judges each person's work impartially, live out your time as foreigners here in reverent fear. For you know that it was not with perishable things such as silver or gold that you were redeemed from the empty way of life handed down to you from your ancestors, but with the precious blood of Christ, a lamb without blemish or defect. He was chosen before the creation of the world, but was revealed in these last times for your sake. Through him you believe in God, who raised him from the dead and glorified him, and so your faith and hope are in God.
>
> Now that you have purified yourselves by obeying the truth so that you have sincere love for each other, love one another deeply, from the heart. (1 Peter 1:13–22)

Commands

Sometimes the Bible gives an instruction based on God's character rather than explicitly on the biblical theology, and we need at that point always to hold the two together. We do not know God outside the biblical theology in that he has revealed himself, and his love and mercy, judgment and wrath must be interpreted in those terms.

A commandment that is not tied to the cross can only kill, because we cannot obey it. But a command that was tied to the cross and then carried by the risen Christ to his throne where I sit with him is a different thing altogether. It can no longer damage me, and I am free to discover its liberating truth. Moreover, the Lord Jesus gives me his Spirit so that I want to obey him without fear. Scott Hafemann says, 'The promises of God are commands in disguise, and vice versa. God commands what he commands because he promises what he promises.'[8]

---

8. Scott Hafemann, *The God of Promise and the Life of Faith* (Wheaton: Crossway 2001), p. 87.

Christians sin because they forget to remember

Why, then, do Christians sin?

The simplest answer is because we forget the gospel, which is why we are continually told in Scripture to 'remember' it, and to remember the way our story is now wrapped up in it.

The voice of the world is loud and seductive. It tells us to be concerned with where we live, whom we live with and what we do with our time and possessions. Giving a biblical-theological reading of that will explain why they are such attractive calls, because Eden speaks that language. As Henry Cloud and John Townsend put it, 'If you think about it, [Eden] was pretty much the life everyone is looking for: a great place to live, the perfect mate, lots of good things to occupy your time, and a job that fits your makeup.'[9]

The fall lost the relationship of each of those things to our creator, and so each of them on its own becomes the heart of an idolatrous quest. The new creation will restore all those things, which is what we Christians have to remember: that our new heavenly home will be so wonderful it will show my desire for a conservatory to be trivial; that I can understand why I am ambitious at work because that is how God has made me; that my work now can never fulfil in the way God's concerns will; and so on.

The heart of my temptation will always be the same as the one in the garden: 'Did God really say . . . You will not certainly die . . . when you eat from it your eyes will be opened' (Gen. 3:1, 4). Only the remembrance of the biblical theology will explain both why temptation is so attractive, and what it leads to.

Christians sin because they deliberately forget

2 Peter gives us another window into the reasons why someone turns from orthodoxy to a deviant form of Christianity.

Before we look at the context, here is his description:

> Above all, you must understand that in the last days scoffers will come, scoffing and following their own evil desires. They will say, 'Where is this "coming" he promised? Ever since our ancestors died, everything goes on as it has since the beginning of creation.' But they deliberately forget that long ago by God's word the heavens came into being and the earth was formed out of water and by water. By these waters also

---

9. Cloud and Townsend, *Grow*, p. 33.

the world of that time was deluged and destroyed. By the same word the present heavens and earth are reserved for fire, being kept for the day of judgment and destruction of the ungodly. (2 Peter 3:3–7)

What is clearly foremost is the desire to sin, and the deviant theology has been constructed in order to allow it: 'in the last days scoffers will come, scoffing and *following* their own evil desires'. Secondly, the theology they must dismantle has biblical theology as its shape: 'Where is this "coming" he promised? Ever since our ancestors died, everything goes on as it has since the beginning of creation.' Their new construction challenges the orthodox Christian framework from its beginning to its end. Thirdly, this reconstruction is possible only by a deliberate refusal to remember orthodoxy: 'they deliberately forget' both creation and God's warning of final judgment on sin.

If we now look at the verses either side of this section, we can see Peter's solution:

Dear friends, this is now my second letter to you. I have written both of them as *reminders* to stimulate you to wholesome thinking. I want you to *recall* the words spoken in the past by the holy prophets and the command given by our Lord and Saviour through the apostles . . .

But *do not forget* this one thing, dear friends . . . The Lord is not slow in keeping his promise, as some understand slowness. Instead he is patient with you, not wanting anyone to perish, but everyone to come to repentance . . .

Since everything will be destroyed in this way, what kind of people ought you to be? You ought to live holy and godly lives as you look forward to the day of God and speed its coming. (2 Peter 3:1–2, 8–9, 11; cf. 1:12–15)

The errorists will entice people to sin by the wilful act of replacing orthodox biblical theology; the solution is to keep reminding people of the proper shape of the story, and the implications of that for the life of the Christian.

A similar pattern emerges elsewhere. In Galatians, for instance, the issue looks to be the reverse: people wanting to live a good life before God rather than excusing sin. But Paul's solution is to reimpose proper biblical theology, with everything done in order: promise and covenant before law, then the cross to keep the promise, and then today. In order to be able to justify themselves before God, the circumcision group had to distort the biblical theology and try to persuade the Galatian Christians that they lived in a different time zone. Although Paul does not use Peter's language of remembering and forgetting, he engages in the activity of making them recall his visit, his teaching about the cross, and their conversion on the basis of that teaching – he shows how their story and biblical theology engage.

This has a critical impact for our preaching. It tells us that biblical theology has primacy in interpreting both the biblical narrative and the Christian life today. Those of us who love biblical theology, as I do, sometimes give the impression that we love it as a clever and fascinating intellectual game, in that we can move from any part of the Bible to its centre. Being able to do that becomes the only goal, and talking about application is seen as a dangerous distraction that puts us, not Christ, at the centre.

Not so. Peter and Paul have shown us that biblical theology being pressed into our lives is the ground on which souls are won or lost, and sin is resisted or embraced.

Therefore, applying the Bible as we preach is not nagging, encouraging self-justification or taking the spotlight off Christ. It is helping people both to see who they are as a result of what Christ has done, and the spectrum of consequences.

Who are Christians? Michael Emlet suggests that 'we address people simultaneously as saints, sufferers and sinners'.[10] That is a helpful three-way description, because if I forget any one of them my preaching will become artificial, denying the reality of either the fall or the cross.

Seeing Christians in that way is another way of describing the *no longer*, the *now* and the *not yet*. In some Christian circles there is such an enthusiasm for God's ultimate promises that there is an unreality about what is taught. And I want to tap my foot on the brake, '*Not yet*, *not yet*, we are sufferers and sinners, sufferers and sinners. We deal with Christians who have broken lives and broken hearts.'

In other Christian circles becoming a Christian is a matter of exchanging one world view for another. Nothing is actually different, other than the way I understand reality. And I want to step on the accelerator, 'There are all sorts of things that are *no longer* true about you, and you need to know who you are in Christ *now*! You are a saint, and that radically changes your approach to both sin and suffering. We can take a risk in forgiving each other. We can step forward to serve each other. We can work at that marriage, that anger, that drug abuse.'

We encourage people to struggle with sin precisely because that is the mark of the victory won. No matter how many times we try, fail and ask for God's power and love, that we continue to aim to live in line with biblical theology is a mark that we have spiritual understanding.

---

10. Emlet, *CrossTalk*, p. 74.

Questions for reflection and discussion

- Chris Green talked about the danger of looking for 'magic bullets'. Which 'bullet' do you find most tempting?
- What can you learn from the way various biblical commands move from general to particular?
- Why does Chris Green suggest that moving from indicative to imperative 'is too narrow at both ends'?
- Why is *no longer*, *now* and *not yet* the foundation narrative for any Christian?
- Why do Christians sin?

16. CHANGE IN FOUR DIMENSIONS

> Woe to you, teachers of the law and Pharisees, you hypocrites! You clean the outside of the cup and dish, but inside they are full of greed and self-indulgence. Blind Pharisee! First clean the inside of the cup and dish, and then the outside also will be clean.
>
> Woe to you, teachers of the law and Pharisees, you hypocrites! You are like whitewashed tombs, which look beautiful on the outside but on the inside are full of the bones of the dead and everything unclean.
>
> (Matt. 23:25–27)

When we looked earlier at the great commandments, we saw the four dimensions of human life that Jesus uses to describe the totality of discipleship: heart, soul, mind and strength. If we slow those down, we can begin to understand how to get inside the life of our hearers.

The heart without the gospel

We saw that the heart is the seat of our sense of identity and values, that inner sense of being 'me'. It is therefore the seat of a rightly ordered relationship with God.

So what happens if we try to address the heart without the gospel?

We become the totality of our relationship with God. We become our own god, barely sufficient to gratify our most superficial desires, and clearly insufficient for our deepest needs. And so we worship ourselves, or creation or even the evil one, because sin drives us to displace God from his throne. To a sinner anything, even Satan, is preferable to being ruled by the living God. That is why, if we address the heart without the gospel, we encourage idolatry.

Because human beings are made in God's image, we are, even at our most fragile moments, capable of the most enormous efforts, and can deliver change. The best example I know is the one mentioned in the previous chapter:

Alcoholics Anonymous. By sheer group self-help AA encourages people out of the gutter and back into life. I have already underlined that we have a lot to learn about the honesty with which their members address their faults, and I do not wish what follows to be taken in the wrong way. I admire AA.

Here are AA's famous twelve concepts:[1]

1. We admitted we were powerless over alcohol – that our lives had become unmanageable.
2. Came to believe that a Power greater than ourselves could restore us to sanity.
3. Made a decision to turn a will and our lives over to the care of God as we understood him.
4. Made a searching and fearless moral inventory of ourselves.
5. Admitted to God, to ourselves and to another human being the exact nature of our wrongs.
6. Were entirely ready to have God remove all those defects of character.
7. Humbly asked Him to remove our shortcomings.
8. Made a list of all persons we had harmed and became willing to make amends to them all.
9. Made direct amends to such people wherever possible, except when to do so would injure them or others.
10. Continued to take personal inventory and when we were wrong promptly admitted it.
11. Sought through prayer and meditation to improve our conscious contact with God as we understood Him, praying only for knowledge of His will for us and the power to carry that out.
12. Having had a spiritual awakening as the result of these steps, we tried to carry this message to alcoholics and to practise these principles in all our affairs.

I find that list moving. First, as someone for whom alcohol abuse is not a personal problem, I am in awe of how deeply a group of non-Christians are taking the attempt to restore their lives.

Secondly, theologically, we have to say that because this solution locks people into idolatry it cannot help them properly out of their problems. It cannot deliver full forgiveness, the new identity in Christ or the resources of the Holy Spirit in the church to replace alcohol addiction. 'Do not get drunk on wine, which leads to debauchery. *Instead, be filled with the Spirit*', wrote Paul (Eph. 5:18).

---

1. Taken from http://www.aa.org/bigbookonline/en_appendicevii.cfm.

Thirdly, I am challenged as a church leader over how shallow and narrow are our patterns of discipling. If someone came to me as a new Christian wanting to read Mark's Gospel, I would book them into my diary, but if they had an issue with alcohol I would be tempted to give them AA's number. However, that is too narrow. And if I took it on myself, I might meet up to chat, and then plug them into a normal small group. But that is also too shallow for such serious issues. If we want to deal with these issues at the level of the heart, we must bring the full resources of the gospel and the church it creates to encourage each other in deep, broad discipleship.

The soul without the gospel[2]

The soul, biblically, deals more with our emotional life. The Bible repeatedly addresses our emotions: Rejoice! Be glad! And it tells us not to be captives of our emotions, but to change them by reflecting on the God of the gospel:

> Why, my soul, are you downcast?
>   Why so disturbed within me?
> Put your hope in God,
>   for I will yet praise him,
>   my Saviour and my God.
> (Ps. 42:5; see v. 11; Ps. 43:5)

The danger lies in attempting to affect the soul's emotions without the gospel, and that is manipulation. Scenes of people being whipped into an emotional frenzy are standard when it comes to seeing the foolishness of religion – and we have to say that where professing Christian churches attempt to do this, they are as idolatrous as any cult. It can be enthusiasm or sentimentality, but it is not the gospel.

More cunningly, some churches attempt to manipulate their members by producing the emotion of guilt. There is true, objective guilt for sin, of course, and the right emotional response to that is to feel guilty. But churches use guilt to get people to sign up for building campaigns, to recruit for the Sunday school, to raise the giving – or simply to turn up. They get so used to guilt that unless they feel it, they don't think they have been to church.

---

2. See Michael P. Jensen (ed.), *True Feelings: Perspectives on Emotions in Christian Life and Ministry* (Nottingham: Apollos, 2012).

Another group of churches is so wary of the dangers of manipulation that they downplay the role of emotions completely. I have been in meetings where the song has ended on a moving note, but the service leader did not acknowledge that, said 'Well done' and gave the announcements for the week. That is manipulative as well.

So we must expect, allow and encourage a proper emotional response with the gospel. We expect it to shape, influence and change us. Our task as preachers is to identify the emotional change the passage expects and align people with that.

The mind without the gospel

We are told to think differently as Christians, to avoid lies and believe the gospel, and to consider every aspect of reality from that perspective.

If we address the mind, without doing it through the gospel, we address people as clever, at least in their own eyes. We encourage them, by their own standards of truth, to evaluate elements of the gospel and its claims. We flatter them with the breadth of their, or our, reading. In simple terms, it produces rationalism, liberalism and intellectual pride.

The evangelical equivalent is to teach people *about* the Bible. We use Greek, Hebrew, history and theology to leave people fascinated by the text. They leave church after our sermon on 1 Corinthians understanding the place and culture of Corinth, the structure of the letter, and the move from cross to resurrection that dominates it. They understand 1 Corinthians.

Paul did not write 1 Corinthians so that the Corinthians would understand it. That is too small a goal. He wrote it so that they would stop squabbling and love each other, stop sinning and live in line with the gospel. If the Corinthians had gone home understanding the importance of seeing chapter 13 between chapters 12 and 14 but not doing anything about it, he would have counted that a failure.

The strength without the gospel

The gospel, as we have seen, both requires and empowers us to change. Paul writes, 'Whatever happens, conduct yourselves in a manner worthy of the gospel of Christ' (Phil. 1:27). But the gospel requires constant repentance as its method.

It is possible for preachers to exhort and encourage people to live a better life without going the gospel way. But just telling people what to do produces

rotten fruit: rebelliousness among the social liberals (often the younger generation) and judgmentalism among the social conservatives (often the older
generation). It produces domineering preachers and cowed churches.

We need to tread carefully here. Take that earlier idea of preaching a series
such as *Ten Steps to Improve Your Marriage*. This would encourage a couple to be
honest and loving, sexually frank, with homework for them to do – all quoting
the Bible but without the gospel. That would be disastrous, and land those
marriages in a worse spiritual state than before.

But would it not be possible to build such a series on the gospel? A broken
marriage is one biblical picture of Israel's relationship with God, and adultery
is not just one sin, but a description of all sin. The new creation sees us as a
bride and Christ as a bridegroom. If our human marriages echo that, can we
not genuinely help marriages by building on the gospel? We will come back to
these issues in chapter 18 below.

What Satan loves and hates

Satan means 'accuser', and accusing Christians, both before God and before
themselves, is what he loves to do. He loves it when we erect our proud self-
justifying religious ladders of heart, soul, mind and strength. One author has
seen this all too often in churches:

> My work with teenagers has convinced me that one of the main reasons teenagers
> are not excited by the gospel is that they do not think they need it. Many parents have
> successfully raised self-righteous little pharisees. When they look at themselves, they
> do not see a sinner in desperate need, so they are not grateful for a Savior. Sadly, the
> same is true of many of their parents.[3]

And Satan loves it when our ladders collapse and we slump in despair and doubt.
All four dimensions without the gospel will produce despair.

What he hates, therefore, is what will stop us erecting those ladders in the
first place because there is no need. And that is the gospel: it both entrances us
with what Christ has done, and inspires us with the hope of what he will do.[4]

---

3. Timothy Lane and Paul David Tripp, *How People Change* (Greensboro: New Growth, 2006), p. 4.

4. On entrancing the Christian, see 2 Cor. 7:6; 2 Thess. 2:17; Pss 34:15, 17; 91:3; 143:3; 145:14, 19; 147:3, 6; Isa. 54:11–14; Eph. 3:16; 2 Thess. 2:17. On hope, Rom. 15:4.

Change in four dimensions

So if all four dimensions comprise discipleship, and if all four without the gospel produce despair, then we must address all four with the gospel, all of the time.

> It is in the here and now that many of us experience a gospel blindness. Our sight is dimmed by the tyranny of the urgent, by the siren call of success, by the seductive beauty of physical things, by our inability to admit our own problems, and by the casual relationships within the body of Christ that we mistakenly call fellowship. *This blindness is often encouraged by preaching that fails to take the gospel to the specific challenges people face.* People need to see that the gospel belongs in their workplace, their kitchen, their school, their bedroom, their backyard and their van. They need to see the way the gospel makes a connection between what they are doing and what God is doing.[5]

And it is working out those connections that is the preacher's task.

Kinds of application

To make sure that we remain faithful as we apply, Haddon Robinson makes this suggestion: 'One key, I believe, to making certain our applications remain in alignment with the text is to distinguish between necessary (if "A" is true, "B" must be true), probable, possible, improbable and impossible implications.'[6]

His concern at that point is that we remain faithful to the text, but this also means we remain faithful to the gospel. This avoids legalism, where I as a preacher take my possible inferences as being as authoritative as the necessary statements in the text. Remember, even Christians want legalism because it seems easier than the humility that grace requires.

A second way to be faithfully creative is to grasp that one command can have a number of possible ways to be put into practice. Take 'Honour your father and mother' – which is the first commandment with a promise' (Eph. 6:2). What does that mean for the following?

---

5. Lane and Tripp, *Change*, p. 4, italics mine.
6. Cited in Daniel Overdorf, *Applying the Sermon: How to Balance Biblical Integrity and Cultural Relevance* (Grand Rapids: Kregel, 2009), p. 69; similarly, Haddon Robinson, 'The Heresy of Application', in Haddon Robinson and Craig Brian Larson, *The Art and Craft of Biblical Preaching* (Grand Rapids: Zondervan, 2005), p. 309.

- A 6-year-old.
- A 16-year-old.
- A 26-year-old on the brink of marriage.
- The retired couple I knew, both in their seventies, and who each had one parent still alive.

As I talk about each of those situations, and what the command means in that life, other people in the congregation mull over what it means for them as well.

Sermons that explode on Monday

So, to conclude. Well, how *do* you conclude a sermon? We can divide the sermon into four parts, like the movements of a symphony as the listener experiences it over time.

1. Why? Why should I invest the next 25 minutes of my life in listening to this, when I have other things that could occupy my attention while I pretend to be listening? Answering that is the task of the introduction, which should grab my attention and start to engage me with the next question,

2. What? What is this passage talking about?

To underline my point, most preachers think that this is all a sermon has to do, but that is not true. What Bryan Chappell says bears repeating:

> Even if the explanation of a sermon were to define every Greek and Hebrew word for prayer, were to quote at length from Calvin, Luther and E. M. Bounds on prayer's meaning, were to cite fifty passages that relate to prayer, and were to describe the prayer practices of David, Jeremiah, Daniel, Paul and Jesus, would listeners truly understand what prayer is? No. Until we engage in prayer we do not really understand it. Until we apply a truth understanding of it remains incomplete. This means that until a preacher provides application, exposition remains incomplete.[7]

Let us take it to the next level.

3. So what? Have I understood the implications of this for my life? Do I perceive what this preacher thought was so worthwhile to get me to listen? What am I supposed to do about this? Again, Bryan Chapell insists on 'Direct application *right between the eyes – with love*.'[8]

---

7. Bryan Chappell, *Christ-Centered Preaching* (Grand Rapids: Baker, 1994), p. 203.

8. Ibid., p. 223, italics his.

4. Now what? Am I clear about the very next action I need to take?[9]

This last step might seem as though it is legalism creeping in through the back door, but it is an important step for two reasons.

First, Jesus taught us that when faced with a hard call in discipleship, our tendency will be to put off responding (Luke 9:59). Expecting people to understand and decide what to do in a sermon is therefore critical. Every lazy spiritual muscle will want us to put off the hard conversation – getting people to the point where they say, 'OK, I need to ring Jean and ask for her forgiveness.' Once again, just because someone's tempted to legalism doesn't mean I don't tell them what to do.

Secondly, I need to put a brake on my own churchiness. Because preachers spend most of their time on church-related business, they see applications easily only in those areas. I live in church world and forget what it is like in world world. Randy Frazee says that in order to apply everything in sermons, he suspects most people would need to quit their job and live in a monastery![10] One experienced preacher said:

> I feel we should make certain that most of our applications relate to Monday, not Sunday. As preachers, our lives centre around the business of the church, so our inclination is to make applications such as, 'You need to volunteer to teach a class. You need to tithe. You need to attend church services.'[11]

That's right. So, when I preach on anger, I need to make sure that it does not just relate to a spat over the coffee rota or a disagreement between two of the children's leaders. People will be rightly thinking of their week ahead and how the gospel affects it, and the meeting they have tomorrow afternoon with the colleague who always winds them up. I need my sermon to explode in their minds on a Monday as they put their hands on the door handle: *in your anger do not sin.*

---

9. David Veerman, editor of the Life Application Study Bible, suggests that application should answer two questions for the listener: 'So what?' and 'Now what?' David Veerman, 'Apply Within: A Method for Finding the Practical Response Called for in a Text', in Robinson and Larson, *Art and Craft*, p. 285. Similarly, see Andy Stanley and Lane Jones, *Communicating for a Change* (Colorado Springs: Multnomah, 2006), throughout.

10. Randy Frazee, 'Helping Preachers Practice What We Preach', in Robinson and Larson, *Art and Craft*, p. 302.

11. Cited in Overdorf, *Applying*, p. 131.

Questions for reflection and discussion

- What happens if we address the 'heart' without the gospel?
- What happens if we address the 'soul' without the gospel?
- What happens if we address the 'mind' without the gospel?
- What happens if we address the 'strength' without the gospel?
- Haddon Robinson delineated five kinds of implication: necessary, probable, possible, improbable and impossible. From a text you are working on, try to find an example of each.
- Chris Green suggests there are four 'movements' of a sermon. Do you recognize them from your own listening or speaking?
- What makes a sermon 'explode on Monday'?

PART 5

HOW DOES THE BIBLE ENGAGE
OUR ATTENTION?

17. OUR LOVE OF QUESTIONS

> When the queen of Sheba heard about the fame of Solomon and his
> relationship to the LORD, she came to test Solomon with hard questions.
>
> (1 Kgs 10:1)

There are broadly three schools of ethics: those that say there are things we
ought to do because some external authority tells us they are true (the *deontological*); those that say there are things it is good to do because of the result they
produce (the *teleological*); and those that say there are things that are good to do
because they feel right (the *existential*).[1] Taken individually or in combination
they form the map on which any ethical theory must be found. It is common,
though, for them to fight, because our duties and rights serve different ends in
a fallen world. Ultimately, only the gospel makes these three cohere: what we
ought to do because God commands it is also what will produce the greatest
possible blessing and – as I am remade in the image of Christ – becomes what
I want to do most in the world and gives me greatest delight. Those three schools
of ethics produce the three principal questions that non-Christians, and ques-
tioning Christians, will ask of any sermon:

---

1. This is obviously a crude summary. For our purposes, 'teleological' encompasses
   'utilitarian' or 'consequential' ethics, where a (good) end can justify (questionable)
   means, and 'existential' encompasses 'virtue ethics', dealing with questions of
   character and behaviour. For an insightful understanding of Christian ethics,
   see Andrew J. B. Cameron, *Joined-up Life: A Christian Account of How Ethics Works*
   (Nottingham: Inter-Varsity Press, 2011).

- The deontological school produces the question *Is what I'm hearing true?* On what authority is this person speaking?
- The teleological school produces the question *Is what I'm hearing relevant?* What would be the result if everybody did this?
- The existential school produces the question *Is what I'm hearing real?* Is this preacher a phoney, or do we get to meet God?

To reintroduce our systematic theology, the reason why they can all be answered in a coherent way is because of the person and work of Christ: as prophet, he gives assurance that his words are truthful and from God, as king he gives assurance that his kingly rule is one of blessing and goodness, and as priest he gives assurance that we will genuinely and uniquely meet God through his sacrificial death. Because he is one, those three will work together.

All hearers have all three questions – or, if they do not articulate them, they recognize them when they are stated. We could usefully follow that for Christians; but in this section I want to look at non-Christians, whose questions we need to address. Timothy Keller puts it like this:

> I'm a Calvinist, and because I'm a Calvinist, I realise belief isn't something people can work up without God's help. So why should I preach as if I think anyone who has any trouble believing what I'm saying is an idiot? It should make me compassionate with those who doubt.[2]

'What shall we do?'

If we ask those three questions, we find they are answered in subtly different ways. 'Is what I'm hearing true?' is answered most plausibly in the area of thought and intellect. 'Is what I'm hearing relevant?' is answered most plausibly in the area of practical consequences. And 'Is what I'm hearing real?' is answered most plausibly in the area of personal relationships and emotions. Each of them therefore is asked with a cultural and contemporary edge that will vary.

Now these are not independent buckets of answers, but I find it helpful to distinguish them. If we push it further and think about the response to the gospel, we can see the result after the sermon on the day of Pentecost. Peter,

---

2. Timothy Keller, 'A New Kind of Urban Preacher', in Craig Brian Larson (ed.), *Prophetic Preaching* (Peabody: Hendrickson, 2012), p. 87.

you remember, has just proved from Scripture that the risen Jesus is both Lord and Christ: 'When the people heard this, they were cut to the heart and said to Peter and the other apostles, "Brothers, what shall we do?"' (Acts 2:37).

'When the people heard this' shows that Peter had been engaging in proper, rational argument, and that his hearers had been persuaded of the truth of his statement.

And 'they were cut to the heart' shows that the full impact of what they had just done was terrible. They had murdered their Messiah and judge, but he had then not stayed dead. God had installed him more certainly in both roles. They therefore engaged with the rational message with their minds but also quite rightly with their emotions.

'Brothers, what shall we do?' shows that they were aware, or Peter had made them aware, that there was a practical claim that this message made upon them, and that demanded that they act.

So there is a triple thread that can run through our apologetic and evangelistic preaching, from the questions of the sceptical unbeliever through to the response of the person who is coming to faith.

The three elements of the thread are related, but distinguishing them helps me see if I am becoming biased in one direction, or away from one. When I ask how we do our apologetics, I suspect we have concentrated most of our fire power into the 'Is it true?' question, and I fear we may be mishearing or not answering some important questions.

Triangles and squares

At this point you may be expecting me to map this triangle onto some of the other big conceptual diagrams we have used. I have to disappoint you. Not all these diagrams line up in one, architectural, model. For instance, it would be lovely if we could map these three questions onto the *heart, soul, mind, strength* diagram. But we cannot.

Similarly, when Christians see the number 3 they will gravitate towards thinking in trinitarian terms. That would also be a mistake here: the doctrine of the Trinity is a beautiful and careful balance of loving relationships, interlocking and mutually defined. The three questions I have identified do not work in that way, and should not be forced into that mould.

They do, however, work well with Christ as prophet, priest and king, as I have noted, and here we can join up two of our triangles.

The *prophets* were those who brought God's Word to bear, words of law and forgiveness, judgment and blessing, warning and promise. As the narrative of

Israel unfurled, they provided God's commentary of ultimate redemption. They bore the *promise*.

The *priests* were those who represented God to the people and the people to God; they brought people into the temple with the sacrifices for sin, and led them in praise and prayer. They guarded, and occasionally entered, the holy of holies. They were the people of the *presence*.

The *kings* were the individuals who sat on the throne of David, or on the rebellious throne of Israel, and guarded, ruled and protected God's people as a nation – or abused their office and the nation. Their concern was the *people*.

So the triangle of biblical theology (God's people, in God's presence, under God's promise) can be focused into the individual Christ, our prophet, priest and king. And since we have seen that those three offices produce answers to the three questions of non-Christians, our biblical theology, Christology, application and apologetics are interrelated disciplines.

Apologetics

Alastair Begg says wisely, 'In our generation people fear persuasion. Anybody who is persuaded is regarded as sort of weird or over the top. You don't indoctrinate children. You leave them to make up their own minds. We don't persuade because it isn't fashionable.'[3] So if we are trying to engage in something that is both implausible and unfashionable, there is no surprise if is hard. Indeed, because we are creatures of our culture, we need to recognize that we will meet resistance in our own hearts over the same two issues.

Timothy Keller nails it perfectly: 'In the early twentieth century, skeptics rejected Christianity because it wasn't true – "miracles cannot be". Today, skeptics reject Christianity because it even claims to be true – "absolutes cannot be".'[4]

But we cannot run away from the task. We need to answer those questions, and ask some hard ones of our own. Because we can answer those three questions coherently, we need to help people to realize the instability of any alternative answer.

---

3. Alastair Begg, 'Preaching to Change the Heart', in Haddon Robinson and Craig Brian Larson, *The Art and Craft of Biblical Preaching* (Grand Rapids: Zondervan, 2005), p. 162.

4. Timothy Keller, 'Preaching Morality in an Amoral Age', in Robinson and Larson, *Art and Craft*, p. 166.

Moreover, because biblical theology and apologetics can be coordinated, we can use the narrative of God's plans to provide the right and attractive alternative to the false narratives that idols tell. We will come back to stories in the next chapter.

Above all, though, we cannot hide behind our fear of people laughing at us because of our unfashionable or implausible strategy: 'Since, then, we know what it is to fear the Lord, we try to persuade others' (2 Cor. 5:11).

As I prepare my sermon, I need to imagine three sceptics sitting by my desk, asking each of these questions. I may not be able to handle all three in any given sermon, but it is a good habit to have each one present and to give at least one of them something substantial to chew on. If I need to find an angle on this, I ask myself, 'What will my sceptical friend find most implausible about this passage?'

Question 1: Is it true?

So at this point, I am going to have a friendly debate, trying to get the person to realize that my answer to their question is not only viable, but better than any they can come up with. To do this, I need to have the courtesy not to mock them for asking questions, and indeed to put their objection with sufficient clarity that they do realize it has been understood. I sometimes imagine my friend, arms crossed, smiling and muttering, 'Yup, that's the question, and I couldn't have put it better myself. If he can get out of that, I'll be interested.'

At that point I need to reply.

The clearest biblical example of this is Paul's evangelistic work in Corinth:

Every Sabbath he reasoned in the synagogue, trying to persuade Jews and Greeks.
   When Silas and Timothy came from Macedonia, Paul devoted himself exclusively to preaching, testifying to the Jews that Jesus was the Messiah. (Acts 18:4–5)

And shortly afterwards, Apollos followed his example, in Achaia:

When Apollos wanted to go to Achaia, the brothers and sisters encouraged him and wrote to the disciples there to welcome him. When he arrived, he was a great help to those who by grace had believed. For he vigorously refuted his Jewish opponents in public debate, proving from the Scriptures that Jesus was the Messiah. (Acts 18:27–28)

My clarifying thought is therefore this: 'What do I want people to *understand* in the light of this passage, and why do I want them to *understand* it?' Andy Stanley came up with this and the next one, and I have modified it only in that he says, 'What do I want people to know?', and that could mean that there was a lack in people's knowledge that I have somehow filled.[5] By using the word 'understand' instead, I am trying to express the 'Aha!' moment: when people get it, the penny drops, the light bulb comes on, they join the dots – you get the idea. They have been persuaded. But Andy Stanley is right, that I need to express to myself: not just *what* I want people to understand, but *why* I want them to understand it.

Seeker small groups

So what could you offer such enquiring minds? One idea might be that by the end of your evangelism course, or whatever you do, you don't just offer the two options of becoming a Christian or not. You could offer another course based on another gospel, giving another author's presentation of Jesus. Or how about addressing the questions they think Christians are too scared to answer: pain, other religions – you know the list. How about offering a series of properly planned Bible studies, aimed at non-Christians, on just one of those areas so you can really go into it? Six small-group studies on whether God can be really loving if he lets small children die of HIV/AIDS. Don't duck the question – tackle it.[6]

Book groups

All around where I live are small book groups, easy to find on the Web or in cafés, where people get together to discuss what they have been reading together, a classic or a new one. I joined one that operated out of a local bookstore.

The reason is not just that I like reading and enjoy discovering new books, although both are true and it probably would not make sense to join such a group if it weren't. The point is this: every time we met, it was to have an intelligent discussion about a book, and there is hardly a book that is worth reading that does not create echoes for the gospel to address. More than that, if you are reading a classic work of fiction, the Christian story is often assumed as part of the culture, and the reader cannot make sense of the story without it. So you can contribute the gospel into the group, as a genuine part of the conversation, to help discussion further. For instance, a modern reader of Tolstoy's *Anna Karenina* sees it as a doomed love story of a woman trapped in a loveless

---

5. Andy Stanley and Lane Jones, *Communicating for a Change* (Colorado Springs: Multnomah, 2006).

6. Gary Poole, *Seeker Small Groups: Engaging Spiritual Seekers in Life-Changing Discussions* (Grand Rapids: Zondervan, 2003).

marriage; a Christian reader, as Tolstoy intended, also sees it as a story of adulterous betrayal and a wronged husband. We read the story better.

My hearty friends tell me about joining hockey clubs to make non-Christian friends and maybe, somehow, to get the gospel across. Join a nice book club and you'll have all the opportunities you want whenever you turn up, without any physical injuries.

Questions

So as I prepare a sermon, I find I ask myself these questions about what is true:

- What is the assertion that listeners would find most problematic?
- What is their objection to that assertion? What is the fundamental belief behind the objection?
- What reasons can I offer that tackle that fundamental belief and then the precise objection?
- What question could I ask to demonstrate the falsity of that fundamental belief?
- What evidence or illustration can I offer to show the validity of the assertion?

Question 2: Is it relevant?

All too often we have successfully managed to force the gospel into a box marked 'religious club', and made it something that occupies a social niche: if you like sport and summer days, join the tennis club; if you like crafts and home-making, join the card-making club; if you like choral music and doing good, join the church.

The question of our non-Christian friends, therefore, is what is the point of our club? Why am I so anxious for them to join mine, when they are not particularly fussed if I join theirs or not. They prefer what their club does.

At this point I am not so much dealing with questions of truth, as of relevance, although they are obviously close allies. And since I believe the gospel is not just news, but good news, I need to work at showing them why it is, and what difference it will make to them if they skip cricket one week and come to us.

At the back of this is the second of Andy Stanley's questions: 'What do I want people to do in the light of this passage, and why do I want them to do it?' But it is of course much easier for a non-Christian than a Christian to answer. Many would say, 'All we can ask a non-Christian to do is repent and believe the gospel,' and I have a great deal of sympathy for that. The question is: How do we present the gospel so that people see its relevance?

One of the most controversial areas of evangelism and what is called 'church growth' is the idea of meeting the 'felt needs' of non-Christians. Its proponents say they are acting as responsive servants, whereas its opponents say they are avoiding Christ's claims; one side says they are making the gospel visible, and the other says they are making it *in*visible.

There is a way of identifying and meeting the needs of non-Christians that is of course quite fake. We could offer diet clubs, first-aid courses and all manner of things that would reinforce the idea that Christians are nice people who like to help out. They need helping out, and that's what we are here for. That is what church is for. It's what God is for.

But here is the genuine dilemma – when you see the world through proper gospel lenses, you see two things with great clarity.

First, it becomes clear that fallen people are so idolatrous and ignorant that they do not know what their real needs are. Phillip Jensen puts it clearly: 'If we are even half as sinful as God tells us we are, we cannot be trusted to diagnose our own problems, let alone discover the required solutions.'[7] That is quite right. We do not know the relevance of the gospel until God reveals it to us, and then we discover our deepest problem is sin (which we never considered), not the things that occupy our minds all day. The fact that something is a felt need does not mean it is important.

Fake churches can make great hay in meeting these fake-felt needs: the prosperity gospel, success gospel and health gospel are all attempts to cash in, meeting superficial needs, superficially. Letting sinners set the agenda with their rights, ambitions and need for approval is a disastrous way to set a ministry. It is what we dread in meeting felt needs.

But the other truth we see with gospel lenses is that sin damages lives, it wreaks havoc in the homes and businesses of everyone on the planet, and causes real pain and real needs. Just because a need is a felt need, does not mean it is fake.

Non-Christians, as fallen image bearers, still carry the defaced image of God; it has not been removed. And that means that sometimes they will rightly identify their needs, and sometimes wrongly; they will not be able to carry the thought

---

7. Phillip D. Jensen and Paul Grimmon, *The Archer and the Arrow* (Kingsford: Matthias Media, 2010), p. 94.

down to its deepest levels in the gospel, but they can and often do identify with the problems sin causes, and the longings for God's right values. When they long for political stability, good families and physical well-being, it is not that those are wrong ideals, but that they are not placed in a gospel light that would make them shiningly true. As they stand, disconnected from the gospel, the ideals become idols.

Billy Graham observed that in every culture where he spoke, people had five things in common: dissatisfaction with material possessions, emptiness and a quest for meaning, loneliness, guilt and fear of death.[8] I suspect the reason those are cultural universals is that they are the cries of the fallen image of God that feels the weight of sin but is not able to articulate the problem. Pastors might wish to add a sixth universal to Graham's list: Why does it hurt?

Rick Warren has a similar list, when he says that there are six things he knows about every crowd he speaks to:

- Everyone wants to be loved (i.e. Billy Graham's point about loneliness).
- Everyone wants their lives to count (Graham's point about meaning).
- No matter how wealthy or successful, their lives are empty without Christ (the same as Graham).
- Many of these people are carrying a load of guilt (the same as Graham).
- Many are consumed with bitterness over past hurts (the additional point about hurt).
- There is a universal fear of death (the same as Graham).[9]

The fact that we can so easily track the connection between those universal felt needs and the gospel means I will be guarded in how I approach this. William Willimon, for instance, is much blunter than I would be: 'One of my problems with so-called seeker services and seeker-sensitive churches is that, in my pastoral experience, whatever most people are seeking it isn't Jesus.'[10] I want to say, 'Yes

---

8. B. Graham, 'Evangels of Grace', in Billy Graham, Eugene Peterson and William Willimon (eds.), *The Pastor's Guide to Effective Preaching* (Kansas City: Beacon Hill, 2003), p. 10.

9. Handbook to Rick Warren's *Purpose-Driven Preaching* conference (http://www. pastors.com: Foothill Ranch, California, 1999), p. 7. Stott uncovers a range of existential questions about meaning (John R. W. Stott, *I Believe in Preaching* [London: Hodder & Stoughton, 1982], p. 151).

10. William H. Willimon, foreword to Frank Honeycutt, *Preaching to Skeptics and Seekers* (Nashville: Abingdon, 2011), p. 11.

and no.' He is quite right that people are not banging on our church doors demanding to be led to Christ. They are happy enough sailing, having a lie in or surfing the Web. Jesus does not cross their mind.

> there is no one who understands;
> there is no one who seeks God.
> (Rom. 3:11)

On the other hand, their lives experience the consequences of sin; their hearts long for God even as they rebel against him; and the idols with which they fill their lives are the good gifts of God that point to him though they do not realize it. 'God did this so that they would seek him and perhaps reach out for him and find him, though he is not far from any one of us' (Acts 17:27).

So there are two tasks for us.

One is, we must identify those felt needs that are a hardly articulated expression of a real need. Daniel Overdorf has a helpful list, matching biblical teaching to the corresponding need:

Biblical teaching	Corresponding need
Christian fellowship	Loneliness
God's grace	Guilt of sin
Sexual purity	Struggle with lust
God's sovereignty	Fear of unknown
Faith	Doubt
God's guidance	Loss of direction[11]

The second task is to unmask the idolatry where people worship the creation and not its creator, distracted by other things from their real need. This means finding what David Powlison calls the 'functional gods'.[12]

Can we counsel non-Christians?

So a couple comes to see you: they are not Christians, and never go to church expect for weddings and funerals. But their marriage is close to its death, and

---

11. Daniel Overdorf, *Applying the Sermon: How to Balance Biblical Integrity and Cultural Relevance* (Grand Rapids: Kregel, 2009) p. 116.

12. David Powlison, *Seeing with New Eyes* (Phillipsburg: P&R, 2003), p. 130.

the wife has said she will not have her unfaithful husband back one more time unless he agrees to see a minister. So here they are, facing you, one fearfully hopeful and one resentful.

What can you say? Can you say anything? Can you apply the Bible to non-Christians?

A *Ten Steps to Improve Your Marriage* pastor could. He would pull out ten top tips, all from Proverbs, and give them to the couple: be honest, recover your love, express your appreciation, and so on.

Should we shut the door regretfully? Their felt need is a broken marriage, but their real need is to come to the next guest service – is that all we have?

Or can we tell the story of the gospel, from creation to new creation in terms of love lost and found, and adultery forgiven. Can we tell them the gospel in such a way that they see the reason for their marriage breaking up is sin, and the gospel puts the proper marriage back in place when we get to the marriage feast of the Lamb, so that our marriages, when they are pointing in that direction, begin to discover their purpose and the power to forgive?

Once again, Timothy Keller is wise:

> Every message and point must demonstrate relevance or the listener will mentally 'channel surf.' But once you have drawn in people with the amazing relevance of the gospel, you must confront them again with the most pragmatic issue of all – the claim of Christ to be absolute Lord of life . . .
>
> You see, until you decide if there is a God, if Jesus is the Son, and other matters, how can you make an intelligent decision about what is right and wrong about sex? Christians believe what they do about sex not because they are old-fashioned, or because they are prudish, but because Jesus is the Way, the Truth, and the Life . . .
>
> [We] must be careful. We can say that morality 'works' but only because it corresponds to reality. And we must preach that sometimes Christian morality 'works' only in the long run. Looking at life from eternity it will be obvious that it works to be honest, unselfish, chaste and humble. But in the short run, practicing chastity may keep a person alone for many years. Practicing honesty may be an impediment to career advancement. This must be made clear to the contemporary listener.[13]

---

13. Timothy Keller, 'Preaching Morality in an Amoral Age', in Robinson and Larson, *Art and Craft*, pp. 168–169.

Questions

So as I think about the plausibility of the passage I am speaking on, here are the questions I work through for my sceptical friend:

- Why would a hearer say that this passage does not work in normal life?
- What evidence would they offer?
- What explanation would they offer?
- Do I wish to challenge their evidence?
- Do I wish to challenge their interpretation?
- What alternative evidence do I wish to offer?
- What alternative explanation do I wish to offer?

Question 3: Is it real?

Most of our friends think we are self-deluded. There is no God, and we are making all this up. Or if there is a 'god', there is no conceivable way to make any truth claims about it. There may be a spiritual reality of some sort, accessible through the arts for some or yoga for others, but there may be nothing in it; the desire for religion is a leftover piece of the evolutionary past, an appendix of the intellect.

Much of what we do as Christians bears that out. There is an apocryphal story of an Anglican bishop who complained, 'Wherever Paul went they started a riot; wherever I go they serve tea.'

There are clues in Scripture that it is not meant to be this way. Lee Eclov puts it like this:

> Have you noticed that some psalms seem sort of emotionally exaggerated?
> Take those imprecatory psalms, for example: 'May his children be fatherless
> and his wife a widow.' I'm almost never that angry with anyone. My psalm would
> be much more restrained: 'Lord, make those irritating people start being nice to
> me.' At the other end of the spectrum, there is that exuberant praise: 'Shout
> for joy to the LORD, all the earth.' I don't even like clapping along with the
> praise songs.[14]

---

14. Lee Eclov, 'Tune My Heart to Sing Thy Grace', in Craig Brian Larson (ed.), *Inspirational Preaching* (Peabody: Hendrickson, 2012), pp. 109–110.

Our task is to teach people what a proper encounter with God is meant to be like, and encourage them into it. What does the Bible mean when it talks about our knowing God, being filled with the Spirit, and so on? What is that meant to be like? What is supposed to happen to me, and how do I know if it has? How do I map my internal life onto what the Bible says about it?

The clarifying question in this area is, what do I want people to *feel*, and why do I want them to *feel* it?[15] Because if people go home thinking they have met God when all they have done is have their body pounded by a good band with a decent sound system, your sceptical non-Christian friend will see through that in an instant. Or if your sceptical non-Christian friends go home thinking they have met God when they are actually just better informed rebels, we are not handling the Bible in line with its purpose.

Cut to the heart

The phrase we noted from the response to Peter's day of Pentecost sermon is 'they were cut to the heart', and that is what I am trying to describe. This was a genuine engagement with the gospel on an individual level, and that phrase describes the moment when a non-Christian realizes, 'This is real.'

Part of our responsibility as preachers, then, is to bring people face to face with the Lord Jesus, and hold them there so that they cannot look away. As so often in gospel matters, we cannot force that to happen, but we can do things that get in the way, one of which is to avoid emotional language.

One common diagram used to explain the impact of the gospel is of a cartoon figure standing on a narrow wall; ahead of him is the word 'Facts', behind him is the word 'Feelings', and he wears the label 'Faith'. Faith, we are told is keeping our eyes firmly on the Facts; if we allow Faith to focus on Feelings, we will fall off the wall.

Much in that diagram is commendable, and in particular the point that if we have to choose between the Facts and my Feelings (say, that I am unforgivable, or that God does not love me), then I must choose the Facts and go straight to the Scriptures. There I will find the assurance and comfort I need.

But we need to be wary of the assumption that our feelings may be fallen but our minds are not; or that our feelings are more fallen, that therefore feelings are *inherently* wrong. That cannot be: that is just secular rationalism. We know

---

15. John Ortberg, 'Authentic Inspiration', in ibid., p. 31.

that as we grow as Christians, our feelings about God are stretched to fit Scripture's shape, just as our mind is. God made our emotions and he remakes them through the gospel. And while my feelings can mislead me, I can lie to myself just as easily.

The proper work of the gospel is quite different from shallow emotionalism. We know and distrust the latter, but that should not make us distrust when the hearers are *cut to the heart*.

The preacher cut to the heart

Notice too that Peter is affected by the gospel. 'With many other words he warned them; and he pleaded with them' (Acts 2:40). He is not presenting a message that can be taken or left, of interest or not. For him this is a matter of life-defining truth, and he is emotionally engaged with it as he presents it.

John Ortberg reports that

> someone once asked the president of [America's] largest speaker's bureau: 'What's the most important characteristic a person needs to be an effective communicator?' I expected her to answer 'articulation' or maybe 'intelligence.' To my surprise, she answered, 'They have to have passion.' She explained that people with passion can overcome any other obstacle, such as a limited vocabulary or even a speech impediment. If they have an authentic passion, they tap into something contagious, something that feeds and inspires the human spirit. Conversely, if speakers don't have authentic passion, they may have great technique or phrasing, but their listeners will only tread water.[16]

Dwell on that word 'authentic', because you and I can tell a fake from a mile. If I preached and worked myself into a lather doing so, you would rightly walk out in disgust. But the gospel deals with big themes, of sin and forgiveness, lavish love and infinite care. If we can talk about the cross without it captivating our hearts, then we are as inauthentic as the tub thumper, and our secular friends can spot that we are phonies too.

Contrast our deadpan delivery with Paul's passion: 'For, as I have often told you before and now tell you again even with tears, many live as enemies of the cross of Christ' (Phil. 3:18).

---

16. Ibid., p. 28.

Questions

So in my thinking I find I ask myself these questions:

- What is the emotional impact that this passage is supposed to have on its hearers?
- Have I made sure that I am talking about the issues that cause that in the passage?
- What is the emotional impact it has on me as a preacher?
- In my study what has suddenly made me stop to pray and praise?

So, to pull this together, we have looked at the three questions of non-Christians and Christians, and thought about how to address them from the passage we are preaching from.

- They ask, 'Is what I'm hearing true?'
- I ask, 'What do I want people to understand in the light of this passage, and why do I want them to understand it?'
- They ask, 'Is what I'm hearing relevant?'
- I ask, 'What do I want people to do in the light of this passage, and why do I want them to do it?'
- They ask, 'Is what I'm hearing real?'
- I ask, 'What do I want people to feel in the light of this passage, and why do I want them to feel it?'

Those are the principal questions lying behind every genuine sceptical query.

Questions for reflection and discussion

- This chapter contains many questions to work through already, so reread and address them as they arise.
- How does Chris Green relate the questions and answers in apologetics to the work of Christ as prophet, priest and king?
- Would you, or could you, run a seeker small group? What would happen at it?
- Try answering the three questions (whether this sermon is true, real and relevant) about the last sermon you preached or heard.

18. OUR LOVE OF STORIES

Let the redeemed of the LORD tell their story –
   those he redeemed from the hand of the foe,
those he gathered from the lands,
   from east and west, from north and south.

(Ps. 107:2–3)

How to lose an audience

I was in New Zealand, speaking at a conference for Christian students, all potential gospel workers. New Zealand is a fabulously beautiful country, but it is short of such workers in many places, and I was enormously encouraged to be speaking to two hundred young people.

On the first night, before my talk, I was interviewed up at the front in a pleasantly relaxed, Kiwi way. I was asked what I liked most about New Zealand. That was easy, and I could talk with enthusiasm about my affection for the places, the people and my memorable, but terrifying, bungee jump in Queenstown.

Then came the harder question. What didn't I like about New Zealand? The room held its breath, and I dared to say that I did not really enjoy the *Lord of the Rings* movies. I know; I know. I might just as well have mocked the *haka*.[1]

I will come back to why I do not enjoy them shortly, but I do realize that I am in a tiny minority. Despite decades of reports telling us that TV is shortening

---

1. The *haka* is a ritualized dance of defiance, performed by the New Zealand rugby team, the All Blacks, at their international matches. No other nation has an equivalent ritual, and some struggle to know how to respond.

attention spans and that preachers need to speak in sound bites, people are watching hours (on the extended DVDs, many, many hours) of a trilogy.

Why? For the same reason I started this section like this – because people across all cultures like stories. They connect with the characters and the drama, and they want to know what happens at the end. I suspect that one reason so much biblical information is given us in a story form is to keep us hooked.

Gotcha!

One of the most powerful aspects of a story is that it is almost impossible not to feel with the most sympathetic character, and we read ourselves into the plot. 'What would I do?' we wonder. 'How would I choose?'

Jesus used that trait to cover the hook in several of his parables. The ending of the good Samaritan in Luke 10, or the prodigal son in Luke 15, shows how people were supposed to be swept along and then find themselves confronted by God. But Jesus was not the first biblical example. Take the way that King David, having committed adultery and then murder, was confronted by Nathan:

> The LORD sent Nathan to David. When he came to him, he said, 'There were two men in a certain town, one rich and the other poor. The rich man had a very large number of sheep and cattle, but the poor man had nothing except one little ewe lamb that he had bought. He raised it, and it grew up with him and his children. It shared his food, drank from his cup and even slept in his arms. It was like a daughter to him.
>
> 'Now a traveller came to the rich man, but the rich man refrained from taking one of his own sheep or cattle to prepare a meal for the traveller who had come to him. Instead, he took the ewe lamb that belonged to the poor man and prepared it for the one who had come to him.'
>
> David burned with anger against the man and said to Nathan, 'As surely as the LORD lives, the man who did this must die! He must pay for that lamb four times over, because he did such a thing and had no pity.'
>
> Then Nathan said to David, 'You are the man!' (2 Sam. 12:1–7)

David had swallowed the bait, and found himself hooked by God's prophet. The story had disarmed him.

We frequently run this idea in reverse, by telling ourselves stories about the idols we choose, to keep ourselves hooked on them. One story about money is that by hard work and saving we will one day retire on a yacht; another is that it gives us power to enjoy ourselves here and now. Save or squander – they are both stories. We idolize sex by telling the story of endless erotic adventures, or of the perfect marriage in the perfect house with the perfect kids. We idolize power with the story of achievement and success, or of liberty and individuality. You probably thought of a movie or a book for each of those.

Why are these stories so powerful?

The seven basic plots

The literary critic Christopher Booker conducted an exhaustive survey of Western literature, and concluded that there are basically only seven basic plots.[2] Every fairy tale, movie and blockbuster uses one or more of these. They are so prevalent that even when we know we are watching one, we still stay in our seats. Often even if we have seen it before.

- *Overcoming the Monster* is the plot of the dark threat that hangs over us and that must be defeated. It can be animate, as in *Beowulf* or *Jaws*, or inanimate, as in a thousand 'earth in peril from passing meteorite' movies. It can be supernatural or alien, but it must be killed.
- *Rags to Riches* is the story of someone who goes from poverty to fabulous wealth or success. It is *Cinderella* and *Aladdin*, but if you ask what happens next it turns into *Citizen Kane*.
- The *Quest* is the need to find 'the thing'. The ticking bomb, the golden fleece, the anti-serum, the code, the assassin.
- *Voyage and Return* is as old as Homer, but do you remember the subtitle of *The Hobbit*? 'There and back again.' In the process of the journey our hero is transformed in some way, normally wounded but ennobled.
- *Tragedy* has a thousand forms, but at heart is the inevitable working out of one simple, small event – a mistake or character flaw – until it consumes everyone in sight. King Lear loves but does not understand his daughters – that is all.
- *Comedy* does not mean that something is funny all the way through. Any of these stories can have humorous variants, but what comedies have in common is their shared, happy ending 'and they all lived happily ever after'. Rom Coms are comedies, as are the Shakespeare plays where all the confusions are cleared up and there are several weddings.

---

2. Christopher Booker, *The Seven Basic Plots: Why We Tell Stories* (London: Continuum, 2005).

- *Rebirth* is the story of the character who changes and starts their story again in a different guise. The Batman movies started off telling that story in a simple way, and finished in a much more complex and dark narrative, but it is the same one. A movie can even do an apparently endless series of rebirth stories, like *Groundhog Day*.

Some stories run more than one of these: *The Hobbit* is all of the first four, and with a hint of the seventh. Others put a twist in the basic plot, but that can cause problems: people once felt so uneasy at Shakespeare's disturbing twist at the end of *Twelfth Night* that they gave the play a 'proper' happy ending. Clever writers tell just a fragment of the story, or change the point of view, or drag so much tension and release into plot laid on plot laid on plot that it keeps us on the edge of our seats, like the movie *Inception* – but once you have seen the list of seven plots, it is hard to escape the conclusion that Booker is basically right.

Now here is an intriguing question, and it is one Booker does not ask – looking at the seven, which one of those is the gospel story?

- Is it the story of overcoming the monster of sin and death?
- Is it the story of the flesh and blood humans who are allowed to sit on God's throne and share his riches?
- Is it the story of a God who was willing to pay any price to restore what was lost?
- Is it the story of a king who went on a journey in disguise and went to the pit of death, but returned with a treasure beyond all value to him?
- Is it the story of a creature so magnificent that it was like a god walking but that was reduced, by one small, simple action, to unimaginable disaster?
- Is it a story that will end, with happy ever after and a wedding?
- Is it a story about being born again?

The gospel is the great story, the one that all the others long for and fail to meet.

Fallen image bearers not only have fragments of their glory that they occasionally see but don't recognize for what it is; they also are trying to put together the story that makes sense of the cosmos. In their stubborn sin they reject the true story and try to make another one – that is the intellectual endeavour of the last three hundred years of the West. But even the most rebellious political and military narratives of left and right can do nothing but present versions of the great story.

Lord of the Rings 2

I am reading *Lord of the Rings* to my two boys. I am not naturally at home in the worlds of elves and dwarfs, but I can recognize the skill and artistry of Tolkien. Here was a man who knew all about those archetypal stories and wrote them repeatedly in the plot, in small and large ways, sometimes with several running simultaneously. It is not just one story, but all of them.

More than that – Tolkien knew the Great Story. The power of the Ring is the temptation that leads to awful living death, there is a wise and miraculous man who dies and rises again, a king who comes to reclaim his kingdom, a servant who suffers – the gospel leaps off the pages. He was writing about Jesus all the time.

As he wrote to his son:

> Of course I do not mean that the Gospels tell what is only a fairy-story; but I do mean very strongly that they do tell a fairy-story: the greatest. Man the story-teller would have to be redeemed in a manner consonant with his nature: by a moving story. But since the author of it is the supreme Artist and the Author of Reality, this one was also made . . . to be true on the Primary Plane.[3]

And I think that is why I found the movies so disappointing, and my reaction so saddened my New Zealand friends. Because it has become a cycle of movies about love and heroism, and ecology and interracial friendship, and nobility and transformation – its makers have cut the thread of connection with the Great Story: it is no longer about Jesus. It is just about a bunch of hobbits.

But if I gave you a bunch of people who loved the movies and the books, and who did not know Jesus, could you show them that what they love and are looking for but fail to find is found, not in fantasy but in reality? Of course you could. And you'd do it by preaching the story.

An open door

That is not just true about *Lord of the Rings*. Most of the last two thousand years of Western culture are built on the explicit knowledge of and assume the truth of the gospel. I have already made the point about books, but it is true

---

3. Humphrey Carpenter (ed.), *The Letters of J. R. R. Tolkien* (New York: Houghton Mifflin, 1981; repr. 2000), pp. 100–101.

more widely in the arts. And if Booker is right, we won't just find this at the top of the artistic tree: we can get from almost any story in any culture to the gospel if we work hard enough. Because it is not that Western culture is a product of the gospel; it is that all cultures are the product of fallen image bearers.

But it does mean we should become more comfortable with describing God as the most attractive being there is, the creator of the world we would love to be true:

> O afflicted city, lashed by storms and not comforted,
>   I will rebuild you with stones of turquoise,
>   your foundations with lapis lazuli.
> I will make your battlements of rubies,
>   your gates of sparkling jewels,
>   and all your walls of precious stones.
> All your children will be taught by the LORD,
>   and great will be their peace.
> In righteousness you will be established:
> tyranny will be far from you;
>   you will have nothing to fear.
> Terror will be far removed;
>   it will not come near you.
> (Isa. 54:11–14)

And as preachers we are saying not only that it is a fabulous story you long for to be true; it is true.

Questions for reflection and discussion

- Think of the last two movies you watched or novels you read. Do they fit the theory of the seven basic plots?
- How would you relate each of those to a longing for Christ?
- Chris Green argued that sins are related to stories we tell – how would understanding that help a preacher?

PART 6

HOW DOES THE BIBLE APPLY TO
DIFFERENT KINDS OF PEOPLE?

19. APPLYING THE BIBLE TO NON-CHRISTIANS

> Your iniquities have separated
>   you from your God;
> your sins have hidden his face from you,
>   so that he will not hear.

(Isa. 59:2)

At some stage we will need to preach about 'sin'. But it is a word with so many wrong assumptions surrounding it that any preacher has to clear the decks:

- For some of our hearers, when we talk about sin they think we are talking about sex, and therefore we are against sex, and against them.
- For some of our hearers, when we talk about sin they think we are talking about them, not us, and saying they are not good enough for God, but we are.
- For some of our hearers, when we talk about sin they think we are talking about religion, not going to church or about being good and giving to charity.

These are all common views, however mistaken or misplaced, and they all have in common their lightness. Sin is redefined as a trivial matter that God could just forgive if he wanted to, without the complex mechanisms of sacrificial atonement. What is all the fuss about?

To present sin clearly, we can use the two triangles we have developed, as well as our biblical theology.

Sins of the head are to do with the area of truth. We wilfully or ignorantly believe lies, and reject or suppress the truth. And this can be over any area, whether God, ourselves, each other, our public life. The religious variants of these sins take the form of offering alternative gods and gospels, wrapped up in theological language. The secular variants are rational and wilfully atheistic.

Sins of the heart lie in the area of love and hate, and the fact that we love and hate the wrong things: sinners hate God and other people, and love sin and themselves. So the biblical writers frequently use the language of 'lusts' for this love of sin, and where our culture uses that simply for sexual desire, we insist that biblically it is much broader, and is used for every wrongly placed love (Gen. 6:5; Num. 11 – 25; Eccl. 9:3; Rom. 13:14; Gal. 5:16–17; Eph. 2:2–3; 4:18–19, 22; Jas 1:14–15; 4:1–3; 1 Peter 1:14; 2 Peter 1:4; 1 John 2:16).

We can see too that these categories of sin infect each other. So Paul writes about 'deceitful desires' (Eph. 4:22). Our lusts will deceive us about truth, and our lies will deceive us about both good and wicked feelings. Religious versions of them will seek to self-justify what we feel as being normal, and not needing to be put right with God. Secular versions will not need to self-justify – that we feel the desire for something is proof of its authenticity and normality, and requires satisfying.

Sins of the hands lie in the area of actions. Wilful disobedience and inability to obey come here, but so does a pride in visible self-control, or forcing others to do our will.

Each of these aspects of sin has a number of variations, some that are expressions of running away from God, and some that are self-congratulatory for not being bad. In terms of Jesus' parables these two forms represent the younger and elder brothers in the parable of the prodigal son (Luke 15:11–32).[1] While one form is rebellious and self-indulgent, the other is conformist and self-justifying. Both need to be restored to a relationship with their father.

The younger and less socially conformist your hearers, the more they will identify with the younger son – and identify you, the preacher, as the older son, accusing them of not being as good as they could be, and preferring that they stay wallowing in the pigsty where they belong.

The older and more socially conformist your hearers, the more they will identify with the older son – and cheer you, the preacher, as you point out the sins of the younger brother and congratulate them for not being in a pigsty.

What a terrible position for a preacher to be in: that we are responsible for neither brother coming home. Take a moment to identify a sin from each of

---

1. See Timothy Keller, *Prodigal God: Recovering the Heart of the Christian Faith* (London: Hodder & Stoughton, 2009).

the three aspects, think of a younger brother and older brother equivalent, and what should be the generous father's response.

	Younger brother version (rebellious and self-indulgent)	Older brother version (religious and self-justifying)	Father's reaction
Sin of the head			
Sin of the heart			
Sin of the hands			

So far we have seen sin as an internal matter, as an aspect of our condition. But our condition is that we reject Christ, and that is its external aspect. People can be extremely religious, and affirm a number of truths about God, but God insists that he has installed Christ as Lord and judge, and our reaction to him determines our eternal destiny (Ps. 2; Acts 2:36–37; 17:31–32).

We can see the external results of sin if we consider our second triangle, with Christ as prophet, priest and king.

The rejection of Christ as prophet

Jesus claims to be the ultimate truth about God and how he is to be known. The Son was called a teacher, and he exercised a teaching ministry both before and after his death and resurrection. He has now been established as the ultimate validator of truth, as universal judge.

This correlates to sins of the head: to reject God's truth is to reject Christ as prophet. Since there is no other way of cohering truth but through Christ, such rejection is a preference for irrationality, meaningless lies that prevent us from knowing him.

Identifying this aspect of sin and showing its conclusions means we will need to show the incoherence of any claim to truth without Christ. Our secular friends will say that they can be good without God, and we will have to argue that they cannot be consistently good, or explain, without reference to God, why being good matters. Since in their self-justification they will want to show that they are wise, we will have to show that in their sin, 'Although they claimed to be wise, they became fools' (Rom. 1:22).

In rejecting Christ as prophet, sin is foolishness.

The rejection of Christ as priest

Since Jesus claims to be the one who sacrifices himself for sin for us, rejecting his priestly ministry is trying to find another way into God's presence, and be our own priests so we can worship what we want to. It correlates to the sins of the heart, whereby we do not love God but love everything he has made, and are so fallen that we even prefer to love it in its distorted fallen forms rather than God himself.

Identifying this sin will mean that we show what it means to worship something other than someone who wants to bless. If I worship something other than me, it will dominate me and I will be its captive; if I worship myself, I will crush you as a rival. Worshipping anything other than God will result in despair or dominance, suicide or murder.

We can also see that rejecting Christ in one of his offices will spread to others: 'They exchanged the truth about God for a lie, and worshipped and served created things rather than the Creator – who is for ever praised. Amen' (Rom. 1:25; see Col. 3:5; Eph. 5:5; 1 John 5:21).

In rejecting Christ as priest, sin is idolatry.

The rejection of Christ as king

Christ's third office covers his right to rule, and his laws and standards. As king over his subject people, he determines every aspect of our lives, and because he is our loving king that means he does it for our benefit. He is a good king, and since he is almighty and eternal, he is the only one we will ever have.

Any other laws we prefer to his will work to our harm, but even so they come under his rule. Notice how in Romans 1 the consequences of our foolishness and idolatry do not take us out of his rule:

> For although they knew God, they neither glorified him as God nor gave thanks to him, but their thinking became futile and their foolish hearts were darkened. Although they claimed to be wise, they became fools and exchanged the glory of the immortal God for images made to look like a mortal human being and birds and animals and reptiles.
>
> *Therefore God gave them over* in the sinful desires of their hearts to sexual impurity for the degrading of their bodies with one another. They exchanged the truth about God for a lie, and worshipped and served created things rather than the Creator – who is for ever praised. Amen.

Because of this, *God gave them over to shameful lusts* . . .

Furthermore, just as they did not think it worth while to retain the knowledge of God, so *God gave them over* to a depraved mind, so that they do what ought not to be done. (Rom. 1:21–26, 28)

These correlate to the sins of the hand, and issues of obedience and disobedience. This is the area we most naturally gravitate to when we talk about sin, and it is right that we use this language because it too is properly biblical.

In rejecting Christ as king, sin is rebellion. Rejecting Christ in any one of his offices is to reject him completely, because they relate to each other. And rejecting Christ means we face his final judgment, and our eternal death.

Repentance

Now we can see why repentance can never be a matter of trying harder to do better. The root idea behind repentance is of changing one's mind, but it is too light to say I used to think lying was a useful idea, but now I've realized I was wrong. That is simply remorse, in that I changed one idol (how to advance my career by careful lying) to another (how to advance my career by being straight with my boss after he caught me out).

No, what we need to change our minds about is Christ, and therefore about me. Our sin is foolish disbelief of what God's prophet has said, blasphemous idolatry against the priest he has provided, and open rebellion against the king he has installed. Repentance is turning from ignorance to acknowledge the truth, from idols to serve the true and living God, from rebellion to obedience.

Put it like that, and no longer do we see him as the God of the gaps, making up by his death for the good we failed to do, added on to the good we have managed. There is no neutral ground here. We are utterly ruined before this holy God. We come before him with nothing, holding on simply to his promise of mercy.

Why do the nations conspire
    and the peoples plot in vain?
The kings of the earth rise up
    and the rulers band together
    against the LORD and against his anointed, saying,
'Let us break their chains,
    and throw off their shackles.'

The One enthroned in heaven laughs;
 the LORD scoffs at them.
Then he rebukes them in his anger
 and terrifies them in his wrath, saying,
'I have installed my king
 on Zion, my holy mountain.'

I will proclaim the LORD's decree:

He said to me, 'You are my son;
 today I have become your father.
Ask me,
 and I will make the nations your inheritance,
 the ends of the earth your possession.
You will break them with a rod of iron;
 you will dash them to pieces like pottery.'

Therefore, you kings, be wise;
 be warned, you rulers of the earth.
Serve the LORD with fear
 and celebrate his rule with trembling.
Kiss the son, or he will be angry
 and your way will lead to your destruction,
for his wrath can flare up in a moment.
 Blessed are all who take refuge in him.
(Ps. 2:1–3)

When we encourage people to come to Christ in this way, we have managed to avoid repentance being self-improvement, or a trivial raising of a hand or ticking of a box. Repentance will mean acknowledging that Christ has the right to reorder our lives, which is how repentance and deeds are connected.

Some parts of that will be marked by what we stop doing. Peter preached, 'When God raised up his servant, he sent him first to you to bless you by turning each of you from your wicked ways' (Acts 3:26). We have seen that we need to be painfully specific in describing those ways. Others will be marked by what we start: Paul explained his ministry to King Agrippa in these terms: 'First to those in Damascus, then to those in Jerusalem and in all Judea, and then to the Gentiles, I preached that they should repent and turn to God and demonstrate their repentance by their deeds' (Acts 26:20). Here again we must be unmissably clear. In both cases repentance is marked by a humble life change that acknowledges the authority of the risen Christ over our lives.

Peter said that this turning from our wicked ways was God's way of blessing us. Repentance is not a way of pleading favour from a reluctant God, as if we could make bad news into good news. It is a mark of his rich kindness that he loves us so much to turn our hearts. That is good news. That is why when Levi repented, he proved his repentance by throwing a party:

> After this, Jesus went out and saw a tax collector by the name of Levi sitting at his tax booth. 'Follow me,' Jesus said to him, and Levi got up, left everything and followed him.
>
> Then Levi held a great banquet for Jesus at his house, and a large crowd of tax collectors and others were eating with them. But the Pharisees and the teachers of the law who belonged to their sect complained to his disciples, 'Why do you eat and drink with tax collectors and sinners?'
>
> Jesus answered them, 'It is not the healthy who need a doctor, but those who are ill. I have not come to call the righteous, but sinners to repentance.' (Luke 5:27–32)

Just ask

What do I want people to understand? That Christ was crucified for them and he is now their risen king for eternity. Why do I want them to understand it? Because coming into his kingdom will transform everything for ever, and rebelling against him will be an eternally irrevocable decision.

What do I want people to feel? Fear and awe before this high and holy priest, and loved, and forgiven, and eternally sacrificed for. Why do I want them to feel it? Because the guilt and shame we rightly feel before him can be stripped away and replaced with the robe of his guiltless perfection.

What do I want them to do? Repent, and prove their repentance by their deeds of obedience to their new and eternal king. Why do I want them to do it? Because the way he has designed for us to live under his rule is the way things were always meant to be.

Have you done all that? Then invite people to repent.

Questions for reflection and discussion

- How is sin an expression of rejecting Christ as prophet, priest or king?
- Can you give a concrete example of each? Can you think of a kind of sin that does not fit that pattern?
- How would you explain 'repentance'?

20. APPLYING THE BIBLE TO ONE ANOTHER

> I charge you before the Lord to have this letter read to all the brothers and sisters.
>
> (1 Thess. 5:27)

Until this point, what we have basically been working with is a model that takes the Bible, expounds it and delivers it into the life of the individual, applying it at home, at work, at church, in society, and so on. In a way, as someone who is being preached to, it is a bit like an older Christian taking the trouble to have a quiet time with me to guide me through the passage, to show me things I could not have seen or understood on my own, and help me put it into practice.

This model does exactly what most preaching textbooks say. Bryan Chappell, in his excellent *Christ-Centered Preaching* puts it like this:

> Expository messages require preachers to ensure that the applications they make will answer four key questions: What does God now require of me? Where does he require it of me? Why must I do what he requires? and How can I do what God requires?[1]

Terry Carter, Scott Duvall and Daniel Hays encourage us to 'exegete the audience' as well as exegete the text. This involves knowing the background, maturity, culture, and so on, of the people we speak to, and they conclude their chapter on the subject with a question:

---

1. Bryan Chappell, *Christ-Centered Preaching* (Grand Rapids: Baker, 1994), p. 204.

Take one of your sermons and ask the following questions about it. How might this message, the illustrations and applications sound to: a young mother, fourth-grade girl, freshman soccer player, father who recently lost his job, recent widow, person struggling with an addiction, spiritual seeker, retired couple, and mature believer?[2]

I hope by now you realize I have a great deal of sympathy with that approach. It takes a preacher out of the study and into the lives of people who are in a kaleidoscope of contexts. One minister I know kept a list on his desk of the people he had met that week, and ran through it for his sermon, making sure as far as he could that there was something for each one of them.

But I am troubled by two repeated words in Bryan Chappell's list: 'What does God now require of *me*? Where does he require it of *me*? Why must *I* do what he requires?' and How can *I* do what God requires?' And I am troubled by a question that, at the end of 'exegeting the audience', ends with a series of individuals.

Because a church is more than an audience of individuals: it is a body of believers, assembled by God to hear from and respond to him. A significant amount of the New Testament was written to churches, not just to address individual matters, but corporate ones too: their relationships, gullibility, hard-heartedness, soft-headedness. Which means they need to attend to God's Word together. If one of our tasks is to understand the individuals who turn up to church and their lives outside the meeting, another is to understand their relations as a church, and their lives within the meeting.

Speaking to the church

If it is true that much of the New Testament was written to churches, then one part of application will be to apply God's Word to the whole church. That is where the language of 'me' or 'audience' is so distracting. It takes us away from thinking of corporate application.

The individual and the corporate both need to exist, and sometimes it is the case that the individual is addressed in a corporate context. The refrain in each of the seven letters at the beginning of Revelation stresses both: 'Whoever has ears, let them hear what the Spirit says to the churches' (Rev. 2:7, 11, 17, 29; 3:6,

---

2. Terry G. Carter, J. Scott Duvall and J. Daniel Hays, *Preaching God's Word: A Hands-on Approach to Preparing, Developing, and Delivering the Sermon* (Grand Rapids: Zondervan, 2005), p. 98.

13, 32). In fact it goes further, because this says that I as an individual can also hear what God said to all seven churches.

So part of the privilege of preaching is that we not only address matters of individuals in the congregation, but also matters *between* individuals in the congregation, and matters concerning the congregation as a whole.

Because I travel a fair amount, I often find myself preaching in churches I do not know. In one sense that does not matter because God's Word is his Word, and it will have its relevance whoever speaks it. But I often approach such sermons with a sense of unease: I don't know if this is a church where a senior member has just been diagnosed with a critical illness, or if there is infighting among the elders, or if there is a habit of meanness or criticism. All three zones are the preacher's territory, but I cannot bring God's Word to bear if I do not know what is going on.

Preaching to ourselves

Our first duty is to preach to ourselves, otherwise we are frauds. We also sit under God's Word, and are members of the church before we are leaders in it. We must be seen to sit under our own preaching.

If we do not, then we fall into the trap Jesus described so vividly: 'You experts in the law, woe to you, because you load people down with burdens they can hardly carry, and you yourselves will not lift one finger to help them' (Luke 11:46). It is a terrible wrong to weight people down with guilt and activity, while we allow ourselves not to serve on the coffee rota because we are too important or busy.

Hear instead what the Bible says we do: Proverbs 23:12 says:

Apply your heart to instruction
　　and your ears to words of knowledge.

Although I have talked freely of application, the Bible rarely uses the term, but when it does, it uses it of the idea of self-application: press the Bible into your own soul.

Only then can we allow God's Word to pass through us to others. We can see that modelled in the ministry of Isaiah, who nine times preaches a message containing 'Woe' to other people in the first five chapters (Isa. 1:4; 3:9, 11; 5:8, 11, 18, 20–22), and fifteen times in the remainder of his book (Isa. 10:1, 5; 17:12 [twice]; 18:1; 24:16; 28:1; 29:1, 15; 30:1; 31:1; 33:1 [twice]; 45:9–10), but whose heart cry in meeting the holy God is 'Woe to me . . . I am ruined!' (Isa. 6:5).

Older preachers knew this. Here is Calvin:

Seeing that the assembled flock ought to hear the word of God by the mouth of a man, he that speaks must certainly testify that it is all in good faith, and that he has such a reverence for the teaching he proclaims that he means to be the first to be obedient to it . . . and that he wishes to declare that he is not only imposing a law on others but that the subjection is in common and that it is for him to make a start.[3]

That is what Paul meant by being 'an example' (1 Tim. 4:12).

The seventeenth-century English theologian John Owen said, 'A man preacheth that sermon only well unto others, that preacheth itself in his own soul. If the word does not dwell with power in us, it will not pass with power from us.'[4]

This habit of self-examination and appropriation has several consequences for us as preachers, but let me highlight four I have found.

First, if I am honest with myself in private it makes applying the Bible to others a whole deal easier. I extend to others the courtesy that they believe in Jesus as I do, and struggle with sin as I do. It is a great leveller. I will no longer look down on people, and they will not think I do. If I honestly, in my study, map out how the Bible presses itself on me, both to wound and to heal, I will be able to help those who need the Bible pressed on them in the same way. Proverbs 20:5 says:

> The purposes of a person's heart are *deep waters*,
>   but one who has insight draws them out.

My tentative experience is, the more we allow God's Word to plunge to the depths of our hearts, the more we will enable it to plunge deep into others', and we will draw out their inner purposes.

There is a time to shut the commentaries and do business with God.

Secondly, it helps me to pray:

> But who can discern their own errors?
>   Forgive my hidden faults.
> Keep your servant also from wilful sins;
>   may they not rule over me.
> Then I will be blameless,
>   innocent of great transgression.
> (Ps. 19:12–13)

---

3. Quoted in T. H. L. Parker, *Calvin's Preaching* (Edinburgh: T&T Clark, 1992), p. 116.

4. Quoted in E. Alexander, *What Is Biblical Preaching?* (Phillipsburg: P&R, 2008), p. 28.

One of my practices as a pastor was to turn verses like that into my prayer for our church, 'Lord, please don't let my sin get in the way of your blessing your people.'

Thirdly, it stops me from becoming a preacher whose primary note is denunciation. There is a time to denounce, but it should not be our default setting. Identifying the sins of other churches and the faults of other people in the church can easily become an excuse for me to start to make myself look good in my own eyes and those of my fans; and you will gather a fan base if you denounce.

And fourthly, it helps me in my relationships. I might take the instruction list from Titus 2:1–8, and ask myself, 'Who is younger and the same sex as me? Older and the same sex as me? Younger and the opposite sex to me? Older and the opposite sex to me? Am I teaching and relating to all four fittingly?'

Addressing them as individuals

Our second duty is that we need to address people as individuals, noticing their different contexts; that is what Carter, Duvall and Hays call 'exegeting' the congregation.

At its simplest, I take a verse like 1 Thessalonians. 5:14: 'And we urge you . . . warn those who are idle and disruptive, encourage the disheartened, help the weak, be patient with everyone.' There is a particular background to that verse in the letter, of course, but there is a general truthfulness in it that makes it useful for this exercise. And I sketch a little grid of nine boxes.

People:	Who are the *idle* and *disruptive* in our church?	Who are the *disheartened* in our church?	Who are the *weak* in our church?
Messages:	How from this passage will I warn them?	How from this passage will I encourage them?	How from this passage will I help them?
Ways to conduct myself:	How can I do that with patience?	How can I do that with patience?	How can I do that with patience?

I aim to have names in those top three, and think hard about how I apply to each of them.

And I underline the patience point because the Bible does so. Paul tells Timothy to teach, rebuke and encourage 'with great patience and careful instruction' (2 Tim. 4:2; see too 1 Thess. 2:7–12; Titus 1:10–13; 2:15). Church people are saints, sinners and sufferers – we struggle. And sometimes we are stupid as well. I know that because I am. So I must cut them the slack I cut myself.

On other occasions I use different life categories the Bible explicitly addresses:

- Male/female
- Older/younger
- Child/parent – at what age? Childless?
- Married/single/divorced/widowed – at what age?
- Wealthy/poor?
- Sick/healthy?
- Powerful/powerless
- Independent/indebted
- Tenant/property owner/ homeless?
- Resident/alien (guest/refugee?)
- Employer/employee (Unemployed? Retired? Student? Vocational/ 'just a job'?)
- Christian/non-Christian (at what stage? At what age converted?)

Sometimes we need a yet bigger picture. J. I. Packer suggests that one Puritan practice was to think in terms of the different forms of biblical address:[5]

- Instruction in doctrine
- Refutation of false doctrine
- Encouragement to obedience
- Challenge and call to repentance
- Comfort
- Self-examination

Alternatively, they considered the different spiritual states of the people in front of us, of which they identified seven: ignorant and unteachable, ignorant and teachable, informed but proud, humbled and desperate, believers going on with God, believers in error, discouraged believers.

---

5. J. I. Packer, *Among God's Giants* (Eastbourne: Kingsway, 1991), pp. 377–378; the horizontal axis comes from *The Westminster Directory for Publick Worship*, and the vertical axis is developed by Packer from *The Art of Prophesying*, by Richard Perkins.

If we combine them in a grid we end up with the representation below.

	Instruction in doctrine	Refutation of false doctrine	Encourage-ment to obedience	Challenge and call to repentance	Comfort	Self-examination
Ignorant and unteachable						
Ignorant and teachable						
Informed but proud						
Humbled and desperate						
Believers going on with God						
Believers in error						
Discouraged believers						

I make that forty-two kinds of sermon! Now not every box can be filled. I doubt if we would ever want to comfort the ignorant and unteachable. But even if we blocked out one or two, it is still a useful exercise to see how many boxes we could tick in our next sermon series. It would help to prevent us being stuck in a rut.

And it does not matter that not every box can be ticked, because not every verse of the Bible applies to me. I will never, as long as I live, be a widow. So I have to develop the category of not being so much a hearer of God's Word as an *over*hearer. I overhear what God says to widows and discover how he treats them, and therefore how I should. A non-Christian overhears a sermon on Christian parenting and discovers how grace and forgiveness mirror God's patience for his stubborn children. Once she learns that even God's perfect parenting has to deal with rebellious kids like us on a daily basis, she will learn why we can be kind to each other as well. A Christian overhears an evangelistic talk and learns how to answer the questions of her colleague in the staff room.

Even within that massive range there is the commonality of being redeemed sinners, which means there is nothing I cannot learn from or grow into. As Haddon Robinson puts it, 'The surprising thing is that the more directed and personal a message, the more universal it becomes.'[6]

Earlier we saw the survey that Willow Creek Community Church conducted across 80,000 people in 376 churches.[7] The authors' conclusion is that what people most want and need is a pastor who

- provides sound doctrine rooted in biblical accuracy
- challenges people to grow and take next steps
- models and reinforces how to grow spiritually.[8]

And they conclude:

> As church leaders, we need to give people a place to belong and a pathway that guides them on their spiritual journey towards intimacy with Christ. We catalyze their spiritual growth by helping them understand the Bible in greater depth, by challenging them to apply the Scriptures with specific next steps and modelling how we are taking those steps ourselves.[9]

Those are dauntingly high standards, which few churches reach. But we need to aim even higher.

Addressing them as related individuals

The people hearing a sermon are not just related to me as hearers to a speaker; they are related to each other as fellow hearers who are addressed by God's Word in their relationships with each other. That is critical to stress to ourselves as preachers, because we see people as individuals, soaking up our words and then taking them away.

---

6. Haddon Robinson, 'Preaching to Everyone in Particular', in Haddon Robinson and Craig Brian Larson, *The Art and Craft of Biblical Preaching* (Grand Rapids: Zondervan, 2005), p. 116.
7. G. L. Hawkins and C. Parkinson, *Focus* (Barrington: Willow Creek Resources, 2009), p. 53.
8. Ibid., p. 84, bullet points in the original.
9. Ibid., p. 87.

But we are not a bunch of isolated people, coming together for a weekly event we all happen to enjoy together. Our relationships as Christians are not just to be better than the world's on some sliding scale, but must be markedly different because of the gospel. With very occasional exceptions the normal biblical pattern is for Christians to be part of (not go to) a church, and to demonstrate to the watching worlds, both natural and supernatural, that Christ's victory has been won. That is demonstrated by our relationships (1 Cor. 3:16–17; 2 Cor. 6:16; Eph. 2:14–22; 2:21–2). So whether someone has something against me or I have something against them, I take the initiative and go to sort it out (Matt. 5:23–24; 18:15).

The word *allēlous* appears fifty-four times in the New Testament, as the most frequent word for 'one another'. Translating it by the same English term consistently is close to impossible, and there are other similar concepts, but the texts below are where that word appears.

The Gospels
'be at peace with each other' (Mark 9:50)
'wash one another's feet' (John 13:14)
'love one another' (John 13:34–35; 15:12, 17)

Paul's letters
Romans, 1 Corinthians, 2 Corinthians
'Be devoted to one another in love' (Rom. 12:10)
'Honour one another above yourselves' (Rom. 12:10)
'Live in harmony with one another' (Rom. 12:16)
'love one another' (Rom. 13:8)
'let us stop passing judgment on one another' (Rom. 14:13)
'Accept one another, then, just as Christ accepted you' (Rom. 15:7)
'Greet one another with a holy kiss' (Rom. 16:16; 1 Cor. 16:20; 2 Cor. 13:12)
'I appeal to you, brothers and sisters, in the name of our Lord Jesus Christ, that all of you agree with one another in what you say and that there be no divisions among you, but that you be perfectly united in mind and thought' (1 Cor. 1:10)
'when you come together to eat, wait for one another' (1 Cor. 11:33 ESV)
'have equal concern for each other' (1 Cor. 12:25)

Galatians, Ephesians
'serve one another humbly in love' (Gal. 5:13).
'If you bite and devour each other . . . you will be destroyed by each other' (Gal. 5:15)

'Let us not become conceited, provoking and envying each other'
(Gal. 5:26)
'Carry each other's burdens' (Gal. 6:2)
'be patient, bearing with one another in love' (Eph. 4:2)
'Be kind and compassionate to one another' (Eph. 4:32)
'forgiving each other' (Eph. 4:32)
'speaking to one another with psalms, hymns, and songs from the
Spirit' (Eph. 5:19)
'Submit to one another out of reverence for Christ' (Eph. 5:21)

Colossians
'Do not lie to each other' (Col. 3:9)
'Bear with each other' (Col. 3:13)
'forgive one another if any of you has a grievance' (Col. 3:13)
'teach . . . [one another]' (Col. 3:16)
'admonish one another' (Col. 3:16)

1 Thessalonians
'you yourselves have been taught by God to love each other'
(1 Thess. 4:9)
'encourage one another' (1 Thess. 4:18; 5:11)
'build each other up' (1 Thess. 5:11)
'Live in peace with each other' (1 Thess. 5:13)
'seek to do good to one another' (1 Thess. 5:15 ESV)

Hebrews
'encourage one another daily' (Heb. 3:13)
'spur one another on towards love and good deeds' (Heb. 10:24)
'Keep on loving one another' (Heb. 13:1)

James, 1 Peter, 1 John, 2 John
'do not slander one another' (Jas 4:11)
'Don't grumble against one another' (Jas 5:9)
'confess your sins to each other' (Jas 5:16)
'pray for each other' (Jas 5:16)
'love one another deeply, from the heart' (1 Peter 1:22; 4:8)
'love one another' (1 Peter 3:8)
'Offer hospitality to one another without grumbling' (1 Peter 4:9)
'clothe yourselves with humility towards one another' (1 Peter 5:5)
'Greet one another with a kiss of love' (1 Peter 5:14)

'But if we walk in the light, as he is in the light, we have fellowship with one
another, and the blood of Jesus, his Son, purifies us from all sin' (1 John 1:7)
'love one another' (1 John 3:11, 23; 4:7, 11; 2 John 5)

It is obvious, then, that Christianity is a corporate experience, where relating to
each other is a proper concern. If we move from a simple word study to looking
at the concept, this becomes even clearer. For example, the word for 'one
another' is absent from Paul's letter to the Philippians, yet the issue of relationships is close to its centre:

> in humility value others above yourselves. (Phil. 2:3)

> Do nothing out of selfish ambition or vain conceit. Rather, in humility value others
> above yourselves, not looking to your own interests but each of you to the interests
> of the others. (Phil. 2:2–4)

> to be of the same mind in the Lord. (Phil. 4:2)

Lists like that often feature in books for church members, encouraging their
healthy relationships, and rightly so. As preachers we should also take this to
heart, but closer to our issue is that the relationships between the Christians in
our churches are a proper concern for our preaching.

Addressing them as a body

And finally, we address them as a body, a unit, called together and shaped by
God's Word, our lives and relationships being increasingly interlocked in his
plan. Paul describes the foundation of God's Word and then the building of
God's temple on that foundation in these terms:

> Consequently, you are no longer foreigners and strangers, but fellow citizens with
> God's people and also members of his household, built on the foundation of the
> apostles and prophets, with Christ Jesus himself as the chief cornerstone. In him
> the whole building is joined together and rises to become a holy temple in the Lord.
> And in him you too are being built together to become a dwelling in which God lives
> by his Spirit. (Eph. 2:19–22)

The interplay between our relationships, the place of God's Word and the
dwelling place of his Spirit must not be missed. We do not come to church to

hear sermons. The sermons are the connecting rods between the foundation of God's Word and the construction of his temple.

The concept of 'building' is related to the English word 'edify' (from the Latin word *aedificare*, 'to build'). Mostly that passes us by, and when we think of an edifying sermon we think of one that was informative, or heart-warming – or possibly incomprehensible. But biblically edification is a function of God's Word, and we engage in it together (Acts 20:32; Rom. 14:19; 1 Cor. 14:4–5, 17, 26; Eph. 4:11–16; 1 Thess. 5:11). It does not just mean better informed, but that we are better informed about why and how we need to love and serve in the body of Christ. It is a relational concept, based on the gospel.

Here again is Calvin:

> Do we want, then . . . to profit in the school of our God, so that his teaching may be useful to us and we may be edified by it? Let us always have this foundation – it is that we try to devote ourselves to the obedience of our God, that he may be exalted in the midst of us, that he may have the reverence he deserves. When that happens we shall be building well.[10]

Our task, then, is not merely to build up individuals, but to build them together.

Questions for reflection and discussion

- Consider the diagram from 1 Thessalonians 5 in the light of a Bible passage you are reading, and identify people, messages and ways to conduct yourself.
- If you are a preacher, which of these boxes do you normally preach about, and which do you avoid? Are there any that we would never address at all? How could sermons better address relationships within the church as a body?

---

10. Quoted in Parker, *Calvin's Preaching*, p. 51.

21. APPLYING THE BIBLE TO THE CHURCH

For Ezra had devoted himself to the study and observance of the Law of the
LORD, and to teaching its decrees and laws in Israel.

(Ezra 7:10)

There is one final aspect of application to consider, and it takes us in an
unexpected direction. Until now we have considered applying the Bible to
individuals, whatever their spiritual state, and to their relationships as a body.
The final element is how the Bible teaches us to apply the Bible to the church
as a whole unit, and to its overall direction. In other words, we need to consider
the relationship between applying the Bible and leading the church.

In the air

'Leadership' is one of the cultural buzzwords of our day. Whether in politics,
businesses, education, charities or the public sector, its presence, or absence, is
said to have made the decisive difference between failure, success and being
outstanding. And although the word may be new, the subject has been fascinating
people for thousands of years. The classic ancient Greek account of leadership
is Xenophon's thrilling account of a military expedition through hostile territory
in Persia, and it is still in print.[1] Xenophon's Chinese contemporary Sun Tzu

---

1. Xenophon's *Anabasis* is accessible in Rex Warner's translation for Penguin Classics,
   The Persian Expedition (London: Penguin, 1949; repr. 1972).

produced a book on military tactics, *The Art of War*, which now finds itself rebranded as a handbook for business leaders, *The Art of War for Executives*.[2]

Christian leadership

Step into almost any Christian bookshop and you will also find a section marked 'Leadership', and although it is a relatively new phenomenon it is a flourishing one. John C. Maxwell notes that his personal files contain over fifty different definitions of leadership, and highlights his personal conviction that 'Leadership is influence. That's it. Nothing more; nothing less.'[3] According to Bill Hybels, the senior pastor of Willow Creek Community Church, 'Leadership in church is one of the biggest challenges that the Church is facing, because without strong leadership, the church rarely lives out its redemptive potential.'[4] The Christian journal *Leadership* has been published every quarter since 1980.

After a while, though, those two worlds, of secular and Christian leadership, seem to merge. The business gurus Jim Kouzes and Barry Posner who wrote a bestseller called *The Leadership Challenge*,[5] subsequently edited *Christian Reflections on the Leadership Challenge*,[6] to which John C. Maxwell contributed a chapter and a forward. Ken Blanchard, who wrote the bestselling *One-Minute Manager* series, has become a Christian and written *Leadership by the Book* with Bill Hybels and Phil Hodges.[7] Hybels hosts a Global Leadership Summit at Willow Creek every summer, at which Christians such as Maxwell and Blanchard share the stage with leading non-Christian writers, thinkers and practitioners.

Some of that merging is natural, because we need to outline how a Christian might act in a secular company. And it is surely right to invite high-profile leaders

2. Sun Tzu, *The Art of War*, tr. Roger T. Ames (New York: Ballantine, 1993); Donald G. Krause, *Sun Tzu: The Art of War for Executives* (London: Nicholas Brealey, 1996).

3. John C. Maxwell, *Developing the Leader Within You* (Nashville: Thomas Nelson, 1993), p. 1. Warren Bennis and Burt Nanus note over 850 definitions in *Leaders: Strategies for Taking Charge* (New York: HarperCollins, 1997), p. 4.

4. At Willow Creek's *Global Leadership Summit*, 2005.

5. James M. Kouzes and Barry Z. Posner, *The Leadership Challenge* (San Francisco: Jossey Bass, 1995), pp. 8–9.

6. James M. Kouzes and Barry Z. Posner, *Christian Reflections on the Leadership Challenge* (San Francisco: Jossey Bass, 2004).

7. Ken Blanchard, Bill Hybels and Phil Hodges, *Leadership by the Book: Tools to Transform Your Workplace* (London: HarperCollins, 1999).

who are Christians to explain how the gospel shapes their work, and how it gives them those high ultimate values that secular leadership craves but cannot grasp. But some of the merger is unnerving. John Stott is right to note that '"Leadership" is a word shared by Christians and non-Christians alike, but that does not mean that their concept of it is the same. On the contrary, Jesus introduced into the world a new style of servant-leadership.'[8]

But is embedding even the best of secular practices in the running of a church, an assault on the rights of the Lord Jesus to define how he wants the church to be run, by Scripture? That too is not a new concern. It has been said that the oldest book explaining to a Christian leader how to apply the best of both secular and Christian thinking to his task is *The Prince* by Niccolò Machiavelli, who taught the fifteenth-century Florentine rulers that Christianity was of no use in the public sphere, whatever good it might do in private, and different rules for leaders need to be sought. The family for whom the book was written, the Medici, later produced popes.[9]

So at this point we need to ask whether there is such a thing as 'the gift of leadership', and if so how it is to be recognized, developed and exercised in a biblical way. In particular, for our purposes, we need to ask how it relates to the task of applying the Bible.

Is there a 'gift of leadership'? Romans 12:1–8

On the face of it there should not be much disagreement here: Paul lists a number of gifts in Romans 12, and in the context of testing of gifts and personal humility (v. 3), and his usual argument about the critical importance of the gifts and place of every member of the body (v. 4) says that we must use those gifts to serve others, including 'if it is to lead, do it diligently' (v. 8). Paul does not say over what this person leads, which has led some to suggest that this person oversees the management of the generous donations of the previous person in the list, the one with the gift of generosity. But Paul does not use the word (*proïstamenon*) elsewhere with that financial meaning, and twice explicitly uses the word of the church leadership (1 Thess. 5:12; 1 Tim. 5:17).

So although Paul does not yet outline what leaders are to do, they are to do it 'diligently', with passion and commitment (Rom. 12:8; 2 Cor. 7:11–12;

---

8. John R. W. Stott, *Calling Christian Leaders* (Leicester: Inter-Varsity Press, 2002), p. 9.

9. Niccolò Machiavelli, *The Prince*, tr. George Bull (London: Penguin, 1961; rev. ed. 2003).

8:7–8, 16). This is a task that will bring the best out of people, and constantly call them to take higher steps of faith in calling others to follow God's will.

Paul does not say how we would identify someone with that gift, but common sense would suggest that this is the person who makes things happen, and who can be trusted with demanding corporate tasks. But there is one more passage we need to explore before that will become clear.

Do pastors have the 'gift of leadership'? 1 Timothy 3:1–7[10]

There is a general requirement for pastors to be mature Christians, and a specific requirement for them to be 'able to teach'. Deep in the list of qualifications from 1 Timothy 3, though, is a second intriguing qualification: 'He must manage his own family well and see that his children obey him, and he must do so in a manner worthy of full respect. (If anyone does not know how to manage his own family, how can he take care of God's church?)' (1 Tim. 3:4–5). This is similar to what we saw in Titus, in chapter 9 above, and it needs unpacking.

The church in Ephesus, where Timothy was based, was being disrupted by the presence of false teaching. The precise contours are not clear, although it was some aspect of the way we are to read Old Testament law (1 Tim. 1:6–7), but the consequence was evident in the lives of those who obeyed it. There was a curious and evil marriage between a world-denying asceticism (4:1–4) and a craving after material excess (6:9–10), both of which depended on a denial of the gospel. It was rooted in a love of endless debate that Timothy is to avoid (6:20–21). But as Paul laid out his conversion story in chapter 1, as an example of the correct use of the law in convicting sin, he described the law as being for

> lawbreakers and rebels, the ungodly and sinful, the unholy and irreligious, for those who kill their fathers or mothers, for murderers, for the sexually immoral, for those practising homosexuality, for slave traders and liars and perjurers – and for whatever else is contrary to the sound doctrine. (1:9–10)

So this was a false teaching that taught disrespect for Timothy, the teacher, and the breaking of the moral code of the Old Testament. This, then, became

---

10. Most commentators see 'pastor', 'elder' and 'overseer' as synonyms, with perhaps some variation in what the title describes: role (shepherd), maturity and task (oversight). See Acts 20, where the same group are described as elders (v. 17), overseers and shepherds/pastors (v. 28).

precisely the issue in the household of the future pastor under consideration: Are the children showing the kind of attitude and behaviour that show they have come under the influence of the false teachers? And if so, what has this potential pastor done about it? Because if someone cannot exercise discipline over this matter at home, there is no reason to expect them to be strong enough to exercise it in the church. The issue in the family is the same issue as the one in the church: if the children have not been disciplined, neither will the church be.

The connection of a future elder with leadership is critical here because twice here Paul uses the word from Romans 12:8: 'He must manage [*proïstamenon*] his own family well and see that his children obey him, and he must do so in a manner worthy of full respect. (If anyone does not know how to manage [*prostēnai*] his own family, how can he take care of God's church?)' (1 Tim. 3:4–5). Paul expects future pastors to display the leadership gift at home, to demonstrate their suitability for church leadership, where exactly the same gifts are required.

The 'double gifting' of the pastor

So here is the conclusion if we put Romans 12 alongside 1 Timothy 3. In Romans 12 Paul describes a series of gifts, including the gifts of those who teach and those who lead. It is not a requirement that anyone has either of those gifts, nor that if they have one they must have the other. There are people who are superb at organizing a series of evangelistic talks, but who cannot give those talks, and there are those who can be persuasive evangelists, but who cannot organize the rest of the team to make the events occur. Teaching and leadership are – like all gifts – separate, and in the body of Christ we need both.

But in 1 Timothy 3 Paul takes those two gifts and says that we need to find them in the same person, if that person is to be a pastor. Why? Because for the pastor they are intimately connected: from God's Word the pastor can teach what truth is, show errors and call for repentance. That is the teaching gift. And when the pastor considers with the other leaders what to do about the erring members, that is the leadership gift. The teaching gift is expressed in the leadership gift, when the Bible is applied to the church.

This is supported elsewhere. So Hebrews 13:7 says, 'Remember your leaders [a different Greek word: *hēgoumenos*], who spoke the word of God to you'; and a few verses later, 'Have confidence in your leaders [*hēgoumenos* again] and submit to their authority, because they keep watch over you as those who must give an account' (v. 17). The pattern is the same, even where the language has changed: leading and teaching are the double tasks of the same people.

So if the passage to be preached on is Ephesians 5:18, 'Do not get drunk on wine, which leads to debauchery. Instead, be filled with the Spirit', both gifts will be needed. In the morning there is a sermon to be preached and changed lives to be called for; in the afternoon there is a private conversation with an individual who is struggling in the area of alcohol abuse; and in the evening there is an elders' meeting where there will be discussion about setting up a support group for Christians who struggle with this issue, and who will run it, how it will be funded, how it will feed into existing patterns of growing disciples.

Leadership, then, is not to be exercised out of the sphere of the teaching gift, because leadership is an indispensable partner for the pastor/teacher, but nor is it to be collapsed into teaching, as if all pastors have to do is preach sermons. We can align these two gifts, and come up with a definition like this: *biblical leadership is the application of God's Word to the structures, habits and plans of the church, so that there is corporate, as well as individual, obedience.* That is why the two tasks are intimately connected.

Because God's Word is the driving force of this idea of leadership, a faithful Bible teacher will never let us rest with our current habits of idleness and sin; the theme of the application is, 'Together we can obey God's Word, and this is how we are going to do it.'

Questions for reflection and discussion

- How would you define 'the gift of teaching'?
- How would you define 'the gift of leadership'?
- Chris Green defines leadership like this: *biblical leadership is the application of God's Word to the structures, habits and plans of the church, so that there is corporate, as well as individual, obedience.* Do you agree?

CONCLUSION: TEACHING THEM TO OBEY

Therefore go and make disciples of all nations, baptising them in the name of
the Father and of the Son and of the Holy Spirit, and teaching them to obey
everything I have commanded you.

(Matt. 28:19–20)

Death by popcorn

So, preachers, let's go to it. Dig deep in your Bibles for the treasures of Christ,
and show them to us so that love for him drives out love of sin. Entrance us
with his wisdom, grace and power; measure for us the breadth, length, depth
and height of his love; and defy us not to pay attention to him and his ways.
Help us see the richness of God's plan for his church.

But please, show us why it matters.

Haddon Robinson skewers featherweight preaching when he says:

It's like what the Roman Catholic priest said about listening to confessions from nuns
– it feels like being stoned to death by popcorn. Or, as Peter Marshall said, the church
is like an army of deep-sea divers marching triumphantly to pull the plugs out of
bathtubs. There are heavy applications needed to maintain the dignity of the gospel
... Application-driven sermons are trivial. But concept-driven sermons do business
in deep waters.[1]

---

1. Cited in Daniel Overdorf, *Applying the Sermon: How to Balance Biblical Integrity and
Cultural Relevance* (Grand Rapids: Kregel, 2009), p. 87.

The flip side of every sin is the gospel that explicitly and exactly meets and heals the need that sin has caused; the flip side of every act of obedience is a sinful reflection of it that distorts the image of God to the opposite of what it means to be like Christ. Don't leave that thought at the level of generality: push down to the deepest level of sin and you will find the grace that precisely answers it. We don't need to be afraid to deal with sin.

So next time you wield the sword of God's Spirit, his Word, drive the point of it deep down into the human heart, because it makes a wound that God promises he will heal.

INDEX OF PRINCIPAL BIBLICAL PASSAGES

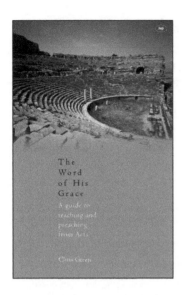

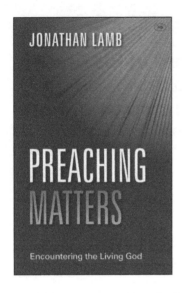

related titles from IVP

Preaching Matters

Encountering the Living God

Jonathan Lamb

ISBN: 978-1-78359-149-7
192 pages, paperback

Preaching matters. It is a God-ordained means of encountering Christ. This is happening all around the world. The author recalls the student who, on hearing a sermon about new life in Christ, found faith which changed his life and future forever; and the couple facing the trauma of the wife's terminal illness who discovered that Christ was all they needed, following a sermon on Habakkuk.

When the Bible is faithfully and relevantly explained, it transforms hearts, understandings and attitudes, and, most of all, draws us into a living relationship with God through Christ.

This is a book to ignite our passion for preaching, whether we preach every week or have no idea how to put a sermon together. It will encourage every listener to participate in the dynamic event of God's Word speaking to his people through his Holy Spirit. God's Word is dynamite; little wonder that its effects are often dynamic.

'A book for both preachers and listeners … a fitting manifesto not just for the Keswick Convention, but for every local church.'
Tim Chester

Available from your local Christian bookshop or **www.thinkivp.com**

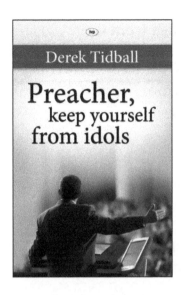

related titles from IVP

Preacher, Keep Yourself from Idols

Derek Tidball

ISBN: 978-1-84474-496-1
208 pages, paperback

'Preachers' and 'idolatry'. Surely these two words don't belong together? Or do they?

The apostle John ends his first letter with the plea, 'Dear children, keep yourselves from idols' (1 John 5:21) – an exhortation to believers to keep alert to insidious temptations of all kinds.

What is true of Christian life and ministry in general is true of preaching in particular, and John's warning may be taken as a specific warning to preachers who can easily fall prey to various forms of idolatry associated with their calling.

With insight and wisdom, Derek Tidball reviews a selection of idols to which preachers are particularly vulnerable, under four headings: the self, the age, the task and the ministry. His aim is not to condemn – for the task is perilous enough – but to alert, and thereby help us to avoid those factors which, although good in themselves, become idolatrous, deposing God from the throne which is rightly and exclusively his. Our preaching should be offered up as a worthy sacrifice to the one, true, living God.

Available from your local Christian bookshop or **www.thinkivp.com**

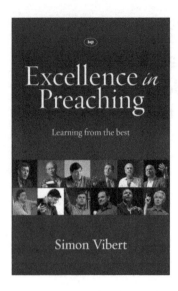

Excellence in Preaching
Learning from the best
Simon Vibert

ISBN: 978-1-84474-519-7
176 pages, paperback

What makes some preaching gripping – unforgettable even?
What can we learn from the best preachers?
How can we appreciate great preaching, often at the click of a mouse,
without devaluing the role of the local church minister?

*'Without creating a guru mentality, I focus on one positive aspect from
each preacher and offer ideas on how other preachers might emulate
them,'* says author Simon Vibert. He also looks at the Bible's own take on
good preaching, and focuses on the exemplary models of Jesus and Paul.

This is not a how-to manual, nor a biblical theology of preaching, nor
even a critique of the subjects. Rather, it is a focus on modern-day
practitioners, from whom all preachers can form a composite picture
of excellence, and from whom all preachers would do well to learn.

*'An inspiring, accessible and engaging book for preachers, at whatever
stage in their preaching ministry ... The examples of good preachers, in all
their diversity, challenge us to review how we preach. We are encouraged
not to try to be like clones, but instead develop our own style of good
preaching. A must-read for anyone who takes preaching seriously.'*
Revd Clare Hendry

For more information about IVP
and our publications visit
www.ivpbooks.com

Get regular updates at **ivpbooks.com/signup**
Find us on **facebook.com/ivpbooks**
Follow us on **twitter.com/ivpbookcentre**

Inter-Varsity Press, a company limited by guarantee registered in England and Wales, number 05202650. Registered
office IVP Bookcentre, Norton Street, Nottingham NG7 3HR, United Kingdom. Registered charity number 1105757.